THE SPORTS WORKSHOP

Team work, research,
technology, passion
and social value

edited by Fondazione Pirelli

Illustrations by
Lorenzo Mattotti

Go on, I'll stay and wait for Bartali
Quivering in my sandals
Around that curve will come
That sad nose of a cheerful Italian…

Paolo Conte, *Bartali*

Apart from the wonderful single moments that fate can bestow on you, loving your work […] represents the best, most concrete approximation of happiness on earth.

Primo Levi, *The Monkey's Wrench*

CONTENTS

INTRODUCTION

10
Marco Tronchetti Provera

Our Values Between Enterprise and Sport

14
Giovanni Malagò

The Power of the Olympics that Goes Beyond Borders

18
Evelina Christillin

The Educational and Social Role Enshrined in the Constitution

22
Stefano Domenicali

Formula 1 Captures Minds and Hearts

PIRELLI FOR SPORT

TRAINING THOUGHTS

32
Antonio Calabrò

A Story of the Future, Between Power and Control

52
Joe R. Lansdale

Batman's Punch is a Guide to Life

STORIES OF OUR ACHIEVEMENTS

66
Mario Isola

What a Team, Behind a Driver in the Race

76
Ambrogio Beccaria

The Energy of Research and the Wind in the Sails

88
Daniele Pirola

Those Sports Fields Next to the Factory

TALKING ABOUT CHAMPIONS: MUSIC, TECHNIQUES, IMAGES…

106
Eva Cantarella
The Epic of Competitions That Create Myths

118
Emanuela Audisio
Being Together Dreaming of the Same Horizon

130
Giuseppe Lupo
Popular Heroes in the Cycle Sprint

146
Giuseppe Di Piazza
Music and Choirs to Celebrate the Podium

162
Darwin Pastorin
The Passion for Writing About Champions and Dreamers

182
Massimo Sideri
Innovation Redeems the 'Blue Spot'

196
Sandro Modeo
Neurosciences for Training

TESTIMONIES FROM ALL PIRELLI SPORTS

214
Athletics

224
Motorsport

234
Football

242
Cycling

252
Motorcycling

264
Rallying

276
Skiing and Mountaineering

284
Tennis

288
Sailing and Water Sports

FINAL NOTES

298
Fondazione Pirelli

302
Authors' Biographies

306
Bibliography

308
Index of Names

INTRODUCTION

OUR VALUES BETWEEN ENTERPRISE AND SPORT

Innovation and a job well done are essential to win today and be even more competitive tomorrow. The horizon of social and environmental sustainability

by Marco Tronchetti Provera

Executive Vice Chairman of Pirelli and Chairman of the Fondazione Pirelli

T he values shared between sport and business can be conveyed in essential words, linked to a more general human predicament. The first word is competition, to bring out the talents of the best and teamwork, which is important even in competitions where a single athlete is the hero. Then there is the disposition to innovation, as a commitment to the unrelenting progress of people and structures, be they sporting or productive, as well as that extraordinary inclination for research and work well done, with the awareness that today's results will have to be made even more competitive tomorrow.

In the age of the great mass movements, in which a greater attention is also being drawn to the values and interests of individuals, the special relationship between sport and business takes on original traits that go beyond market success and wins in competitions. They involve the ways of being together, the spirit of community, the languages that connect people and social groups, the sense of sharing in a common adventure, be it sporting or economic.

The corporate enterprise, at the time of the primacy of the values of sustainability, both social and environmental, has a growing responsibility towards all its stakeholders, the citizens of the territories and communities on which the enterprise has operations, its employees, customers and suppliers: a special attention to the wellbeing created and shared. The relationship of sport with its stakeholders is similar: not only to build support and cheer, but above all to promote supportive passion, a sense of involvement and the importance of social inclusion. All this to encourage people to actively engage in sport and to be sportsmen and sportswomen deep in their souls, far beyond the status of mere viewers of an event. 'History is us', sang a great musician of our times, Francesco De Gregori. So is the history of sport and business.

It is from these thoughts, which are widespread and deeply felt in our Pirelli community, that the decision arose to have the Fondazione Pirelli's latest book on *The Sports Workshop*, explored in all the aspects that surround and go beyond the fundamental moment of competition: the research laboratories and technologies, the work sites, the training of athletes and teams, but also the languages, rituals and myths of the fans, the psychological and cultural mechanisms of commitment. And the roots and topicality of playing sports as a metaphor for a growing quality of life, both individual and collective. In the pages you will read, you will find the ideas and testimonies of leading figures from sporting institutions, economic and sporting leaders, writers and journalists, women and men from business and culture. It is a special, polyphonic, choral account, which provides a boost for the continued growth of business and sports culture as pillars of community spirit.

The relationship between Pirelli and sport is an old one, almost contemporary with the company's birth in 1872. It initially concerned cycling, but then rapidly expanded to include all motorbike and automobile competitions and other disciplines, tennis and sailing, football, athletics, skiing and mountaineering.

The Peking to Paris raid in 1907, the Targa Florio and Mille Miglia races, the Giro d'Italia and the Tour de France, and then Formula 1, support for Inter and regattas, right up to the performances of *Luna Rossa Prada Pirelli* and *Alla Grande-Pirelli*, with Ambrogio Beccaria at the helm, are just a few examples of our commitment.

The photos in this volume, taken from the Pirelli Historical Archives, confirm an energy that has lasted for over a century and that continues to be forward-looking with confidence. It is the confidence of those who, as a large company that is very Italian and at the same time well-rooted in various international settings, have as their values and reference practices innovation, research, quality, as well as a commitment to sustainability, safety in the workplace, and the full exploitation of the talents and skills of the women and men working at Pirelli.

The race tracks are genuine open-air laboratories for rigorously testing the quality and performance of products that will later go on the markets. The new digital technologies that reinforce the research and development efforts and help boost the drive for top performance on the road and on those special waterways, the sea routes, on which Pirelli continues to support those seeking to achieve records of excellence.

There is an overarching tenet, which for Pirelli remains constant over time: to provide excellent products to teams and champions, but also, as a sponsor and direct player, to grow the widespread culture of the values of playing sports, with fairness, loyalty, commitment to the spectacular nature of competition and to the beauty of performance.

Here is the summary: quality and beauty, ethics and technique. These are all values that are implemented in our daily commitment as a responsible company

The game of rules is interwoven with the rules of the game, thereby a special relationship is established.
Here is the summary: quality and beauty, ethics and technique. These are all values that are implemented in our daily commitment as a responsible company on the international markets where our presence has grown.
A choice of passion, but also a choice of reason: sport is one of the most selective laboratories of personality, culture, technology and production.
The sports of those who compete, excel, weave the web of team play, of those who know how to build dreams of victory and make them come true, courageously facing the sense of limit and pushing the human adventure forward towards unprecedented goals of achievements, successes but also participation and knowledge. Sport, therefore, as a great and generous metaphor for life.
There is a motto in which we continue to fully identify: 'Power is nothing without control'. It was the pay-off of a famous campaign in 1994, starring the extraordinary athlete Carl Lewis, Olympic champion in running and long jump, photographed by Annie Leibovitz in a pair of red stilettos. An original image, ironic, full of strong values, to emphasise the fundamental relationship between power and its control. A relationship that is as true for business as it is for sport, as well as for various social and cultural, ethical, and political values.
Other great men and women athletes have interpreted it, from French Olympic champion Marie-José Pérec to Ronaldo, with the soles of their feet marked by the tread of iconic tyres, the P3000 and P6000.
Still today, in Pirelli advertisements, that catchphrase reminds us all of a sense of responsibility in life, in business and in sport.
There is another facet, which marks our commitment: the social perspective of playing sports, as an essential component of corporate welfare policies. It is a characteristic that has its roots in time, in that long 20th century when, on Pirelli's sporting grounds, not only did champions emerged (one for all: Adolfo Consolini, gold medalist at the 1948 Olympics for discus throwing) but above all, among employees and their children, there was a commitment to grow, compete, and try to give the best of themselves as individuals and as members of cohesive teams.
Sport as a form of participation, public involvement, and civic engagement. Sport as passion and as the joy of the game. Sports provide a sense of community of which, in all our global pursuits, we are truly proud.

THE POWER OF THE OLYMPICS THAT GOES BEYOND BORDERS

Sport is a language that bridges distances, unites beyond differences and builds a better society. Talent to be recounted as a social value

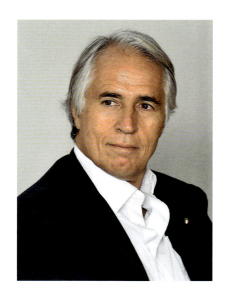

by Giovanni Malagò

President of CONI, of the Fondazione Milano Cortina 2026 and member of the IOC

Introduction

Sport's unrivalled power opens up horizons that can extend beyond all borders. It possesses the strength of an activity that bridges distances, helping to unite people despite their differences. It knows no divisions, but only encounters and exchanges to transform critical issues into opportunities, a powerful drive that helps build a better society because it is permeated with the values that characterise the system and make it special.

The five rings are the most eloquent expression of the significance of the movement, a symbol that embodies the Olympic spirit and unites the world in the name of brotherhood, making it the only relevant paradigm. There is a legacy that is handed down from generation to generation, a tradition that has its roots in the authentic message that passes through time without losing its effectiveness, rather renewing it in the name of an identity that is the common denominator of athletes, technicians, managers, volunteers and enthusiasts.

Sport is a banner to be proudly raised; it is embodied in many exclusive stories, in many different ways of living and practising it, expressed through behaviours adopted spontaneously, out of a sense of belonging, and as a result of dynamics to be discovered and appreciated. The backstage of a victory has to be decoded through the nuances that characterise it; talent is the fundamental requirement, but by itself it does not suffice unless the desire to train it intervenes, to create the conditions to progress by pursuing increasingly ambitious goals, cultivated with application, perseverance, sacrifice and a concern for detail.

An athlete wins by a far-sighted choice epitomised by a trajectory studied on a monitor, by a new material adopted instead of conventional ones, by tests repeated to the bitter end in the search for the most efficient aerodynamics. A matter of millimetres, hundredths, a sigh that reflects years of tough preparation. It is extraordinarily difficult to schematise what lies behind feats that are in the annals, burnishing the achievements of Italian sport at a universal level.

Behind it there is a technical trademark that is the result of know-how built on the genetics of the system, which many seek to replicate but without particular success, due to the qualities from which it draws its originality and strength, with its architrave resting on the activity of amateur associations and clubs and without effective planning related to motor activity in the schools, an area that by statute, mission and purpose lies beyond the jurisdiction of our universe. This is the machinery that I am honoured to explain to my two hundred and five colleagues from the other Olympic Committees

of the world, when they ask me about the secret of our model. This gives a sense of the uniqueness of Italian sport and the exceptional nature of the results achieved, thanks to the ability to interpret the role with a competence dictated by passion and osmosis that produces a combination—between CONI and the various sports bodies—destined to make the difference. There exist assets that can give us an inestimable added value, such as the School of Sport—established in 1966 by Giulio Onesti, the longest-serving president of the institution—a training school that gives continuity to the movement, handing down the secrets in the sector and providing the resources for a highly specialised preparation of essential protagonists called on to find the right keys in the technical, scientific and methodological field.
Sixty years ago, the Institute of Sports Medicine was also founded by Antonio Venerando, our showpiece, providing a frame of reference for Italian athletes, placing at their service the professionalism of doctors and experts of world calibre for diagnosis, care and personalised treatments, joined in the 1970s by the Institute of Sports Science, supporting federations on a scientific level with a constant action in depth in terms of research and development to respond to the growing need to optimise performance, exploiting synergic relations with institutions and universities to follow the most successful paths in the fields of physiology and biomechanics.
The Giulio Onesti Olympic Preparation Centres in Rome, Formia, Tirrenia and now—by virtue of a recent, specific memorandum of understanding signed with local organisations—also Livigno, are outposts for optimising training and ensuring performance.
This is the legacy that we have inherited and that we seek to nurture day by day to enable Italian sport to remain among the world's elite, thanks to those successes that in recent years have enabled us to rewrite history with new peaks, from the record number of medals won at the Tokyo Olympics to the ideal podium gained for two consecutive years at a global level, thanks to the overall results obtained in the Olympics and in the world and continental competitions. A trend that is not fortuitous, rewarding the horizontal work performed with tenacity and courage, leaving no one behind, with a vocation that gives us jurisdiction over 373 disciplines, a cultural hallmark that we seek to nurture to continue to certify the credibility and depth of the whole system.
Its ambassadors are the champions whose successes enthral us, examples of strength and great moral stature out of respect for the ideals that are part of our genetic code. The fourteen million members who come under the aegis of CONI are a heritage to

Its ambassadors are the champions whose successes enthral us, examples of strength and great moral stature out of respect for the ideals that are part of our genetic code

be valued, if we consider a process that is inexorably eroding our base. The figures are merciless in this respect. Since 1995 we have lost five million Italians between the ages of eighteen and thirty-five, the age group eligible to identify the talents that represent Italy at the Olympic Games and in high-level sports competitions. In 2038, the youth population (15–34 years old) is expected to shrink further, providing us with an alarming picture of the future of our country, which competes with Japan for the record for the most long-lived population.

These numbers help us understand how complex it will be to continue to achieve the levels of excellence that distinguish us, due to demographic contraction and the simultaneous growth in competitiveness of other countries in sports, given their considerably larger reservoir, as shown by the statistics of the last editions of the Olympic Games, with more nations winning medals.

The danger is concrete, but it certainly does not diminish our desire to continue to explore horizons that will enable us to give a voice to the qualities that are part of our DNA, by strengthening the teamwork between the various components and launching effective measures—with the help of other institutional bodies—that will at least mitigate the problems in question.

The culture of sport needs to be rooted ever more deeply to enable people to understand its importance, to permeate the community and open up munificent prospects for moral, physical and competitive development. Beyond the beauty of victories, there is an inestimable intangible value, the benefits it can confer, the Pole Star to be followed without reservation. The finest way to pursue a bright future, by making sport a part of our way of life.

THE EDUCATIONAL AND SOCIAL ROLE ENSHRINED IN THE CONSTITUTION

The rights of sport 'for all and of all', and respect for the rules of the game by athletes and spectators: the commitment to improve the quality of life

by Evelina Christillin
-
President of the Egyptian Museum of Turin

Introduction

Sport has always held an important place in my life. I would say a central place. And I have constantly done my utmost to have the word 'sport' given its rightful place in the Italian Constitution. I argued this before President Sergio Mattarella in October 2022, during the inauguration of the academic year at the School of Higher Military Training in Turin, when I delivered the inaugural address on *Sustainability, Rights and Values in Sport and Culture in the Third Millennium*. Rights, above all, are central. We cannot permit discrimination, whether based on gender, skin colour, religion or ethnicity. And respect has to be the rule of the game, both among the players on the pitch and the spectators in the stands. Hence the Department of Sport states that: 'In the Constitution, sport is the first step on a path that expresses, in a few words, a profound significance and an inestimable value, which we can sum up in the hope of "sport for all and of all", as a part of the indispensable "social immune defences" and an important contribution to improving the quality of life of individuals and communities'. And since September 2023, Article 33 of our Republican Constitution has a new paragraph declaring that: 'The Republic recognises the value of sporting activities in all their forms in fostering educational, social and psychophysical well-being'.

Sport is also a family passion. My father, a racing driver, took part in five editions of the Mille Miglia. In 1950, together with Egisto Corradi, at the time a correspondent of the *Corriere della Sera*, he competed aboard a Lancia van in the Algiers–Cape Town Rally. He was also a great skier, instilling in me a passion for alpine skiing. I remember I was just over ten years old when he and Carlo De Chiesa, the father of Paolo, a great friend of mine, took me to the 1968 Grenoble Olympics. There we saw Jean-Claude Killy win his third gold medal in the fog. He was the most beautiful, the best, the most successful of skiers: a legend. I never thought that I would meet him, yet thirty years later I was sent by Gianni Agnelli to interview him—as a member of the International Olympic Committee (IOC)—in our promotional campaign to bring the 2006 Winter Olympics to Turin. I went to see him in Geneva. A hopeless amateur and very excited, I could hardly open my mouth at first. 'No one ever wins at the first attempt', he told me right away. Today we're close friends. He was later appointed president of the IOC Coordination Commission for the Turin Games. A passion for skiing led me as a child to enjoy winter sports, in which I went so far as to compete in the National B Team together with my friend Claudia Giordani. I remember that I used to set off from Turin and pick her up in Milan. The other girls were all from northeastern Italy, between Cortina and South Tyrol. We were 'the city folk', arriving from outside. Yet we still lived a communal life, sharing everything from morning till night, all the same, from our uniforms to our training. Because sport unites people in the effort, beyond the individual achievement, beyond the result recorded by the stopwatch. Then you return to the team. The first thing you learn is that you lose much more often than you win. You race, you set your time, and sometimes you make mistakes. And the next morning you start training all over again. Of course, it was a little more difficult for me as one of the 'city folk' and with my commitments at a classical high school. My parents made me face my limitations and accept my responsibility to myself. They got me to see that, despite my talent, I was not on the same level as Claudia Giordani and sooner or later I would have to decide what else to do in life. So playing team sports taught me to take the measure of myself. And it confirmed that in sport—at least in skiing—sexism doesn't exist. In the same way, I never had any problems as a woman when I entered the world of work, first with a position in the Fiat press office and then with the chair of Modern History at the University of Turin. Meanwhile I also worked with Valentino Castellani on the campaign to get him re-elected mayor of Turin. In the fateful year of 1998, the Torino 2006 Organising Committee was formed to present the city's candidacy for the Winter Olympics. Of course, personalities such as Gianni Agnelli and Mayor Castellani were on it. However, an executive chairperson had to be chosen, a figure with an active role. Perhaps because of my past in skiing, or because I'd just organised the exhibition for the Juventus centenary, perhaps because they needed a free spirit, or because I had a good relationship—never political—with the city authorities, Agnelli and the mayor asked me to act as chair. I said yes with enthusiasm and a fair dose of healthy recklessness. I have to admit that at the time the candidacy of Turin and its mountains seemed like mission impossible. We had to start from scratch. But I had the support of Gianni and Umberto Agnelli, of Fiat, of my husband Gabriele Galateri, and then a certain experience—gained at Fiat itself—in organising a working party. I took leave of absence from university and said to myself: 'You wanted this. Now put your shoulder to the wheel'. And the Committee began its arduous work. The following year came the corruption scandal at the IOC, which led to a ban on Olympic candidates contacting other federations. There could be no exchanges of visits with those who would later be the voters. So, we hired a communications agency, which organised a tour of interviews with the international media. Since I speak a number of languages, it was not difficult for me to travel around the world—I must have covered a hundred thousand kilometres—to meet all the possible influencers who could help us in our candidacy, at least by reporting on it in the media. And so, in June 1999, in Korea, we beat the Swiss town of Sion, which had already applied three times, and to everyone's surprise we managed to bring the Games to Turin. The rest,

The first thing you learn is that you lose much more often than you win. You race, you set your time, and sometimes you make mistakes. And the next morning you start training all over again

in the role of the deputy vice-president of Toroc, the Turin Organising Committee, was the crowning achievement of a story that lasted nine years and ended with that 2006 edition of the Winter Olympics. I think it was a success. Then I was appointed to the presidency of the Teatro Stabile di Torino and the Egyptian Museum. On the official opening of the museum's new premises in March 2015, I invited some prominent figures I knew in the world of football to attend: Carlo Tavecchio, Michele Uva, the members of the Federal Council of Federcalcio. Afterwards we all went to watch the Italy v England match, played that night at the Juventus Stadium. As fate would have it, a short time later there was the upheaval caused by the FIFA scandal, with Gianni Infantino replacing the outgoing president Sepp Blatter and, in a global revolution, the statute also changed. Starting from 2016, each continental Confederation would have to elect at least one woman among its members. So, perhaps because of my Olympic experience, or the awards and accolades received from CONI, the IOC and the Presidency of the Republic, or my great passion for football, particularly associated with Juventus, and, of course, a fair dose of luck, at the UEFA Congress in Athens I was the first European woman to be elected to the FIFA Council, the world's most important football organisation.

Apart from sport, my working life has brought me cultural appointments, with the presidencies of theatres and museums. This showed me that sport and culture—basically two ways of spending one's leisure—are both bearers of values that rest on the key term of respect. Respect for different cultures, as stated in Articles 3 and 9 of the Constitution. Respect as the creation of bridges and not barriers. In the two fields in which I have worked, sport and culture, I have always tried to limit exclusion as far as possible, whatever the reasons for it. Another key word on which the sport–culture pair rests, as I see it, is freedom. Freedom to meet, first of all, and freedom to share, which is a much stronger resource than any temptation towards political or territorial rigidity. Leaving aside racism and scandalmongering, we can recall Livio Berruti, among much else one of the Italian athletes who carried the Olympic flag in Torino 2006, and his relationship with the American sprinter Wilma Rudolph at the Rome Olympics in 1960. In conclusion, I would like to recall what was said in the Senate during the examination of the bill amending Article 33 of the Constitution: 'It becomes the duty of the Republic to ensure that the practice of sport is truly universal, accessible to all, without distinction of sex, race, language, religion, political opinions or personal and social circumstances. And at the same time it is appropriate to adopt all the measures to ensure their protection and safety, and strengthen the guarantees for the protection of minors, for an integral and healthy organisation that also guarantees gender equality'. This is the lesson of sport: always strive, never exclude.

The Sports Workshop — 22

FORMULA 1 CAPTURES MINDS AND HEARTS

From its beginnings in post-war Europe to its current status as a global phenomenon with five hundred million fans. Our platform as a sustainable technology leader

by Stefano Domenicali
-
President and Chief Executive Officer of Formula 1

Growing up at Imola it is hard not to fall in love with motorsport. I have worked for Ferrari, Audi, Lamborghini and now Formula 1: what more could a kid from Imola ask for? Motor racing has been part of my life for as long as I can remember, but I could not have predicted the development it has had in recent years, especially since I took over as CEO of Formula 1 in 2021.

Formula 1 is the most prestigious expression of motorsport, and for decades now it has captured the hearts and minds of racing fans: from its beginnings in post-war Europe, when a conflict-torn continent was trying to reinvigorate its passion for motorsport, to the global phenomenon it is today, with a calendar spanning five continents and more than five hundred million fans. It is an ever-evolving sport, where innovation and entertainment are two sides of the same coin.

In its more than seventy years of existence, Formula 1 has gone through various phases. The fascination of racing has remained constant, with the heroes that have been created and the legends that have always existed. It has grown steadily from an elite and super-fan sport at its inception in 1950 to a global phenomenon that reaches over 1.5 billion people each season.

In 2017, with the advent of Liberty Media, Formula 1 came into an exciting new era. The US group's investment, commitment and passion have taken the sport to an unprecedented level, increasing its visibility and accessibility and providing fans with more entertainment. The strategy has focused on creating more races, fuelling the passion they inspire. On the track, new regulations have been introduced to promote closer racing and to develop new formats that offer fans more competitive events during race weekends. Away from the track, there is a drive to reveal our sport, to invite fans behind the visor and into the cockpit, to understand who the drivers are and to show how immense the feat of driving a Formula 1 car is.

It seems odd to think back today to a time when Formula 1 had no social media coverage, while other sports had already recognised the power of the various platforms. This is one of the first changes made by Liberty. Teams, drivers and Formula 1 itself are granted the licence to use social media to invite fans into the paddock three hundred and sixty-five days a year, opening up to them a world that was previously the sole prerogative of drivers and crew chiefs, and showing highlights of the latest races directly on their phones or tablets. This is a breakthrough, not only for fans but also commercial partners, who can use our platforms to communicate directly with millions of fans.

Another winning choice is *Drive to Survive*. The docuseries takes viewers backstage at the Formula 1 Championship and is enjoying huge success, which continues to grow. The fifth season outperformed the fourth, which is very rare in television, and, upon its release, spent many weeks in the world top ten.

Its success is based on telling the stories of the drivers. Formula 1 is one of the few sports where the champions are hidden behind helmets while they race, and a way has to be found to bring out their personalities. *Drive to Survive* not only shows them on the track, showcasing the highs and lows of a season, but also takes viewers inside their private lives. All this has evolved the relationship of fans with the drivers and introduced Formula 1 to the media networks even outside motorsport. In short, it's a true game changer.

This is proven by the commercial deals that champions are getting beyond their teams, launching personal brands and securing global sponsorship contracts. In my opinion, this is a virtuous circle for our sport, which benefits everyone.

We, as rights holders, benefit from the fact that our heroes are better known around the world; the teams have two global superstars they can involve in marketing campaigns, generating commercial value; and the drivers have the freedom to develop their own brands and cultivate passions outside Formula 1.

This doesn't just apply to the drivers: I don't think anyone expected the team principals to have such an impact either, with Guenther Steiner, Toto Wolff and Christian Horner becoming popular names.

The effect of Netflix is often overstated, but it has undoubtedly played a significant role in increasing our fan base. It has introduced Formula 1 to a wider audience, sparking interest in a younger demographic. One in seven of the new fans in the last four years has cited *Drive to Survive* as the main reason for following Formula 1 and this has certainly had a positive effect on commercial growth as well.

Our strategy, however, goes far beyond social media: on-track developments have also been key to growth. We have pandered to the fans' demand for more overtaking and introduced rules that allow cars to follow each other closely and overtake more easily. This has led to a 30% increase in overtaking from 2021 to 2022, and we expect the same in 2023.

The F1 Sprint Race is another example of success and shows how our sport can innovate. In 2023 we went from three to six Sprint events, introducing a new format that amplified the level of intensity and action during the entire race weekend. This increased the TV audience and increased Friday race attendance on Sprint weekends by an average of 30% compared to standard race weekends.

We are talking about one of the few sports in the world where the new fans are mainly young people and the female audience: an exciting aspect to take into account in order to continue to grow

We also wanted to make sure that the Grand Prix is not just about racing. For example, at many of our events, once races are over, tens of thousands of fans attend concerts by world-famous artists such as Bruno Mars, Ed Sheeran, The Black Eyed Peas and Calvin Harris. This added value is combined with the expansion of interactive fan zones, where it is possible to drive simulators, practise pit stops and, crucially, listen to the stars, the drivers. In fan zones we work with our commercial partners to further promote their presence in the sport by sponsoring activities or setting up their own fan-facing stands, creating new opportunities to engage their target audience.

Identifying key growth markets has allowed us to expand the calendar to a record twenty-four races in 2024, reaching millions more people. This has led to an increase in commercial agreements with broadcasters and companies interested in our global reach. We have expanded the number of official partners, with an impact on the entire grid, where there are now more than three hundred sponsors collaborating with our teams, a huge increase compared to 2020.

In a further strategic development, we have enhanced our hospitality offering, improving the premium space in the Paddock Club and launching a new product, 'garage', a place where fans, for a fee, can experience the race from inside a luxury garage in the pit lane. These services had a record year in 2023 and reached such level of popularity that they attracted high-value partners: the Formula 1 paddock became a meeting point for CEOs and opinion leaders from all over the world.

Being able to involve the fans more and more is a crucial issue for us. We are talking about one of the few sports in the world where the new fans are mainly young people and the female audience: an exciting aspect to take into account in order to continue to grow.

Off the track, in addition to *Drive to Survive*, we are bringing Formula 1 to Hollywood: with Apple Studios, the highly anticipated film with Brad Pitt is in production. Filming took place at several races in 2023, with a stage team filming on the track, operating from their garage, and even lining up their cars on the grid before the race.

Just as Netflix introduced Formula 1 to a whole new audience, we believe Apple's film will broaden interest in our sport to an even wider audience in the US and around the world.

Finally, we are bringing Formula 1 to our fans in the cities where they live, through our new licensed experiential venues, F1 Arcade and F1 Exhibition. F1 Arcade, where you can drive Formula 1 simulators in a social environment with friends, food and drinks, is already in place in London, and twenty more venues will open over the next

As important as growth is, the focus on being net zero by 2030 is very clear to us. Sustainability is a vital component in the future of all sports

five years, starting with a second in the UK, in Birmingham, followed in 2024 by new US locations in Boston and Washington DC. The first F1 Exhibition, which offered fans a unique journey behind the scenes of Formula 1 history, opened in Madrid in April 2023, and was the largest temporary exhibition of the year in Spain. Vienna is the next stop on the ten-year global tour, offering immersive experiences and bringing Formula 1 to life for our fans even if they cannot come to a race.

As important as growth is, the focus on being net zero by 2030 is very clear to us. Sustainability is a vital component in the future of all sports and is embedded in every part of our business. I also believe that we can use our global platform as a leader in innovative technologies to contribute significantly to reducing carbon emissions beyond our racing events.

Formula 1's commitment to using 100 per cent sustainable fuels and next-generation hybrid engines in 2026 aims to achieve a major impact on the world around us. There are currently 1.4 billion vehicles on the road with internal combustion engines, and they are increasing. The fuel we are developing for our cars is specifically designed as a 'drop-in' fuel, i.e. it can be used in any car without requiring changes. The effect on society could be enormous.

We have taken significant steps to reduce our emissions, introducing a new fleet of biofuel trucks in 2023 to support freight movements in the UK and Europe.

We are also experimenting with low-carbon power generators within the racetrack, using a combination of alternative fuels and solar energy. An experiment conducted this year in Austria is estimated to have reduced emissions from paddock and team operations by more than 90%.

By embracing these new technologies, we are not only reducing our carbon footprint, but promoting their use beyond our sport, with potentially huge effects. We are not done yet: our next step will be to look at the way travel takes place at competitions; we have already made changes to our calendar to help with the movement of goods for 2024, and we hope to implement this for future calendars. We are also looking at the benefits of different types of transport, for example air or sea, which equipment has to travel with us and which can be stored or purchased locally. All these changes contribute to our net zero commitment and we leave no stone unturned.

In addition to our sustainability commitments, we continue to make great strides to make our sport more accessible. In 2022 we announced the creation of F1 Academy, our all-female racing series, which completed its inaugural season in October 2023, becoming part of the Formula 1 calendar at the US Grand Prix in Austin, after six competitions in Europe. The final saw Marta García crowned champion and was the first race to be broadcast live, in over a hundred countries, thanks to the support of our global broadcasters. Marta's success was rewarded with a fully-funded place in FRECA (Formula Regional European Championship by Alpine) for next season, while F1 Academy achieved its goal of creating higher opportunities in the single-seater pyramid.

Next season, all seven races will be included in the Formula 1 calendar and will be broadcast live; in addition, all ten Formula 1 teams will have their livery on a car and a driver participating in the racing series, further promoting the initiative worldwide. Away from the track, we are creating opportunities for those interested in Stem careers, which are at the heart of our sport. In 2021 we unveiled a scholarship program to support engineers at universities in the UK and Italy. Each scholarship covers the full cost of tuition fees together with living expenses, and in 2022 we extended this funding until at least 2025.

During their second year of study, scholars gain work experience at one of the Formula 1 teams, as well as access to career seminars and mentoring.

The programme is part of our commitment to make motorsport more accessible, with the aim of increasing career opportunities for students from less affluent socio-economic backgrounds and underrepresented groups. Since the start of the program we have been able to support twenty students from five partner universities, with the aim of involving another thirty in the coming years.

In conclusion, I would say that Formula 1 has never been healthier, and it is our responsibility to ensure that it continues to be better and greener in the future.

There has never been a more exciting time to be a fan of the sport.

PIRELLI
FOR SPORT

The Sports Workshop

by Antonio Calabrò
-
Senior Vice-President Culture and Director of the Fondazione Pirelli

A Story of the Future, Between Power and Control

From the image of Carl Lewis in red shoes to the new frontiers of artificial intelligence: the renewal of the historic link between Pirelli and sport

Nuvolari is short of stature
Nuvolari is below normal
Nuvolari has fifty kilos of bones
Nuvolari has an exceptional body
Nuvolari's hands are like claws,
Nuvolari has a talisman against evil.

— Lucio Dalla, *Nuvolari*, 1976

'Power is nothing without control'. An advertising slogan must have an extraordinary strength and a symbolic quality that goes beyond the formal limits of the wording, in order to withstand the wear and tear of time, overcome the historical circumstances of the communication for which it was created and evoke, thirty years on, a universe of values that strike, generation after generation, the understanding in the hearts of millions of people, thus leaving behind the chronicle of the message and entering the historical lexicon of a civilisation.

What, then, links 'power' and 'control'? And why does that slogan still today not only continue to conjure up, like a background sound, Pirelli's campaigns but is used in other social and cultural contexts?

To try to understand, let us take a step back in time. It is 1994 when photographer Annie Leibovitz portrays one of the greatest athletes of the time, Carl Lewis, as standing at the starting blocks of the 100 metres. The champion is not, however, wearing race shoes. But a pair of elegant pumps with high stiletto heels. Red. And the pay-off is, indeed, 'Power is nothing without control'.

The success is overwhelming. Leibovitz is one of the most famous American photographers, portraying Meryl Streep and the Rolling Stones (she also signed two Pirelli Calendars in 2000 and 2016). Lewis is one of the greatest athletes of all time, for running and long jump, with four gold medals at the 1984 Los Angeles Olympics, two more in Seoul in 1988 and then two more in Barcelona in 1992 (the ninth would come in Atlanta in 1996). He proudly holds his nickname, 'son of the wind'.

Those red shoes, in fact, are not just a shimmering play on a colour charged with complex symbolic values (the red of emotions, of changes, of the intensity of blood and the power of fire and, today, symbolising commitment to violence against women). They are also a political and cultural statement. A declaration of life. A real outing of the homosexuality by one of the most popular and beloved athletes (this will only be fully known, however, a few years after the campaign began).

The impact, on the entire world of sport and communication, is disruptive. Language, semantics, style indications reveal the start of a new era for advertising: in the foreground is not a product, but a character evoking value systems that go beyond the product referred

The Sports Workshop — 34

Young & Rubicam,
Carl Lewis for the Pirelli tyre
advertisement, poster, 1994,
photo Annie Leibovitz

to. With an added detail: the choice of irony, in those paradoxical stilettos. And irony is an trenchant cultural key to reading reality: it elicits a critical and self-critical spirit, a sense of limit, an awareness of a special ability to measure that relativises reasons and passions.
Irony as a way of life.
For Pirelli, after the great crisis of the early 1990s (the failure of the attempted takeover of Continental), this is the moment of revival: new corporate choices, a radical renewal of the entire industrial process and relations with the markets. The imagery of the critical and virtuous relationship between power and control expresses the new corporate culture very well. In an operation that, while preserving the group's Milanese roots (hence its elegant understatement), has international overtones.
Lewis, told with Leibovitz's sophisticated gaze, is the appropriate interpreter.
Extraordinary performance. And awareness of the limit. To be acknowledged. And to strive to overcome. In the race. But also, by extension of meaning, in business. In technological innovation. In life.
Here is a key point: the sense of limit. Which cannot but feature every human dimension. Beyond the conceits that are shattered also in myths (the disaster of Icarus, the futile labours of Sisyphus). And firmly anchored, on the other hand, in Ulysses' sense of travel and desire for discovery, 'to follow virtue and knowledge' and in the awareness that every creation, every discovery and invention, every sporting record, every artistic composition and every scientific achievement are steps beyond the acknowledgement of human frailty. They are stages of a journey that, precisely between limits, goes towards infinity, which we will never, humanly, achieve and to which, always

humanly, we aspire. Sport itself offers extraordinary metaphors for this.
One can go even further by reading history and politics. In the first half of the 1990s, the world is changing. The collapse of the Berlin Wall and the implosion of the Soviet empire profoundly changed geopolitics, with the unrivalled triumph of liberal democracy and the market economy. The spread of ICT (Information and Communication Technology) is subjecting production and trade to dramatic changes. The gates of globalisation open. International intellectual circles are stirred by a buzz of euphoria, so much so that even influential historians and economists are prompted to write about the 'end of history'.
Later years would tell us that all those changes had limits, critical points, cracks that would also dramatically unravel over time. That the new forms of power would require brakes, counterweights and, indeed, controls. And that to the even brutal evidence of the manifestation of the power of the leading players of the new political and economic choices, the new forms of power would have to be subjected to the same constraints.
The Pirelli campaign, the image of Lewis, the claim 'Power is nothing without control' are not, of course, a political manifesto, they do not claim to be masters of new global socio-cultural balances. But they do reveal the wind that blows.
They become, although not entirely consciously, witnesses to the times. A time that still lasts today, in which, after financial, environmental, health and geopolitical crises, we continue to ask ourselves how to write new maps of knowledge and action. How to drive change.
This is why that quote we began with in our story

remains topical. Because of the strong link between power and control, that is, for that dimension that we now call sustainability, both social and environmental, and for the relationship between the power of technological innovation, starting by shattering new frontiers of artificial intelligence, and human awareness (Sandro Modeo and Massimo Sideri write about this).

In any case, in those 1990s, Lewis, an Olympic champion, strengthened and relaunched a historic link, stretching into the future: that between Pirelli and sport.

Shortly afterwards, under the same tagline, came other champions: the French athlete Marie-José Pérec (gold medallist in the 400 metres at the 1992 Barcelona Olympics and in the 200 and 400 at Atlanta 1996) and then Ronaldo, extraordinary soccer player, photographed by Ken Griffiths balancing on the top of Corcovado, in place of the statue of Christ the Redeemer, in Rio de Janeiro. The soles of their feet are the tread of the P3000 tyre: grip, road holding, pragmatism. The game continues.

Like few other international companies, Pirelli has a special bond with sport. In several disciplines. Car and motorbike racing. And bicycle racing. Football and tennis. Athletics and sailing. Skiing and several other mountain-related activities. As we report in these pages, the 'long P' is a recurring trademark in the most popular competitions around the world and also in support for sporting activities experienced as fundamental components of the sense of corporate sociality and welfare promoted by the company (as written by Daniele Pirola). Sport, in short, in all its dimensions, as a cultural and social choice and a lifestyle that binds the company to its communities of reference, in countries all over the world.

Competition and community. It is precisely in these two words, related by a Latin prefix, *cum*, i.e. together, that the gist of the book you are reading lies. Clear right from its title, *The Sports Workshop*, and from the illustrations that come with the essays, signed by Lorenzo Mattotti, one of the most brilliant and sensitive contemporary artists, committed here to depicting people and environments, competitions and contexts. Workshop. The special place where 'thinking hands' play the leading role. Quality workmanship, with the skill to make excellent use of all technical tools. And creativity. Technological intelligence. And passion. Special aptitude of the individual maker. And articulate teamwork. Engineering. And humanistic wisdom of balance and beauty.

Polytechnic culture, to use a phrase historically close to the Pirelli world.

And conscious memory of those exceptional pages of Leonardo da Vinci's *Atlantic Codex*, which depict machines and gears (hydraulic structures, excavators, special screws and cogs, devices for flight such as a prefiguration of a helicopter or an aeroplane wing) and tell of creativity and experimentation, sophisticated engineering techniques and new balances to be imagined. Knowledge in motion, in Leonardo's pages, in large format, surprising in terms of innovation and fascinating in terms of figurative beauty, preserved in the rooms of the Biblioteca Ambrosiana in Milan. And which Pirelli has contributed, with other sponsors, to exhibit and make known in the United States, the home of technology, with an exhibition promoted by Confindustria, in the summer of 2023, at the Martin Luther King Library in Washington.

It is all there, in *The Sports Workshop*.

And much more. That is to say—scrolling through the

Pirelli for Sport — 37

A Pirelli technical assistant, 1954

Nino Farina and Fausto Coppi with an Alfa Romeo 1900, Sestriere, 1953, photo Publifoto

The Sports Workshop — 38

Costante Girardengo portrayed by the artist Manlio in an advertisement for Wolsit bicycles with Pirelli tyres, wall poster, 1925–26

Ezio Bonini, advertisement for Pirelli winter tyres, proof print, 1953

summary of the contributions, fact sheets and essays full of accurate news and original interpretations—the story of everything that happens before and around the moment of competition. A sport that goes beyond the albeit fundamental sporting act, revealing much more about itself than it may appear.
Technical structures. The materials. The research. But also, the excitement of the athletes and teams. The physical and psychological preparation of those who race and the indispensable role of coaches and trainers (to give just one example, *Chariots of Fire* made a poignant portrait of them in the cinema, which Emanuela Audisio writes about with great insight). The social dimensions in which the passions of competition are embedded. The Olympic epic (recounted by Eva Cantarella) and the literary dimension of the athletes, whether champions or wingmen. The symbols and rituals. The voices, choirs and music that define traditions and new imagery (described by Giuseppe Di Piazza). The chronicles, laden with words and images that, in the best of cases, dodge the traps of rhetoric and contribute to the contemporary epic (the memory of twentieth century masters of sports journalism such as Luigi Barzini, Gianni Brera, Orio Vergani, Sergio Zavoli, Giovanni Arpino and Nino Nutrizio offers exemplary testimony, with Darwin Pastorin's recollections). History and the powerful urge to challenge the future and build, as far as possible, a better one.
A scientific, technological and sentimental universe (Joe Lansdale's story, in the next few pages, deals with precisely these themes, also insisting on the relationship between sporting practice, martial arts in his case, and meditation, between personal, mental and physical training and inclination towards literature).
Courageous women and men, in competition and in the workshop. Talent, resourcefulness and mastery. Engineering and poetry. Power and control. In a dimension that unites athletes, coaches and the public 'because our dreams occupy the same horizon', to quote Audisio again.
The link between Pirelli and sport began immediately after the company's foundation, in the years that swiftly glided from the end of the nineteenth century towards a twentieth century in which industry played a leading economic and social role.
According to Giuseppe Berta, an authoritative historian of business economics: 'It is natural, after all, that the course of modern industry intersected with that of sport in mass society. Industry, like sport, has mobilised, gathered and organised great social energies. Both have helped to stamp their mark on some of the largest and most impressive events of our contemporary times. In Italy, then, the advent of industry coincided with the expression of the spirit of the twentieth century, which, not by chance, was to be shaped by the will to enterprise and a sense of competitive spirit. The history of Pirelli itself bears witness to this'.
The first patented bicycle tyre, the 'tipo Milano', in 1890. And immediately, in 1895, the first road race, Milano-Cremona-Brescia-Milano, restricted to cyclists using tyres made in the factory in Via Ponte Seveso: the debut of a long series of races that, after the successes of the first Giro d'Italia in 1909, would come to the glories of Alfredo Binda and Costante Girardengo ('great champion', Francesco De Gregori would sing of him, remembering his bandit friend), Gino Bartali and Fausto Coppi who, riding a Bianchi-Pirelli, triumphed in 1952 at the Giro d'Italia and the Tour de France, to come to the present day, when Pirelli tyres equip bikes for the most sophisticated

The Sports Workshop

Women workers making Pirelli tennis balls, 1950

amateur sporting performance (Giuseppe Lupo writes about this).

The step towards motorcycling and motor racing is fast and overwhelming. It starts with the Peking to Paris race in 1907. It moves on to the Targa Florio and the Mille Miglia. And it comes to Formula 1, Superbike and contemporary rallies. The first success came in an Itala 40-horsepower car fitted with Pirelli tyres and driven by Prince Scipione Borghese, with journalist Luigi Barzini (who wrote memorable chronicles of it in the *Corriere della Sera*) and mechanic Ettore Guizzardi, with a spectacular comeback in Paris, twenty days before the second competitor, to the notes of a fanfare intoning the triumphal march from Verdi's *Aida*. Then came the spectacular races with drivers named Antonio Ascari and Tazio Nuvolari (nicknamed 'the Devil'), Piero Taruffi and Manuel Fangio, Sandro Munari and Carlos Sainz, Giuseppe Farina and Nelson Piquet, to name but a few. Until Pirelli took over as sole supplier of Formula 1 in 2011, with a renewal that will run until 2028.

Racing is spectacle and experimentation, in that great open-air laboratory that are racing tracks and roads all over the world. Sophisticated technologies (the pages written by Stefano Domenicali and Mario Isola describe them well). And passions of sports teams and the public. Business. And virtuous intersections of values and economic value. Images that feed emotions. And emotions that translate into attention and participation. A fantastic sentimental, choral, plural game. It is a tale that can also be told for other popular sports, in which Pirelli has played and still plays a major role. Football. And sailing. Tennis. Skiing and athletics. Innovation and competition, the backstage of which we continue to describe in these pages. Technology that improves products and production mechanisms intersects with sporting prowess. The resourcefulness that drives the company's development is reflected in the way sport is experienced, also conveying a kind of civilised mindset for the public interest, that is the needs of a community. In 1877, just five years after it was founded, Pirelli started producing rubber items made for sport.

At the beginning of the new century, the game of football, after its aristocratic birth, proselytised in ever-widening crowds. In 1909, Piero Pirelli, eldest son of Giovanni Battista, the company's founder, became president of the Milan Cricket and Football Club, founded ten years earlier and already popular on the national scene. In 1925, there came a leap forward in

The resourcefulness that drives the company's development is reflected in the way sport is experienced, also conveying a kind of civilised mindset for the public interest

innovation, with new Pirelli patents for the shells and inner tubes of footballs. A season of events and turning points. The year before, on the Milan bench, Vittorio Pozzo was appointed coach (who would later lead the national team to World Cup successes in 1934 and 1938). The following year, in 1926, Piero Pirelli, still president of Milan, promoted the construction of the new San Siro stadium.

In 1961, at the height of the economic boom, the Pirelli brand was again chosen for the stadium roofing, with the Visqueen Pirelli Plast, which a couple of years later was adopted on all A and B League football pitches in the cities of northern and central Italy. In 1995, there was a radical change involving business and fans: Pirelli became sponsor and then shareholder of Inter. Shortly after, a phenomenal player came along, Luis Nazario de Lima, Ronaldo, 'Ballon d'Or', idol of the crowds, advertising icon (portrayed on the summit of Corcovado, with the Pirelli P3000 tread as the sole of his foot and the famous tagline: 'Power is nothing without control'; we have already written about it in previous pages).

It was the long season of Inter's international successes, up to the 'triplete' in 2010, with José Mourinho as coach: Scudetto, Coppa Italia and Champions League. The 'long P' on the Nerazzurri jersey is a world-famous symbol. 'Inter!', they answer you smiling admiringly in Moscow and Beijing, in Istanbul and Mexico City, when you say 'Pirelli'.

Sporting focus is a passport to popularity. Still now, when the sponsorship, from 2021, has been replaced by the role of Global Tyre Partner, but the alliance for the Pirelli Inter Campus, an initiative to introduce young people to sport and its moral, cultural and social values in all the countries where the company is present, is still alive.

In the same sporting and social mood, we go to sea. Innovation and resourcefulness. Adventure and team spirit. With an eye for change, we develop a vision and know-how for sea-maps and sailing gear. Yet, we couple it all with a technical outlook, with maps and means of travel as well as with a poetic vision, open to emotions, to feelings.

Mindful of Antoine de Saint-Exupéry: 'If you want to build a ship, don't gather men to gather wood and distribute tasks, but teach them the nostalgia of the wide and endless sea'.

'Water Is Just Another Road', claims Pirelli's support campaign in its commitment to the America's Cup, since 2017. Go, make a boat, build a team and race. Try and try again, before coming to a victory. And then, start again.

Since the end of the 1940s, Pirelli dinghies, the small Nautilus and then the more demanding Laros, which power short trips between beaches and reefs but can also stand up to the challenge of racing sail the waters. All this happens in Italy, from Milan to Trieste in 1968. Later on also on the challenging ocean waves, with the Celeusta, fitted out well with sails and skippered by Mario Valli, Sergio Croci and Vittorio Macioci, to cross the Pacific in the autumn of 1969, in three months, from Peru to French Polynesia, 4,400 nautical miles of great adventure.

That's it, the passion for regattas. Like those that the Yacht Club Italiano organised in Santa Margherita Ligure with the Pirelli-Coppa Carlo Negri competition. And then with *Luna Rossa Prada Pirelli*: 'We have chosen to be part of this project because it is a challenge, both sporting and technological, that can take Italy and the Pirelli brand all over the world', said Marco Tronchetti Provera, Pirelli's Executive Vice Chairman.

The Sports Workshop — 42

NAZZARO, VAINQUEUR DE LA TARGA FLORIO
Le vainqueur du Grand Prix de l'A. C. F. de 1907 vient d'effectuer sa rentrée dans la Targa Florio. Il remporta la victoire, couvrant les 1.000 kil. en 19 h. 28 m. 40 s. (Pneumatiques Pirelli).

Felice Nazzaro and his navigator aboard the Fiat car fitted with Pneus Pirelli tyres, winner of the 8th Targa Florio, 1913

Piero Taruffi's speed record aboard the Gilera Rondine on the Brescia–Bergamo motorway, 1937, photo Fumagalli

The Sports Workshop

Advertisement for Pirelli
bicycle tyres, 1957

Advertisement for Pirelli tennis
balls, 1950s

New materials, sophisticated high-tech choices, original hull and keel shapes and the foil system that makes the boat sail over the waves like an elegant flying fish. And a crew that knows how to combine diversity and unity, special skills and a prodigious 'all for one' blend. A complex world, before and after the race. A workshop, indeed, of techniques and temperaments.
A workshop is also the yard for *Alla Grande-Pirelli*, the boat with which Ambrogio Beccaria, since last year, race after race, has sailed 'the wide and endless sea' and about which, in the following pages, he writes about himself.
To go to sea, after all, is also to sail within ourselves. To discover ourselves as travellers of enchantment and knowledge. To put ourselves to the test. And finding ourselves, with a scar, a nostalgia, a will to rebuild, a gaze that once again challenges the horizon.
'Free man, you will love the sea' were the favoured verses of Charles Baudelaire by Leopoldo Pirelli, a passionate sailor. And sailing under the pull of the wind is the sport that most enthuses Marco Tronchetti Provera. The sea the colour of wine, when the day comes to an end, prompts confidences and memories. Then, when the sun rises again, you start again.
The restart, indeed. In business and in sport, it's all a restart.
In tennis, with the patent for Pirelli's Super Extra tennis balls, licensed in 1938 by the Italian Federation for official competitions, and then with the P1 and Nox, in the season when the Italian team, led by Adriano Panatta, won the Davis Cup in 1976.
In skiing, with Blossom, the first carve ski, in 2017, with an anti-vibration rubber layer inside and with the sponsorship of the World Championships in Saint-Moritz.

In athletics, with Pirelli's sports facilities being made available to great athletes such as Adolfo Consolini, gold medallist for the discus throw at the 1948 London Olympics, and Teseo Taddia, silver medallist for the hammer throw at the 1950 European Championships in Brussels.
There is one peculiar feature linked to these successes: the Pirelli Group's commitment to invest in sport as a phenomenon of wide participation, both among employees and their children. Sport as welfare and education for participation and the values of competition.
A social and ethical value that is still topical.
There is an overriding question, which we must now come to terms with: why does industry commit energy and resources to sport? Is it only for the communication benefits, since sport remains one of the most conspicuous sides of our lifestyle?
The long vision of a historian such as Giuseppe Berta provides evidence of the pioneering link between a large company, Pirelli, the forerunner of Italian industrial development, and sport, when this relationship was at an avant-garde frontier: 'Industry acts as a forerunner of modernity, involving sport because it perceives the elements of affinity and contiguity'.
Then, when the production system permeates, as a leading player in economic and social development a large part of society, it then finds 'in the mass manifestations of sport an obvious counterbalance'.
Now, when industry is no longer the regulating element of social life, does industry face the consequences of the globalisation of production cycles and markets, when it is no longer a phenomenon of mass presence while retaining in Italy, an extraordinary productive relevance?

The Sports Workshop

European Rowing Championships, Lake Malta in Poznan, Poland, 1958

Has sport become a complex and sophisticated world, marked by the consequences of all aspects of show business? 'Sport and leisure define themselves as central constituents of our age. Like in the past and more than in the past, they attract and urge the ability to innovate, creativity and the will to experiment. All this, with the drive towards new records, prestigious results, increasingly impressive performances of excellence, which require delicate organisational procedures, sporting activities continue to be a horizon for the industry to measure itself against'.

The values that guide contemporary sport, according to Berta, 'are the same values that permeate today's economic action. The ability to work as a team, the search for competitive quality that results in a test of excellence, the drive to bring out and reward talent, are conditions for success in sport as in today's industry'. This, then, is why sport is 'an important constituent of the lifestyle that all complex organisations have to deal with'. And, precisely in the Italian context, 'it is also an indicator of a collective and individual taste and sensitivity, which that core of the business economy that is most rooted in the history and civilisation of our territory cannot do without. Sports involvement holds symbolic and communication values that are anything but extraneous or extrinsic to forms of enterprise driven, in a renewed way, to seek harmony with social change and collective orientations'.

We are living through seasons of great changes, both economic and social and of crises in the conventional relationships between political structures, welfare systems and market economies. These are actual productive metamorphoses, in the environmental and digital transition that recombines production and products, customs and consumption.

But it is precisely the assertion of the special characteristics of the so-called 'knowledge economy', accelerated by the critical deployment of all aspects of artificial intelligence, and the spread of the values of social and environmental sustainability, not only as an ethical dimension but also as a real competitive advantage of the most attentive and sensitive companies, that are forcing new choices on economic and political actors and on the target audiences, i.e. the citizens.

Pirelli for Sport

Young & Rubicam, Ronaldo in the advertisement for the Pirelli P3000 tyre, 1998, photo Ken Griffiths

Young & Rubicam, Marie-José Pérec in the advertisement for the Pirelli P6000 tyre, 1997

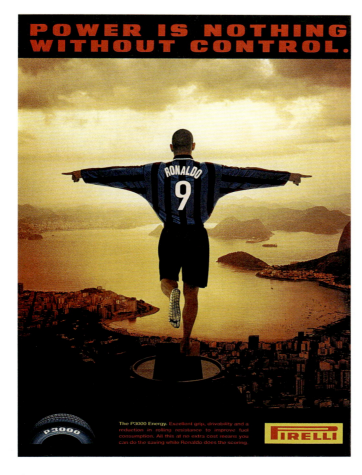

We are moving, in economics, from the primacy of shareholder value (accumulating profits and increasing stock market values for shareholders, as corporate responsibility) to that of stakeholder values, the interests and values of the communities and territories on which the enterprise is based, of citizens, employees, consumers and suppliers. These are all economic values, linked to wellbeing and therefore welfare, also in corporate terms as well as social and moral values, according to the standards of a sustainable, circular, civil economy.

The relationship between business and sport must be inscribed in this new paradigm shift. Hence, we need to emphasise the aspects of sporting activity as opportunities for fair and well-regulated competition, dialogue, cultural and civil exchange.

Sport means knowledge, acceptance of the other's vision, reading the world outside provincial and nationalistic schemes, inclusion.

Sport means involvement, as well as the pride of supremacy of victory.

Sport means a set of moral and civilised values, essential precisely in times of raging conflicts and dramatic imbalances.

Sport is an especially important measure precisely at a time in history when, thinking about the power of artificial intelligence and the difficult and controversial control over its evolution and applications, we fear the absolute dominance of technology and the ghosts feared by Martin Heidegger seem to be taking shape.

Sport is humanism and technique, no matter how sophisticated, cannot win over intelligence, will, strength of character and the very poetic spirit of sporting endeavour.

The Sports Workshop, which we are describing here, is the place where all this is held together in the horizon of the growth of knowledge and community spirit and is the venue of a new humanism that, from industrial and digital, takes on its historical connotations of societal culture once again.

Carl Lewis' red shoes and that catchphrase about the essential relationship between power and control continue to have an extraordinarily intense relevance.

TRAINING THOUGHTS

The Sports Workshop — 52

by Joe R. Lansdale
-
Writer

Batman's Punch is a Guide to Life

True practitioners of martial arts learn to understand they are anything but powerful. Actions are a balance, a kind of meditation in movement

Training Thoughts

One step at a time, one punch at a time, one round at a time.
— *Rocky Balboa*, directed by Sylvester Stallone, 2006

Batman threw the first punch. He performed the first throw. I think Robin may have tripped me, and Bathound may have bit me. Can't say I minded much. Batman started something that is still part of my life and hopefully will be until they carry me out on a board, wearing my favorite blue jean jacket with the outline of Batman's cowl on the back. Mask-rimmed eyes looking out over Gotham City. Batman's punches and throws, Robin's trip and Bathound's bite were metaphorical. Their impact was not.

Here's how the sneaky bat devil did it to me.

As a child I was fascinated with Batman. I couldn't be Superman. I didn't come from another planet where our planet's sun gave me super powers. I didn't have an alien power ring like Green Lantern, and I wasn't a good enough swimmer to be Aquaman. Running fast as the Flash would wear out a lot of tennis shoes. Wonder Woman, was, well, a woman. And so on.

But Batman, he didn't have super powers. What he was, was a curious guy. Studied everything and knew everything. Sherlock Holmes in a cape.

Chemistry. He aced it. He knew about insects, fingerprints, astronomy, geology. He could note the differences in one kind of dirt from another at a glance.

I truly wanted to be like Batman. He caused me to expand my interests. The problem was, when it came to chemistry, with my kid's chemistry set, I could only turn water blue, purple on a good day. Once I mixed outside ingredients into my chemistry set, which it instructed me not to do, and caused a fire. I had an insect collection, which was a bunch of sad-looking bugs pinned to a board after being killed in a killing jar containing a cotton wad soaked in alcohol. Beneath each of them I had little signs with pithy information written on them. Moth. Butterfly. Spider. Grasshopper. Cricket. Daddy Long Legs. June Bug. And so on.

I collected minerals. Or tried to. A lot of rocks looked alike to me, and if dirt wasn't boldly a different color, I couldn't tell one kind of soil from another. It all looked like dirt.

I could identify a few constellations, but was never able to straighten out the difference in the Big Dipper and the Big Bear.

My curiosity was strong in all those areas, but the depth of my understanding sucked.

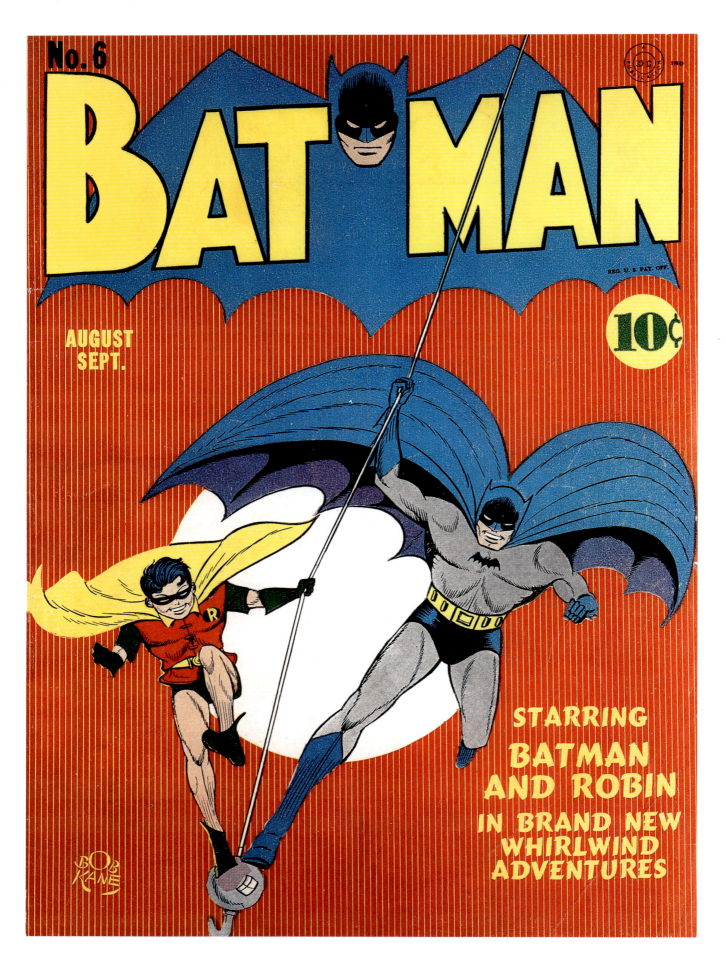

Batman, no. 6, 1941, Christie's Images Limited

Batman was also a master of the martial arts. He was always flipping some villain or another over his shoulder, throwing a right cross to their chins, using a variety of martial techniques from an assortment of systems to conquer the bad guys. These were human skills. I decided to keep the curiosity about all manner of things, but to focus on something I might be able to do. Martial arts.

his prowess as a fighter I was unaware of. When I was eleven years old, and wanting to learn self-defense, I went to my mother and asked if I could study Judo or Karate. She didn't know of any place that taught such things, but she said: 'You know, your dad boxed and wrestled for money, and he knows a lot of things about self-defense. I've seen him in action a few times. You should ask him'.

Batman's punches and throws, Robin's trip and Bathound's bite were metaphorical. Their impact was not. Here's how the sneaky bat devil did it to me

My father, Bud Lansdale, was illiterate. He was a hard worker and a mechanic. He became a mechanic by taking an old car my mother bought him apart, and then putting it back together again. Before long, he was aces at the work and he loved it.
Bud liked boxing, and he would lie on the floor and watch it on TV. I would lie down in front of him and we would watch. He would explain the punches, the foot work, body positioning, the rules and so on. I didn't ask for that, but he told me anyway. Fortunately, I enjoyed the information.
It's odd that when I truly wanted to learn something about self-defense, I didn't think of my father who I had seen snap belts wrapped around his chest by taking in a deep breath of air, or squash an apple in either of his thick hands. I knew he was strong, but

Dad was the right guy to ask. He was in his fifties then, or close to it, starting to wind down physically, but he had done a bit of boxing and wrestling in carnivals for money. He often won his bouts. He had used what he knew in a few real-life situations. I had at this point seen one of those, when I was much younger, but had never thought of him as a hand-to-hand teacher. He was just dad.
Fact was, he had developed a reputation that I had totally missed knowing about.
He also grew up in a tough environment. He went to work in the fields when he was eight, and worked grown men's jobs picking cotton, plowing, etc. Think about it. My father was born in 1909, a year before Mark Twain died. Wyatt Earp was still alive. As was Bat Masterson and Annie Oakley. Cars and electricity

Portrait of Mark Twain, from *L'Illustrazione Italiana*, year XXXVII, no. 18 bis, 1 May 1910, Biblioteca Ambrosiana, Milan

Elvis Presley, *Elvis: That's the Way It Is*, 1970

were still considered new. Airplanes were in their infancy. Indoor plumbing in the rural parts of the country were rarer than hen's teeth. A different world. Later, he went through the Great Depression, but fortunately, could always find work. He supported his family, which consisted of my brother John and my mother, O'Reta. Nearly seventeen years later, I was added to the family.
My mother had thought she was long past child-bearing age.
Surprise!
This meant my brother was grown and out of the house when I was a baby. He married in his teens, and is still married to the same woman, who graduated high school with Elvis Presley in Memphis, Tennessee. That's another story.
As for learning to protect myself, even when I was young, a disagreement could often be settled with straight talk, and if not, it wasn't uncommon to settle grievances by fisticuffs.

Teeth could be lost, bones could be broken, but mostly you just got a black eye, or gave one. Perhaps there was a bloody or broken nose, or you might end up temporarily unconscious, face down in a pool of blood, out back of the grade school with a shoe missing and two of your teeth in a mud puddle. People shot people less, and the guns they used weren't designed to kill every human being in a shopping mall. There weren't any shopping malls. Self-defense was a skill worth knowing.
Turned out my dad was knowledgeable, but a terrible teacher. This was partly due to he worked long, tough hours for a trucking company. A trouble shooter who went out to repair broken down trucks, wherever they were. There were occasions, my mother told me, when he had jobs where he worked under trucks in the cold, and would come home with icicles in his hair.
Tough was Bud Lansdale's middle name.
Dad did decide to teach me. He had no idea he had

awakened a dragon. I loved it. He taught me when he could. No formal classes. Little sessions here and there. After work, when his hours were reasonable. Even then, he was often exhausted.

He taught me the basics of boxing and wrestling, as well as jujitsu tricks he had picked up. What he taught me mostly was the difference between a school yard fight and a real fight. He taught me confidence.

Being a good martial arts student I developed greater confidence. I felt I could accomplish whatever I wanted

I'm sure he was elated when I discovered, while taking lifeguard classes for a Boy Scout merit badge at the Tyler, Texas YMCA, that they taught judo there. It let me continue to study martial arts, and it gave him a deserved break.

Judo became my new passion. Over time, other martial arts showed up at the YMCA. There was a junior college in Tyler, and new people were constantly passing through, a few of them with martial skills, and the YMCA provided teachers of the arts as well as a place to train.

Then, all of a sudden, there was an explosion of martial arts. There was judo, hapkido, tae kwon do, a bit of thai boxing, an introduction to yudo, which was Korean judo, a maverick form of kenpo, as well as different systems of karate; they were all on the menu at least for a while.

I studied martial arts because they were fascinating and because I wanted to learn self-defense. I wasn't plagued by bullies, but they existed, and I loathed them. If they did show up in my life, I wanted to be ready.

They did eventually show up. I was already by nature the kind of person that would fight to the death, but just not well. At least not until I trained in self-defense. In short time, at school, it was understood not to bother me. If you did, you might end up with a knot on your head. For me, early on, this was all martial arts was about. Protecting yourself.

But things changed.

Being a good martial arts student, I developed greater confidence. I felt I could accomplish whatever I wanted, even things outside of martial arts. This, of course, may have been a myth, but it was a concept that I could and did embrace.

As the years rolled on, I was able to study other arts beyond my YMCA introduction. I spent hours a week on all manner of techniques. I began to learn greater life lessons as well.

It taught me greater patience, though I still would not be considered a patient man. But as far as writing and martial arts were concerned, I could compartmentalize and find my zone.

In times of personal stress, financial dips, sickness

in the family, losing parents, this ability to compartmentalize, was a life saver. Instead of going through all the stages of grief, I went from the first to the last. It was an application of economy of motion. A fundamental element of martial arts training.
I learned to stick to whatever I was doing, and not have the false attitude I had mastered anything. In martial arts, you are always a student. You may receive a black belt, be given the title of master

I spent hours a week on all manner of techniques. I began to learn greater life lessons as well

or grandmaster, but in truth, you have only learned more than you knew before. There is still so much more to learn. It's that way in life as well. It's the wise person who realizes this, because now they have an opportunity to become wiser.
Instead of teaching you that you are invincible, a real martial artist learns you are anything but all powerful. You can be hurt, and worse, you can hurt someone unnecessarily. You have to be able to instantly measure a situation and come to a solution, and live with your choices.
That's a sort of guide for life in general. Trying not hurt anyone, making choices, and living with them.

As the years have gone by, the actions of the martial arts have become a kind of moving meditation.
In the system I practice, which I founded some years ago, based on all my years of studying martial arts, I practice the moves and teach. It clears the head. It keeps the body flexible, improves endurance and balance.
Balance in martial arts is essential, as it is in life. And not merely physical balance. Life balance. Moderation.
As I move into old age, I continue to practice, and as certain physical abilities slip away from me, I alter my techniques, my mind set, to fit what will accommodate bad shoulders, a slipped hip, strained back, shoulders that have been dislocated numerous times, etc. Martial arts have been good to me, but intense practice has taken a toll.
That toll teaches another important lesson. You are not invulnerable and you are not forever, and neither are those you love. All things are born, live, and die. Martial arts give me the courage to accept and adapt. Even with the injuries, I'd do it all over again. It took some things away from me, but it gave me so many others that are much more important.
Practice keeps me in touch with my father who first introduced me to martial arts. It keeps me in touch with my various instructors. It keeps me in touch with pain and pleasure, the sorts of things life deals you. It's important to understand pain may not be craved, but it is often received. As I always say, 'Life is just full of little disappointments'.
Allowing whoever you are training with to throw you, and you to throw them, to spar them,

Training Thoughts — 59

A moment of the fight between Cassius Clay and Joe Frazier, New York, Madison Square Garden, 8 March 1971

The judo section of the Pirelli Sports Group, 1950s

Training Thoughts

Karate in Tokio, 1958,
Münchner Stadtmuseum,
Munich

to practice a variety of techniques, teaches you to deal with adversity as well as learning to cooperate. As a martial artist, you have a lot more fails than successes before the successes increase. That's an important life lesson. Tenacity. Sweet and sour, pepper and salt. The smoothness

In life, take the gliding step, go with the pull, go with the push, control balance, be in the moment

of technique, when your opponent seems weightless, or you fly through the air knowing you have the knowledge of how to fall correctly is an important skill. You have to learn how to get under the weight of life's disappointments. How to fall and roll with them. How to get up again. It's about not letting disappointment drown you. Kick your legs, move your arms, swim back up to the surface until it becomes an impossibility and your life passes, well lived and well-intended.

One of the great things about the martial arts, is changing people's lives as an instructor. It starts out to be about self-defense, but for those who stick with it, it turns into a lifestyle not only for you, but for them as well.

I frequently receive calls from students, some who didn't acquire a blackbelt, or trained only for a short time, who tell me how much better their lives are for studying the arts with me.

Other students who moved away, are now studying other arts. They've retained their love for learning, and have stayed curious, which is another aspect of the art. Curiosity. The very thing Batman had and inspired me with. A thirst for knowledge. A student for life.

There are a lot of different martial arts, but in my view, there is only one true art. Martial art. They may have different flavors, like different kinds of tasty soups or stews. Yet, they have common ingredients. It's the spices of environment and personality that give them different flavors.

Not everyone profits from its study, but those that do often have better lives. For me, martial arts are at the core of my accomplishments, minor as they may be in the greater scheme of things.

In life, take the gliding step, go with the pull, go with the push, control balance, be in the moment. Batman threw the first punch. I'm glad it hit me.

STORIES OF OUR ACHIEVEMENTS

The Sports Workshop

by Mario Isola
-
Pirelli Motorsport Director

What a Team, Behind a Driver in the Race

A team that takes care of every detail, from car development to logistics, from the workshop to managing the pit stops. The new tools of virtual design

They could never have imagined it, those pioneers who invented the automobile, that it would possess us like this, in our imaginations, in our dreams.

— *Rush*, directed by Peter Morgan, 2013

Yes, it is true. The Formula 1 driver is alone in his car, but how big is the 'team' behind him? A team that takes care of every detail, from the engineers who develop the car to those in charge of the logistics and the others who manage the pit stops. Pirelli supplies tyres to all the Formula 1 teams, but the work with the teams is only a small part of the process in which we are involved. The R&D department designs a new product starting with virtual design, i.e., the creation of a virtual tyre model that is used by all the constructors before starting the phase of making physical prototypes. These are then tested on the track by the teams and drivers who race in the World Championship. We share all information with them and they receive from us, in the first instance, the same data and the same virtual model, which is then refined on the basis of the feedback collected. If we think that this happens not only for Formula 1, but for over two hundred motorsport championships around the world, we can understand that those fifty or so professionals we see on the track at race time are the tip of the iceberg. Just one example: the new car that will debut in the Ferrari Challenge 2024.

Here again, we initially shared a tyre sample that was 'fitted' on a virtual car before starting to make the first adjustments, in order to validate the final product on the track. The process described is one that applies today to the development of any tyre, including original equipment tyres for on-road cars. The difference is that the time available to develop a new product for Formula 1 is less than half, if not a third, of that for road products. In the near future, we will be ready for a new challenge: that of the transition—we are still talking about Formula 1—from 18-inch to 16-inch rims, a development planned for 2026.

One wonders why this downsizing has taken place: the aim is to reduce the mass of the car, making it easier to handle. This weight has certainly increased over the years due to the wheel assembly (tyre, rim, suspension), but also to safety equipment, such as the halo, which protects the driver's head, and the introduction of the hybrid engine, which is heavier due to the batteries.

It is a known fact that since 2005 the minimum weight of a single-seater has risen from 600 to around 800 kilograms. Too much to maintain the agility the drivers need.

To this we have to add the sport's increased focus on sustainability: less rubber obviously means less material in tyre design and production. The issue of sustainability, with regard to Formula 1 and motor racing in general, is a complex and sensitive one. Yet, it is a journey to be made, and it is a journey that involves all of Pirelli's partners. Since 2014 the cars have been fitted with extraordinarily efficient hybrid power units, and from 2026 the fuels will also have to be

In view of new regulations that will study how to reduce the number of tyres used in the race, we have implemented a process that allows us to reuse intermediate or wet tyres, obviously avoiding bead damage in the disassembly and reassembly operation. These are tricks that won't change the world but have their own value: the separate collection of waste materials on the track, the use by us of clothing and shoes made from recycled material,

The issue of sustainability, with regard to Formula 1 and motor racing in general, is a complex and sensitive one. Yet, it is a journey to be made, and it is a journey that involves all of Pirelli's partners

sustainable. For sure, we are not in the pure electric of Formula E, but this choice has been made to ensure Formula 1 maintains its original nature. Because it is obvious that the 'entertainment' factor cannot be deleted, the appeal and identity of Formula 1 itself would suffer. Pirelli has, however, started with an advantage in this race for sustainability. Just think of our tyre factories, which are so far ahead in the process of environmental compliance that they have allowed us to obtain FIA three-star certification for the Environmental Accreditation Program.
Then, the decision to prefer transport by sea over air, as ships produce much less carbon dioxide.

the agreement with local bodies and organisations to redistribute unconsumed catering food. Formula 1 itself is planning to design a calendar that reduces the movement of materials and people as much as possible: it is a long journey, but the one towards sustainability in Formula 1 has begun and promises great results. The rest is up to us in the industry, meaning those of us who arrive at the track on Thursday mornings, if not on Wednesday evenings. I am often asked: 'But what do you do until the Sunday?'. Paradoxically, when the green light comes on at the start of the Grand Prix most of our work has been done. But before that, in those three days

The start of the race during the Formula 1 Pirelli Gran Premio d'Italia 2023, photo Motorsport Images

The Sports Workshop — 70

Sébastian Ogier and Vincent
Landais' Toyota Gazoo
Racing at the 20th Rally Italia
Sardegna, 2023

beforehand, can you guess how much work there was?

Briefings with all the engineers in the teams, first of all. We are sole-suppliers of tyres, so we have to guarantee everyone not only the same product, but above all the same service: each team has its own dedicated engineer, as well as at least one technician, who ensure that the product is used correctly, while collecting data that will then allow the team to maximise its performance. The Pirelli with the allocation assigned by the FIA, defined by a bar code that associates each tyre with the rim supplied by the team and ensures that the product we supply is the same for everyone.

We have to work fast, because you have about a day and a half of work at this stage, but not in a hurry: you can never make a mistake out of haste. For us it is imperative to have no problems. On Friday, the test sessions begin. For the engineers on the track there are the tyres to be measured, analysed, sent

Technology is a great help: each car has sensors that feed more than a hundred telemetry channels and that each team provides to us before, during and after each race

engineer is usually assigned to the team for no more than two years, in order to support all teams in compliance with the procedures established by the manufacturer Pirelli. It's not an intrusion; it's an advantage we offer the teams. And they appreciate it. Scheduled briefings at the start of a race are often virtual meetings: data from the previous year are analysed and forecasts for the current year are discussed, in order to make the best choices during the race. The fitting area—with the tyre fitters—gets underway. There are around one thousand eight hundred tyres to be mounted on the rim, as each team has one hundred and sixty available. Our twenty fitters mount the tyres, taking care to comply to our mobile laboratory in the paddock. It happens, for example, that we have to deal with unforeseen problems, as in the case of the 2023 Qatar Grand Prix where the tyres hitting the kerbs caused dangerous micro-detachments of the rubber from the tyre sidewall. Fortunately, thanks to the computerised analysis and measurement systems that we developed and shared with all the teams, we were able to anticipate the problem, identify the correct solution and allow the race to take place while guaranteeing the integrity of the tyre. Here again, technology is a great help: each car has sensors that feed more than a hundred telemetry channels and that each team provides to us before, during and

The Sports Workshop — 72

A Pirelli engineer at work in
Monza during the Formula 1
Pirelli Gran Premio d'Italia
2023, photo Motorsport
Images

Stories of Our Achievements — 73

Pirelli technicians at work
in Mexico City during the
Formula 1 Gran Premio de la
Ciudad de México 2023, photo
Motorsport Images

A Pirelli engineer during the
November 2022 test days at
Yas Marina Circuit, photo
Motorsport Images

after each race. Thanks to this data, and comparing it with the simulations provided by the teams, we are able to define a series of parameters that must always be complied with when the cars go on track. The Friday before the race is a 'never-ending' day: I personally spend the weekend's sessions in the Pirelli Operations Centre located inside the hospitality area, in radio contact with engineers and technicians who update me after each pit stop, and assessing information on tyre wear and condition, as well as any safety warnings. Anything relevant is immediately reported to the teams, with the chief engineer starting his tour of the teams' garages. Much more data is given to the press and guests. Perhaps we talk about a complicated sport like rallying? Here you need even more versatility: you have to deal with snow, tarmac and gravel. What about grand touring, where tyres have to endure non-stop stress for hours on end, on cars that are closely derived from series production? Perhaps the most evocative race in this discipline is the 24 Hours of Spa, where we carry more than twelve thousand tyres, with about a hundred fitters on duty.
2004, I followed the development of the P Zero tyres for the Maserati MC12, fitted by Pirelli which eventually won the GT Championship the following year. Perhaps it was just a matter of insight.
Or perhaps a matter of fellowship. Or passion.

Perhaps the two hours of racing on Sunday are the quietest in the entire weekend: what needs to be done has been done

the two hours of racing on Sunday are the quietest in the entire weekend: what needs to be done has been done. Our work is done well if nothing happens, if the race was exciting, with overtaking and different strategies.
So far I've only talked about Formula 1. But we at Pirelli follow over two hundred championships on four wheels, a whole universe of motorsport. Shall

The Sports Workshop

by Ambrogio Beccaria
-
Offshore sailor

The Energy of Research and the Wind in the Sails

'To realise how good you can feel at sea, to the point of becoming part of it'. The design team and study of the weather to 'always know where I want to go'

In these places by the sea
With this sky above the sea
When the wind warms the sea in its time.

— Ivano Fossati, *Questi posti davanti al mare*, 1988

Like all sports involving machines —think of car racing or motorcycling—offshore sailing is closely bound up with design, development and research. Building a boat compels one to look for a broad range of solutions and find ways to gain an edge. Competitors are forced to innovate. The *Alla Grande-Pirelli* project has an extremely innovative scope, with a soul one hundred percent Italian. The start-up grew out of the meeting with the yacht designer Gianluca Guelfi in 2017 in La Rochelle, France, where he had moved to work in the studio of Marc Lombard, one of the architects who are the gurus of offshore sailing north of the Alps. I was also in La Rochelle to work on the boat I was going to sail in my first Mini Transat. From then on we cherished the plan to build an Italian Class40. After the pandemic we found ourselves motivated as never before to try to make our dream come true, together with another designer, Fabio D'Angeli. Equally crucial was the meeting with Edoardo Bianchi, who came from his experience working at the Persico shipyard and had recently opened his brand new Sangiorgio Marine shipyard in Genoa. Then Pirelli acted as the cement holding everything together. I immediately realised that we would work well as a team. We all believed in it and shared the same goals.

Offshore sailing calls for complex research, and the technique of the individual sailor counts for a lot. A boat, however good, is not necessarily the best for everyone. It depends on the skipper's preferences, which is why it is essential for the skipper to be part of the design team during trials to choose the most suitable craft. Innovation for its own sake is a two-edged sword; it can be a strength or a form of weakness. By innovating, you run a certain amount of risk, and it is not clear whether the immediate result will be the most efficient.

My role in the design of the boat was mainly as a motivator and consultant. Underlying everything was a very long-term effort, with Gianluca Guelfi and Fabio D'Angeli fine-tuning the project. We created *Alla Grande-Pirelli* trusting not just the numbers but also my experience as a navigator in Class40. By integrating mathematical models, virtual simulations and principles of fluid dynamics with my personal experience and sensibility as a navigator, we tried as far as possible to reduce the margin of error. Of course, personal experience

The Sports Workshop

Alla Grande-Pirelli, the boatyard, 2022, photo Martina Orsini

Ambrogio Beccaria at the *Alla Grande-Pirelli* boatyard, 2022, photo Martina Orsini

is also crucial in research into the ergonomics on board. With *Alla Grande-Pirelli* we did something different from all the other competitors: we designed the whole system around the way I sail. Just look at the cockpit, which is very different from the arrangement on other boats, perhaps rather minimalist, but certainly well protected.

The *Alla Grande-Pirelli* project has an extremely innovative scope, with a soul one hundred percent Italian

Paolo Dessì's consultancy on the structural part was also important. It was essential to keep the aerodynamic factor in the foreground, as well as the collaboration with North Sails Italia and the engineer Michele Malandra. This enabled us to keep adjusting our aim and ensure the hull would coexist with the sails immediately, without needing to install the sails on an existing hull. In this way, we avoided designing a beautiful boat with the wrong set-up. In practice, Gianluca and Fabio designed a hull a day and ran the fluid dynamic models to understand the hull resistance. It took many hours of calculations. We analysed the numbers by combining them with what I had tested at sea, with my experience in terms of trim and rudder angle. Today we are in phase two, which involves optimising the craft, a task that is truly never-ending. Each time you have to work on new details, trying to find less resistance to movement, more ease of control. I have now sailed for more than a year and a half aboard *Alla Grande-Pirelli* and I have learned to be inspired by the other members of the shore team, with their ideas and suggestions.

At the boatyard we have been in close contact with Bernardo Zin—who is responsible for management, organisation and planning—and Bastian Oger, the trainer. With them it is a real team effort: we start with the job list; then we move on to fabricate new pieces in composite materials and work on the ropes to optimise the manoeuvres. Finally there are discussions with the suppliers, to improve the various systems of the boat: solar panels, reliability of the alternator to avoid blackouts and satellite antennas. There are always fruitful exchanges with all the partners. Regattas are prepared as a team. The *Alla Grande-Pirelli* team includes Bianca Bertolini, who is in charge of logistics and organisation, and Valentina Pigmei, the head of communication. Her work is essential: communication, the ability to feed interesting content to the media, is one of the fundamental assets of the project. Valentina protects me from media overexposure, which is a lot of stress.

The last competition I took part in and won last November, the Transat Jacques Vabre, also known as the Route du Café, was a double regatta. With my co-skipper Nicolas Andrieu we also worked together on land, preparing the boat for the race: from the bags to be carried on board to the supplies needed to survive the eighteen days of racing, safety material in case of personal or structural problems and

The Sports Workshop

Class40 *Alla Grande-Pirelli*
ready for launching, 2022,
photo Martina Orsini

Stories of Our Achievements — 81

Class40 *Alla Grande-Pirelli*,
Martinique, 2023, photo
Martina Orsini

The Sports Workshop — 82

Class40 *Alla Grande-Pirelli*,
Ambrogio Beccaria, Transat
Jacques Vabre, 2023, photo
Martina Orsini

the tools and instruments we would need for maintenance. The boat has always to be one hundred percent efficient. When you're sailing, every day is different. It depends on how and where you are, what the light is like, the conditions at sea, whether it's calm or rough. And whether there's a bank of seaweed or a strong current to struggle against, or rocks to avoid if you're sailing close to the coast. The day also changes depending on which part of the ocean you're sailing in. If you're sailing solo, you'll have twenty- or thirty-minute catnaps. If there are we know that we're going to encounter extreme conditions. This is where the question of challenging yourself comes out. Personally I've never considered it a motivation. On the contrary I think of sailing as a way to try to get to know yourself, rather than a challenge. Trying to understand how far you can feel good at sea, to the point of becoming a part of it. For me, this is the real motivation to do things that would seem insurmountable, like facing a storm or skimming across the waves at twenty-five knots. Whenever I think about it, I get gooseflesh, but then

At times, like everyone else who practises the sport of offshore sailing, I wonder why I live this life. It always happens before the start of a race

two of you or a crew, you can sleep a little longer and work shifts with the co-skipper. With Nicolas, for example, we did two-hour stints, during which we had to work the winches, adjust the weights and check the sails. In the case of demanding manoeuvres, of course you have to wake the co-skipper. Then you have to analyse everything on the computer, assessing the strategic plans, both long-term and short. We always do this together, because, as I see it, two people think better.

At times, like everyone else who practises the sport of offshore sailing, I wonder why I live this life. It always happens before the start of a race, when at sea I'm transformed. I try to connect with the world around me. I analyse the clouds, study the currents and plan the rest times. All things that have to be balanced against each other. I don't try to set myself challenges, because it could push me into making mistakes. Instead I try to use my energies sparingly, keep in touch with my rational side, and always know where I want to go. Fear is always lurking, of course, and it plays a key role, but you have to ration your fear, to know when it's good to stop and set limits. It seems paradoxical, but in reality, a storm sometimes puts you at ease. When you're sailing, you know that a problem can always arise, and

The Sports Workshop — 84

Class40 *Alla Grande-Pirelli*, Ambrogio Beccaria and Nicolas Andrieu, Transat Jacques Vabre, 2023, photo Martina Orsini

Stories of Our Achievements

Class40 *Alla Grande-Pirelli*,
Transat Jacques Vabre, 2023,
photo Martina Orsini

The Sports Workshop — 86

The boat-building team of the
Class40 *Alla Grande-Pirelli*,
2022, photo Martina Orsini

for this very reason you need to keep calm, serene and focused. On the other hand, it's the moments of calm that are deceptive. You tend to underestimate things and you can easily be caught off guard. We play at being creatures that understand the sea, the clouds, the currents, in a way verging on magic. We have to predict what the future will be like. In regattas we sometimes meet with very violent done, he filled me with the urge to discover the life of the ocean, and with his advice and encouragement he gave me the means to understand how to cope with it. My other great teacher was the sea. It teaches you to harbour your resources, face your fears and accept failures as part of a journey. In the words of Nelson Mandela: 'I never lose. I either win, or I learn'.

We play at being creatures that understand the sea, the clouds, the currents, in a way verging on magic. We have to predict what the future will be like

weather, but we have to be sure we only accept the risks that we can really face. Danger sets a limit. One step further and it's no longer a game. And you can't play with nature.

In 2020 I was awarded the Ambrogino d'Oro, presented to other yachtsmen in the past, such as Giovanni Soldini in 1996 and Ambrogio Fogar in 2005. The award forms an even closer bond to Milan, my city. Giovanni was the person who inspired me to live this life with his book *Nel blu*. I was in high school and I knew little about sailing. I never imagined it would become my life, too. That book introduced me to a way of life that I didn't think was possible at the time. And even after that, Giovanni was always willing to help me. He was doubly inspirational. By his story and the incredible things he'd

The Sports Workshop

by Daniele Pirola
-
Writer and former researcher
at the Pirelli Historical Archives

Those Sports Fields Next to the Factory

Gyms and race tracks as ways of fostering welfare and community values in the history of Bicocca. Consolini's Olympic gold medal

*One fine day, as he was talking to himself,
He saw her passing by,
White and red, looking like the tricolour flag.
And then he couldn't talk anymore.
He wore tennis shoes, and talked to himself,
Long cherishing a beautiful dream of love.*

— Enzo Jannacci, *El portava i scarp del tennis*, 1964

On Sunday 17 June 1923, the big multi-sports meeting at the Bicocca was somewhat of a naming day for the newly formed Pirelli Sport Club, which had been officially established only a few months earlier. Cavalier Venosta, who had recently been appointed central director of the rubber sector, had been elected president of the club. The vice-president was Giuseppe Vigorelli, also awarded the title of Cavaliere and director of the Lombardy agency Gomme Pirelli. A few years later, he would create the eponymous velodrome in the heart of Milan. The club's honorary president was unanimously elected Commendatore Emilio Calcagni, who, after a lifetime in the company alongside the founder Giovanni Battista Pirelli, had retired while continuing to be involved in sport, as a 'fervent supporter of all forms of physical and moral education'. Under the title *L'adunata sportiva*, the story of the first company sports event at Bicocca is documented in the *Sport Club Pirelli* bulletin, preserved in the Pirelli Historical Archives.

The promotion of sport was a powerful means in the framework of what today we would call corporate welfare, and this was well known by the enlightened entrepreneurs of the early twentieth century. The old model of the exploitation of the workforce that had been a feature of the rise of the Industrial Revolution was by then completely unsustainable, and it was clear that that same workforce was a capital to be valued and preserved both in spirit and in body. Pirelli, in this respect, had been in the vanguard for several years. In the large spaces that the new Bicocca site—opened in 1909 in the area north-east of Milan—had made available over a twenty-year period, the company had gradually built up a network of services for its employees: first and foremost, the Borgo Pirelli cottages, built pursuant to a series of agreements with the Istituto Autonomo Case Popolari and financed by Pirelli to offer employees subsidised rentals and sales. Then, the kindergarten, the school and the Greco railway station, followed by the theatre and the library. Architect Ambrogio Annoni also designed the church next to the fifteenth-century Bicocca degli Arcimboldi on Viale Sarca.

Of course, there were sporting facilities for the 'Pirellians', also due to the historical period, physical fitness was promoted as a source of wellbeing for youth. Thus began the construction—on the other side of Viale Sarca, opposite the plant—of athletics and

Stories of Our Achievements

The football section of the Pirelli Sports Group, 1950s

Archery in the Milano Bicocca sports field, 1950s

The rugby section of the Pirelli Sports Group, 1950s

football pitches, gradually equipped with changing rooms and stands and modern infrastructure. The opening of the Pirelli Sport Club, on the company's 50th anniversary and in collaboration with the legendary sports club Pro Patria 1883, was the ultimate recognition of sport as a corporate value.
Not a casual focus, however. Rather the result of a solid family culture: Piero Pirelli, eldest son of the founder Giovanni Battista, had been chairman of the Milan Cricket and Football Club since 1909, and would remain so for twenty years because he was re-elected by acclamation. It was he who brought the Turin-born Vittorio Pozzo onto the Rossoneri bench, through the intermediary of Ragionier Wilmant, a trusted man of the Presidency but also a team manager: 'I have known Vittorio Pozzo for many years and I regard him as well-read and an expert in commercial matters. He must have a perfect knowledge of at least four languages… He is also involved in journalism, contributing to the Turin newspaper *La Stampa*…', Wilmant wrote to Piero Pirelli in 1924. So, Pozzo received, in addition to the position of coach, also that of advertising manager of the Rubber Sector, which in those days was called propaganda. Sport and work were not meant to be separate at Pirelli. Then history took its course, and Pozzo headed for the glory of the 1934 and 1938 World Cups, the only coach in the history of the Italian national team to win two consecutive world championships.
The sports buff Piero Pirelli was also responsible for construction of San Siro Stadium. Legend has it that the family governess was fed up with those sweaty footballers who, from the Simplon velodrome where they played at the time, came to shower and change in the master's bathroom.

It goes without saying that the company's organisation of skiing days on the snows of Mottarone was also part of the 'welfare package', just as the dense network of holiday camps between the sea, mountains and countryside cheered up the summer of the employees' children.
Inaugurated in the 1920s, the Bicocca sports facilities had their second renaissance in the 1950s. In the post-war period, given the shortage of public facilities, these premises adjacent to the plant gave the many young people employed by the company the chance to play sports. Among these young Pirellians was a young Adolfo Consolini, who joined Pirelli in 1948 from the Veronese countryside. An employee of A.G.A. Articoli Gomma e Affini with the title of 'producer', Consolini travelled around Milan on a scooter offering various rubber articles such as car mats, household goods and toys to shopkeepers.
At five in the afternoon, he was invariably at the sports ground in Viale Sarca, for his regular training session. Because the rubber goods salesman was also an Olympic gold medallist in the discus throw, won in London in 1948. The Pirelli inscription on Consolini's shirt probably remains the icon of the corporate sports welfare concept. A world record holder, Consolini took part in three more Olympic Games, winning silver in Helsinki in 1952. Then Melbourne in 1956 and Rome in 1960 were the honourable end-of-career passes for one of Italy's greatest and best-loved athletes. A champion, like his colleague Teseo Taddia, a specialist in the hammer throw, with a result of 54.73 metres at the Brussels European Championships that earned him the silver medal. Taddia, along with Consolini, also worked at A.G.A. Obviously, Consolini and Taddia were the cover men for the sports reports

The Sports Workshop — 94

Athletes of the Pirelli Sports Group, 1950s

Athletics competitions in the
Milano Bicocca sports fields,
1950s

An athlete in the basketball section of the Pirelli Sports Group, 1950s

in the 1950s company magazines, from *Fatti e Notizie* to *Rivista Pirelli*.

Together with them, on the Pro Patria athletics track, an 'army' of workers, young engineers, secretaries and salespeople gradually gathered: all ready to leave their overalls behind to put on their 'long P' shirts and become hundred-metre runners, hurdlers, roller-skaters and javelin throwers also with remarkable results.

The promotion of sport was a powerful means in the framework of what today we would call corporate welfare, and this was well known by the enlightened entrepreneurs of the early twentieth century

The monthly corporate magazine *Fatti e Notizie* devoted several in-depth articles to sport and the many medals won by Pirellians in the various disciplines. Epic football challenges, with home and away matches with eternal 'automotive' rival Fiat from Turin. It can hardly be said that there wasn't a broad view of the world there: a rare occurrence in Italy, a baseball team was also established at Bicocca.

The corporate sports model at Bicocca was successfully revived at the Settimo Torinese facilities, with the establishment of the local sports group. But in those same years, the phenomenon was also spreading to subsidiaries abroad, with Brazil and Argentina in the lead, of course. Because long before it was codified and institutionalised in the late 1990s, Pirelli's ethical code stated that the company 'promotes social progress in all the communities in which it operates'.

This was already clearly stated as far back as 1946, in the book *La Pirelli. Vita di un'azienda industriale*, by its chairman Alberto Pirelli: 'The company has always encouraged and fostered these events: sports competitions, alpine outings, cycling excursions, fellowship and emulation, esprit de corps'.

Thus, in the Brazilian headquarters in São Paulo, the CAP—Club Atlético Pirelli was founded in the 1950s: from football to cycling, basketball, volleyball, athletics and boxing. The aim of the CAP was to encourage employees to take part in almost any sport, without obstacles of census or ethnicity: a fast track that from the outset linked São Paulo with Milan, a channel through which the same attitudes towards employee involvement, strong interaction with the local social community, and continuous attention to everything that goes beyond the narrow industrial scope and becomes corporate social responsibility could flow. In the articles of the Brazilian company newspaper, it became 'Pirellian pride'. If this sense of belonging in Brazil was made up of brotherhood, especially in sporting terms, between Brazilians and Italians, in Argentina the feeling was that of considering oneself Italian even though twelve thousand kilometres away: very active was the Pirelli Argentina sports group, which in June 1954 formed the Industrias Pirelli—Casa Central football team.

Roller skating competition at the Milano Bicocca sports field, 1950s

As if to prove its aggregating power, corporate sport was not immediately affected by the structural crises of the 1970s. Although gradually handed over to the Milan City Council, finally in 1985, the Pro Patria sports facilities were repeatedly refurbished, upgraded, and made available to new emerging disciplines. The same *Fatti e Notizie*, in addition to the major social reports highlighting the contradictions between capital and labour, continued to devote plenty of space, traditionally in the final pages, to corporate sporting activities. At most, a certain competitive rivalry between the also influenced the organisation and perception of sporting activities, which were sought, and enjoyed, outside the company: a total paradigm shift.

This does not mean that the company had stopped being present in sport, far from it. However, that mission became a 'global' operation, in the role of sponsor—often also technical—for the great top disciplines. So, the rally and Formula 1 seasons, and Superbike, and Motocross came along, putting years of technological research into competition tyres to good use. Then the landing in the world of foot-

Sport became an instrument for the promotion of a sports culture, understood as the promotion of a supportive and ethical society, especially among young people

Group's different industrial sectors was radicalised: tyres versus cables, vulcanisers versus wrapping machines. In between, the historic miscellaneous products played outsiders in the pursuit of corporate tournaments. The crisis of Pirelli's corporate sport, however, came relentlessly with the 1980s and the outsourcing of services. Then a phase of corporate welfare, as it had been known for some fifty years, came to an end. Other strategies became priorities, the scarcity of resources in the 1970s had finally reoriented investment choices.

At the same time, the lifestyles of Pirellians had changed, no longer linked to the vision of the company as a service provider. The trend towards privatisation ball with the stake in the capital of the Football Club Internazionale and the resulting appearance of the 'long P' on the Nerazzurri jerseys: the same for Palmeiras in Brazil, Peñarol in Uruguay, Velez Sarsfield in Argentina, and Basel in Switzerland. And the passion for sailing as well as skiing, and cycling was back with the current revival of the velo line and the sponsorship of the Lidl-Trek team. However, the concept of the welfare of sport, which for decades had been one of the pillars of corporate ethics, was by no means lost. Rather, it evolved into the broader and more global concept of 'sport for solidarity', according to the rationale of a modern and integrated multinational. In this respect, sport

Stories of Our Achievements

The Sports Workshop

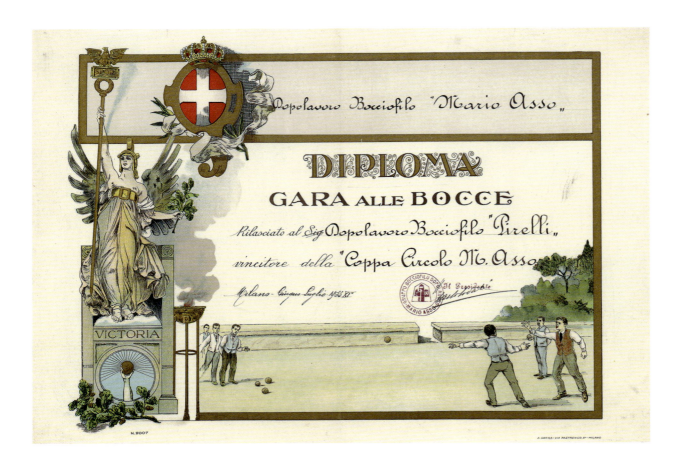

Diploma of honour awarded to the Pirelli Workers' Bocce Club for the 'Coppa Circolo Mario Asso' bowling competition held in Milan in June–July 1933

Pirelli's corporate football team in Milan, 2014

became an instrument for the promotion of a sports culture, understood as the promotion of a supportive and ethical society, especially among young people. In Brazil, the first Pirelli Inter Campus was established at the end of the 1990s, a project carried out in collaboration with the Italian football team aimed at using the values of sport to appeal to young people in at-risk communities in Brazil, from the Capuava favela in Araras in the State of São Paulo, to Recife in Pernanbuco, and Porto Alegre in Rio Grande do Sul. Still in Brazil, an agreement was then signed with the

Contribute to the young pupils' growth by proposing positive values such as friendship, loyalty, perseverance, respect and tolerance

Ministry of Sport and FAMS (Fundação de Amparo ao Menor de Feira de Santana) that provided for the monthly donation of rubber scraps from the local tyre factory to build athletics tracks for children and young people in the different regions of the state.
In turn, the Inter Campus project was then exported to Europe and repeated in 2007 in Romania, another country to which Pirelli—ever since the opening of its first plant—has paid close attention in accordance with its Corporate Social Responsibility policies. In Romania too, football became a strong instrument of social involvement: in the city of Slatina, also home to production plants, Pirelli built another Inter Campus in collaboration with Inter and the Comunità Nuova Onlus association.
In this case, Comunità Nuova was entrusted with the task of following the educational and relational aspects and organising recreational or learning-related activities for kids. More Inter, more football, more Pirelli: in the spirit of the 'solidarity football', the 'Leoni di Potrero—Calcio per tutti' project began operating in Italy, a free training centre supported by Pirelli with the collaboration of Inter's players Esteban Cambiasso and Javier Zanetti, aimed at children aged between five and twelve. The aim is to contribute to the young pupils' growth by proposing positive values such as friendship, loyalty, perseverance, respect and tolerance: a way of teaching the concept of integration to children from different social classes, working to prevent negative situations such as isolation and loneliness.
So far, the 'solidarity football' in the Group's Corporate Social Responsibility policies. But if football is among the most popular sports, it is also true that another sporting discipline succeeds in communicating the values of solidarity and sharing: sailing. Here too, following its more than ten-year sponsorship of the Santa Margherita–Coppa Carlo Negri regattas, Pirelli conceived and supported the 'Matti per la Vela' (Crazy for Sailing) initiative. This project, born in Genoa (Italy) in the late 1990s out of the passion for the sea of a group of health workers, volunteers and professional skippers, set itself the goal of availing of the sport of sailing as a therapeutic tool to help and rehabilitate people suffering from mental illnesses and hardships. Today the story continues, a story of enterprise and sporting feats, of people and values, in the sign of the 'long P'.

TALKING ABOUT CHAMPIONS, MUSIC, TECHNIQUES, IMAGES...

The Sports Workshop

by Eva Cantarella
-
Historian

The Epic of Competitions That Create Myths

Homer's poems tell of a competitive ethic and celebrate the personal and social qualities of champions. The political function of the Olympic Games

In my work, I aspire to find beauty above all, which I believe is not perfect. In fact, it often involves disorder, chaos and imperfection.

— *Black Swan*, directed by Darren Aronofsky, 2010

The most important thing is winning. To understand what sport meant to the ancient Greeks, we first have to forget the cliché that in athletics the most important thing for them was not winning but taking part. A very unfortunate saying, which has unfortunately become celebrated. It expresses (or claims to express, since it is only attributed to him) the opinion on the subject of Charles Pierre de Frédy, Baron de Coubertin, known as Pierre de Coubertin. Born in Paris in 1863 to an aristocratic, very Catholic and deeply traditional family, de Coubertin was firmly convinced that sport ought to have the same importance in the formation of a good citizen as the subjects traditionally taught, such as philosophy or history. And being a great lover of classical culture, in addition to sport, he combined his two major interests by putting forward the idea of reviving the ancient Olympic Games. In describing their characteristics, one day he uttered (or is said to have uttered) the above words. Regrettably, this reflected a serious misunderstanding of Greek culture, of which he was as deeply enamoured as he was profoundly misinformed. Growing up at a time when the myth of Greece was at its height, he had in fact idealised it to the point of completely falsifying its ideals, as his opinions on the Greeks' attitude to sport show clearly and strikingly.

Part I
The ethics of the Greeks
As the Homeric poems show unequivocally, Greek ethics were fundamentally and extremely combative from the beginning.
In the world they describe, the qualities that made someone a hero were those enabling them not just to stand out but to dominate others in all fields, defeating their enemies in war and showing their superiority in social relationships. It is no coincidence that, in the *Iliad*, the teaching that Peleus gives his son Achilles, who is about to set out for Troy, is to 'always be the best and superior to others' (*Il*. XI, 784). It is no coincidence that Hippolytus the king of the Lycians gave the same advice to his son Glaucus (*Il*. VI, 208). This was the legacy that fathers passed on to their children from generation to generation. Just how deeply they absorbed it appear in some famous verses by Pindar. Those who had suffered the shame of defeat, he writes, would return home 'by indirect hidden paths'.

Bronze statue *Boxer at Rest*, attributed to Lysippus, 4th century BC, and Greek sculpture of 'pankratiasts', photographs from the article 'The Olympics in ancient Greece', in *Fatti e Notizie*, no. 8, 1960

Defeat was a sign of inadequacy, victory of valour. The culture of sport was part of this set of values. The importance that it continued to have through the centuries is shown by the prestige throughout Greece of the athletic games held at regular intervals in the various cities. To understand their fundamental political significance a brief historical digression is necessary.

Although we often tend to forget it, ancient Greece was not and never had been a nation (except under Alexander, at the price of its freedom). It consisted of a collection of cities (*poleis,* a term that we significantly translate as city-state), which in the fifth century BC numbered some fifteen hundred, according to the calculation of Mogens Herman Hansen, the leading scholar on the subject. And none of these cities had an institutionalised position of supremacy over the others. Each was autonomous and independent, having its own laws, institutions, and army. Given the competitive nature of the Greeks, it is hardly surprising that they were in a continual state of conflict and war with each other. What else is Greek history, after all—once the Persian enemy had been defeated—if not that of more or less enduring and bloody contests between cities?

The athletic games: nature, political function and history of the Olympic Games
In this context, how can we define the practice of the athletic games between cities that characterised the life of the Greeks from the beginning? Firstly, almost needless to say, it was a manifestation of their competitive ethos. But to limit oneself to this reason would not account for their political significance. The games were the occasion when the awareness of belonging to a common system of values and the importance of this bond prevailed over the natural factiousness of the cities, however briefly. This was, in fact, the fundamental political function of the games. To give an idea of their significance and sum up their social and political dynamics, we have to start from the history of the event that, after

becoming the most famous games in Greece, have become the most famous games in the world (both ancient and modern). As we all know, the Olympic Games were founded according to tradition in 776 BC in the region of Elis, in which Olympia was considered from time immemorial a sacred place, the seat of Zeus. And the games were obviously important for the sparse local population. Olympia was a village; it did not possess a sufficient number

Defeat was a sign of inadequacy, victory of valour. The culture of sport was part of this set of values

of inhabitants to rise to the importance of a *polis*, and it did not become one until much later than the period when the games were first held.
All this raises a point that has posed many difficulties for historians. What happened, what reasons enabled these games, peripheral and rural as they were, to attain the importance that they acquired at a certain point in their history and firmly maintained thereafter? This is a real challenge to scholars. Among the possible solutions I will limit myself to recalling the one that has found the most supporters and could, perhaps, be closest to the truth.
As has rightly been pointed out, the games throughout Greece were organised by the local authorities, so the weaker they were, the less likely they were to gain prestige and political power at the expense of other locations. And Olympia was very weak. Since it could not give rise to any concerns in that respect, is it possible, as has been suggested, that this was the very reason why it was able to slowly acquire the prestige that eventually enabled it to firmly occupy a leading position? This is merely a conjecture, as we have seen, but it might actually explain why the Olympics attained a significant role in the places and at the times when, in the mid-sixth century BC, the so-called *períodos* was held annually. This was literally, the circuit in which the most important games took place. They consisted of the Pythian Games in honour of Apollo at Delphi, the Nemean Games at Nemea in Argolis, the Isthmian Games at Corinth, and the games at Olympia that take their name from the locality.

Rules of participation: the sacred truce
But Olympia was not only one of the most important games in Greece. To remember this alone would be to forget its greatest success, namely the fact that the organisation of its games involved a series of rules that were binding on all the cities taking part. These rules preceded the start of the games, were valid for their whole duration and came to include the time necessary for those who had taken part in them to return to their native towns. A relatively long period, during which, in addition to the fact that armies with weapons were forbidden to enter the region, a 'sacred truce' was proclaimed between the cities that took part, which undertook to forgo all hostilities in those months. The Games,

in short, were an occasion that reminded cities of the importance of feeling united in the name of their common cultural heritage, at least temporarily setting aside misunderstandings and enmities. Just as the people who take part as athletes or spectators in the Olympic Games today do, or should do, for a few days. And ever since, the Olympics have been a reminder that awareness of our shared values is the only means capable of confronting and resisting destructive forces, like those that today are undermining the very possibility of civil coexistence on the planet.

Those who competed in that early phase did so only for the glory. But over time it became customary to pay various honours to the winners, such as giving them free meals for life. Initially the honours were only symbolic, given the high social status of those who could afford to take part in the events. Gradually the prizes and honours were extended, eventually including statues of the victors to be erected in the city of their birth, or commissions to the most renowned poets to compose odes in their honour.

But the event that brought about the greatest change in the spirit of the games was definitely the

What happened, what reasons enabled these games, peripheral and rural as they were, to attain the importance that they acquired at a certain point in their history and firmly maintained thereafter?

Part II
Benefits and social consequences of sport. Prizes
What were the benefits, if any, apart from the political ones, for those who took part in the competitions and were victorious? At first they were only symbolic. The prizes often, not to say customarily, consisted of a wreath, which differed in nature depending on the place. At the Pythian games it was a wreath of laurel, at the Isthmian of pine, at the Nemean of wild celery, at Delphi of laurel, at Olympia of sprigs from an olive tree believed to be sacred…

introduction of a monetary prize awarded to the winners, consisting of 500 drachmas. This measure is traditionally attributed to Solon, the first Athenian legislator, who lived between 638 and 558 BC, and it was a very significant innovation. Some scholars regard this as unhistorical, but it is difficult to question, given its coherence with the policy consistently pursued by Solon in favour of the less well-to-do classes (including—and this was no small advance—the abolition of slavery for debt). This first pecuniary reward was followed by others and, once

Talking About Champions: Music, Techniques, Images...

Discobolus, Roman copy of a bronze original of the 5th century BC by Myron, British Museum, London

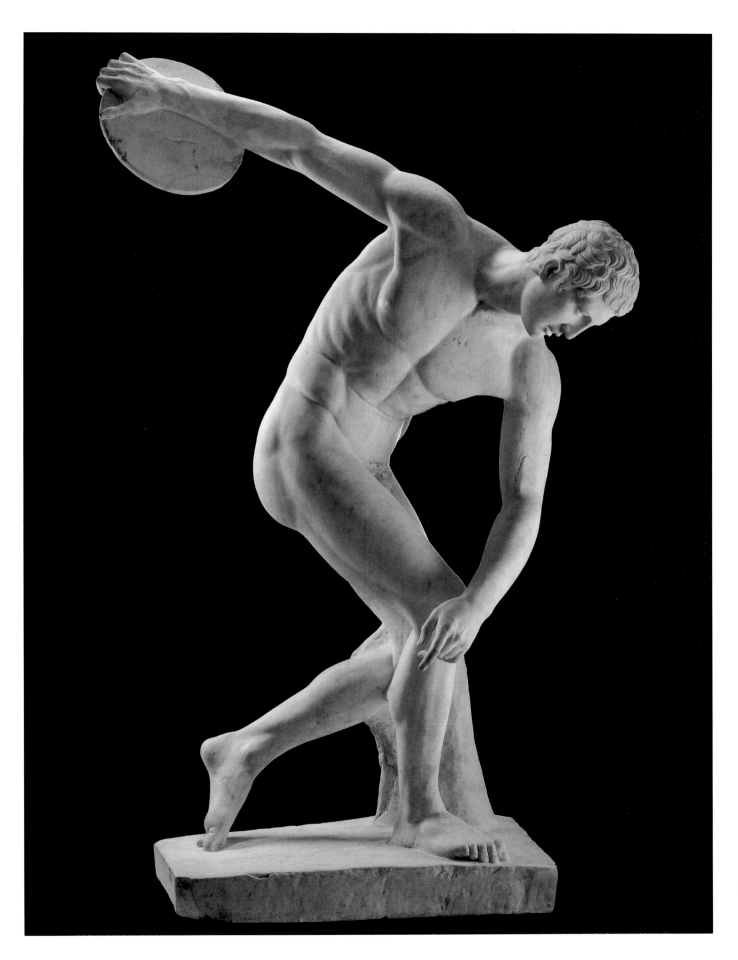

The Sports Workshop — 112

Discus and javelin throwers, image from the article 'The Olympics in Ancient Greece', in *Fatti e Notizie*, no. 8, 1960

Illustration from the article 'The Olympics in Ancient Greece', in *Fatti e Notizie*, no. 8, 1960

introduced, multiplied, as well as other rewards in material goods, which reached very high values. Winning a race, at that point, was no longer just an honour. And this marked the appearance of an important new development.

the most ancient historical sources (needless to say, the Homeric poems), fraud had always existed. This is demonstrated, starting from myth, by the story of the marriage of Pelops (the founder of the Olympics) to Hippodamia. It is worth dwelling on this tale.

The Games, in short, were an occasion that reminded cities of the importance of feeling united in the name of their common cultural heritage

The origin of professionalism and the presumed loss of ancient values
The custom that arose in some cities of giving money to the most promising young athletes from social classes previously compelled to work for a living was an important step in the history of sport. Freed from that necessity, those who had the physical qualities and aptitudes were able to devote themselves to athletics, with consequences from but insignificant. It gave rise to the first professionals and the progressive growth of their number. The effects of these developments have long been discussed. Some hold that this led to the disappearance of the ancient Olympic spirit, the distancing of athletics from the heroic ideals and the growth of behaviour that deliberately violated the ancient rules of fairness. On closer inspection, however, the sources not only fail to confirm this hypothesis, but show that it is groundless. As recorded in both mythical tales and

The father of Hippodamia (who, according to the sources, was in love with his daughter) had made it a condition that those who wished to marry her would have to defeat him in a chariot race in which he would be drawn by his famous invincible horses. But a young man named Pelops defeated him, although, as we learn from the *Bibliotheca* of Apollodorus, only by bribery and cheating on an impressive scale. And, passing from myth to history, we find far from irreproachable behaviour in athletic competitions in the *Iliad*, Book XXIII, containing Homer's account of the games held by Achilles for the funeral of Patroclus. The behaviour of some of the heroes taking part, on the most generous interpretation, is not always ethically exemplary. The violation of the rules of fairness, to close the subject, goes back much further than the birth of professionalism.

Girl with Tambourine, detail from the mosaic of the *Ten Girls*, 4th century, Villa Romana del Casale, Piazza Armerina

Part III
And finally, the other half of humanity. Women and sport

As is customary when dealing with this subject, in the preceding pages we have not dealt with the relationship between sport and women from the viewpoint of the male population. There remains a tenacious belief that women could only practise gymnastics for predominantly eugenic purposes, as preparation for and close to the age when, on reaching puberty, they would marry and so produce new citizens.

Fortunately, for some years now a large body of evidence has irrefutably shown that this theory is erroneous. It is on record that in the second millennium BC in Greece (in the Minoan civilisation, which perhaps was not yet Greek) there were women, like those represented in what is known as the 'bull-leaping fresco', who acted as assistants to the male athletes who performed acrobatics on a bull. Hence women engaged, albeit in a subordinate position, in daring gymnastic feats, which clearly and inevitably required an athletic preparation of an almost professional level.

The iconography, in short, clearly disproves the idea, once dominant, that the only sport practised by women was running, which the Greeks saw as a significant contribution to their physical fitness. It facilitated pregnancy and childbirth, and was clearly fundamental in the performance of their civic task as procreators of new citizens. But this does not mean or entail that its function was solely eugenic. In fact, the sources show this very clearly, if not explicitly, starting with the story of a mythical character who gives us some fundamental information about the subject.

The myth of Atalanta

As often happened, Atalanta was abandoned at birth by order of her father, who had no wish to raise a daughter. After being found by a party of hunters, she grew up happily in the woods, enjoying complete freedom of movement, becoming an extraordinary runner, and without having any intention of marrying. Since an oracle had prophesied that if she did so she would be turned into an animal, she had devised a way of avoiding it by challenging her suitors to a footrace. If a suitor won, he could marry her, but if he failed, he would have to die by her own hand. This regularly happened until one day a young man named Melanion defeated her.

Atalanta kept her promise, married him and they lived happily together until one day when, entering a temple, they made love there, provoking the ire of Zeus, who turned them into lions. The prophecy had come true.

The story of Atalanta is a strange one, with many possible interpretations: a warning to women who failed to respect the rules of life they were meant to follow, perhaps? Possibly, but what is most important to us here is the consideration that running was part of the life experience of women. The sources clearly confirm that this was so in cities such as Sparta, where they regularly ran a race in honour of Helen, or Brauron (near Athens), where they ran in honour of Artemis, and again Olympia, where they celebrated Hera. And contrary to what the traditional literature says, these were not races with an exclusively celebratory function of the goddess honoured in each case. On closer inspection, we see that matters went further than this.

Girls Playing Ball, detail from the mosaic of the *Ten Girls*, 4th century, Villa Romana del Casale, Piazza Armerina

Characteristics and anomalies of racing in Olympia

Every four years at Olympia, to celebrate the marriage between Hippodamia and Pelops, special games were held that differed from the others, called the *Heraia*. As we learn in particular from Pausanias (V, 16, 2-6), this involved a footrace between young women. It was held in the Olympic stadium over a distance (160 metres) about one sixth less than the men's race (192.24 metres).

The iconography, in short, clearly disproves the idea, once dominant, that the only sport practised by women was running

However, although they were, like all other women's races, an initiatory rite, those in honour of Hera were different from the others. At the end, prizes were awarded, and the winners, in addition to a part of the cow sacrificed to Hera in the ceremony, received olive wreaths and could dedicate their portraits to the goddess with their names engraved on them. The memory of them remains in the temple of Hera, where traces of the niches in which they were placed remain on some columns. Although, regrettably, none of these portraits and names have come down to us, the historicity of the information is confirmed. The *Heraia* were *also* competitive in character.

Women's Olympics in Olympia?

It was almost inevitable that someone would advance the theory that parallel Olympics were held in Olympia, reserved for women, and in fact there do exist analogies and similarities. But, even though it is a controversial and debatable issue, on which it is not easy to take up a position, this does not change the fact that, pending the results of the most recent research, it is still an issue that needs to be mentioned.

And so, having analysed the data, here are the conclusions that we seem justified in drawing. Greek women were not precluded from any sporting activity, as was believed for a long time. To be precise: it is not true that only Spartan women were allowed to perform gymnastics. The contrast between Sparta and Athens (and, more generally, between the Doric and other areas) is contradicted by the sources, which show that all young Greek women were able to engage in these activities. Sports and competitions were not only male activities and aptitudes. In both fields, Greek women have much more to tell us than we thought.

The Sports Workshop

by Emanuela Audisio
-
Journalist and writer

Being Together Dreaming of the Same Horizon

The fruitful relationships between champions and coaches, the passing of the torch between generations. And that athletics school as 'the NASA of Italian sport'

But Nino, don't be afraid to fail
a penalty kick
It's not by these details
That a player is judged.
You see a player in his courage
His altruism and imagination.

— Francesco De Gregori,
La leva calcistica della classe '68, 1982

B reasting the tape alone. Before everyone's eyes. An immense solitude, happy or tragic. That's what sport looks like: extreme individualism. A man or a woman alone in the lead. Yet that's not really how it is. It's never the case. You might have the medal around your neck or come within an ace of winning. But behind you there's a world, your village. 'You won the gold medal too!' Niccolò Campriani shouted to his parents over the phone after winning the 50-metre three-position rifle event at the London Olympics in 2012. He recalled when he was a boy and his father would drive him back from competitions and he, filled with rage at not winning, would sulk and turn up the stereo. And then, at one in the morning in London, he sat down to write 150 postcards to thank everyone he felt close to, even the baker in Sesto Fiorentino, his home town.
We all remember the film *Chariots of Fire*, winner of four Oscars in 1981, its title taken from a poem by William Blake. It tells the story of the British athletics team at the 1924 Paris Olympics, but above all the story behind Harold Abrahams' victory in the 100 metres. He was a student at Cambridge, a Jew seeking redemption. His coach Sam Mussabini tells him: 'Only think of two things—the gun and the tape. When you hear the one, just run like hell until you break the other'. Yet Mussabini was not present at the Stade Olympique de Colombes to watch his pupil racing. He was excluded as a professional coach. This was the era of hypocritical, extreme and enforced amateurism. Being paid to coach an athlete violated the rules. Sam, an unconventional type, whom Abrahams always defended, was exiled to a rented room in Paris and heard his athlete's success broadcast over the radio. In the film, he punches out his boater and whispers: 'My son'. Sport creates a family, it creates ties and relationships, even among those who are not kin. We all belong to it because our dreams occupy the same horizon.
The record-breaking duo Mennea–Vittori had a distant relationship. As coach and athlete they were never on first-name terms. During training they were close, but strangers elsewhere. They went to Mexico City with the same aim, to win the 200 metres. And they succeeded on 12 September 1979. Mennea's time, 19.72, is still a European record. It stood as a world record for almost seventeen years, until 1996 when the American Michael Johnson ran

Chariots of Fire, directed by Hugh Hudson, movie set, 1981

it in 19.66. Some records not only shatter times but pierce the years. That day the two men looked at each other. The younger was twenty-seven. They had to part, saying their last words to each other, because there comes a point in life where you come to the parting of the ways. They would meet again; both were on the verge of something. 'I'll do it this time', said the young man. Vittori was astonished. He had never seen him so confident and optimistic. It had just stopped raining. Mennea ran as he had never run in his life and beat the world. He left behind his childhood, his complexes, the south. There are curves that put you off your stride, you falter and feel small, as if walls were rising around you. And there are others where you burst through into happiness. Pietro Paolo Mennea from Barletta ran his curve without losing speed, his left shoulder slightly lowered. And that day Italy discovered another Coppi. He raced, but not on a bike. He came from the south; he was thin, a little crooked, very twisted. Mennea had behind him an Italy that studied; it was no longer amateurish. Homespun, but also competitive. His factory was the National Athletics School in Formia. The NASA of Italian sport. In Formia, they invented, tested and discovered the future. And they developed the science of records. It was also the seedbed for Sara Simeoni's 1978 world-record high jump: 2.01. Abroad they had colleges. Italy had Formia, spartan and somewhat neorealistic. Others who trained there were Baggio, Panatta, Trillini, and the crew of *Azzurra*. It was the destination of the finest youngsters in sport. Simeoni arrived there at twenty-two. 'The room in the guest quarters contained a bed and a wardrobe. It was so dreary that I repainted it myself. There was no gym equipment. We asked the workers there for help. We explained what we needed and they started building the equipment: the sand belt, the iron boot and other equipment. They didn't ask for money in return, just begged us to do well'. Jumping, love and fantasy. Made in Italy advanced in the world of sport. All together with passion. The Azzurri have won the Davis Cup after forty-seven years, and you realise that the tennis team, like many other champions, comprises numerous specialists, from the nutritionist to the

with leading teams. His advanced research and training lab also attracts tennis, golf, sailing and skiing champions. His discovery is that all sports performance depends on the brain, the real engine of the body. And the secret is that the mind can be trained to perform by calm. This is the 'easy-going approach', a kind of education of the mind that learns to associate high performance with serenity. Agitation can be overcome by stillness.

The English mile is 1609.36 metres and to the British it is the equivalent of a passage of Shakespeare on the track: endurance and speed. The crowd roared with happiness, everyone running, cheering, hugging each other

physiotherapist, mental coach, athletic trainer, bodyguard, strategist, coach and communication expert. NBA basketball players even have a chef at home to make sure they don't overstep the line at mealtimes. At twenty-two, Jannik Sinner is imperturbable. A nerveless player. What goes on in his head? What lies behind his gestures? How can he not feel nervous, when a single shot might sink or save the team and a whole season's work? He uses FM, Formula Medicine, which is not a medicine, but a method that helps build Formula 1 champions. It was created in 1993 by Riccardo Ceccarelli, a sports doctor in Viareggio who works

But to understand the multitude of people behind the winner breasting the tape, you have to look at an image from 6 May 1954. Iffley Road, Oxford. Roger Bannister, at the age of twenty-five, succeeded in the feat compared to sailing beyond the Pillars of Hercules or rounding Cape Horn. He ran the mile in under 4 minutes. The announcer, Norris McWhirter of the *Guinness Book of Records*, was unable to finish the sentence: 'Ladies and gentlemen, the time is 3 minutes...'. Only that mattered: the word three. Commenting on the radio for the BBC was Harold Abrahams, the Olympic champion in Paris. The English mile is 1609.36 metres and

Di record in record

SEMPRE PIU' FORTI SEMPRE PIU' VELOCI

Continueremo a correre sempre più in fretta, a saltare sempre più in alto e lanciare sempre più lontano? Gli esperti dicono di sì.
Anzi, secondo i loro calcoli, record dopo record, ogni barriera sarà abbattuta e l'uomo diventerà sempre più un autentico superman. Ma esiste o non esiste un limite invalicabile alle possibilità umane?

Il salto in alto di Sara Simeoni, quello in lungo di Carl Lewis e la corsa ad ostacoli di Gianni Ronconi.

Nove secondi e ottantadue centesimi nei cento metri; diciannove secondi e cinque centesimi nei 200; cinque metri e novanta nel salto con l'asta; ventitrè metri e trenta centimetri nel lancio del peso; diciotto metri e quaranta centimetri nel salto triplo. Sono misure che sembrano impossibili, non è vero? Eppure saranno raggiungibili nel 1990. Lo dicono gli esperti di statistica. Possibile? Impossibile? Certo che nello sport, oggi, le prestazioni eccezionali sono quasi all'ordine del giorno e non c'è meeting che si rispetti che non sforni un primato. La domanda, quindi, nasce spontanea: esiste un limite umano? Un risultato oltre al quale l'uomo non potrà andare, una misura invalicabile? I fatti finora hanno detto di no.

Proprio di recente, Ulrike Meyfarth, 26 anni, tedesca occidentale, ha stabilito il nuovo record del mondo del salto in alto, salendo a 2.02 e migliorando così di un centimetro il 2.01 di Sara Simeoni; Marita Koch, un'altra tedesca si è laureata donna più veloce dei cinque continenti nei 400 metri con uno splendido 48"15; l'inglese Thompson ha portato a quota 8744 il punteggio massimo dei decatleti; lo statunitense Carl Lewis ha compiuto un salto in lungo di 8.56 che lo pone, unico uomo sul globo terrestre, a soli 34 centimetri dal mitico primato di Bon Beamon raggiunto alle Olimpiadi di Città del Messico; un altro negro, Edwin Moses, ha fatto fermare i cronometri a 47"17 nei 400 hs, riuscendo a compiere tredici passi tra un ostacolo e l'altro; i due fondisti inglesi Steve Ovett e Sebastian Coe hanno fatto impazzire tutti gli statistici nella stagione scorsa rubandosi l'un l'altro, nel giro di pochi giorni, i primati negli 800 e 1500 metri.

E' una vera e propria corsa al record, un inseguimento costante e destinato a non esaurirsi mai. "Apparentemente l'uomo ha dei limiti fisici", afferma Enrico Arcelli, medico e consulente scientifico della Federazione Italiana di Atletica Leggera. "Determinate strutture umane non dovrebbero poter sopportare più di certi carichi, alcuni muscoli non dovrebbero poter fornire più di tanta forza. Eppure la capacità di adattamento del nostro corpo è sorprendente e non è stata ancora quantificata. Ecco perché tutto appare possibile".

"I progressi compiuti fino ad oggi sono dovuti a tre fattori", prosegue Arcelli, "in primo luogo, i nuovi metodi di allenamento, la cura degli stili e l'affinamento dei particolari; in secondo luogo, una maggiore selezione dovuta al fatto che il numero di chi pratica lo sport è aumentato, l'alimentazione è migliorata, le condizioni igieniche e mediche anche; in terzo luogo, al mutamento di certe condizioni esterne come i materiali, le piste, gli attrezzi...".

Nel sostegno dello sforzo fisico, la medicina sportiva svolge poi un ruolo importantissimo. In passato ha rasentato talora l'illecito. Ora, invece, punta molto sulle strategie alimentari capaci di dare agli atleti le proteine necessarie togliendo però quegli alimenti come lo zucchero e gli amidi che possono provocare un aumento dell'insulina. Per incrementare la resistenza sono stati poi messi a punto test personalizzati, come quello di Francesco Conconi, che determinano la capacità di ciascuno e aiutano a predisporre programmi su misura.

Se poi ci si dà un'altra occhiata intorno, si scopre che in Svezia gli

E C'E' ANCHE CHI DICE CHE LE DONNE....

"Nello sport, le curve delle prestazioni uomo-donna tendono ad avvicinarsi e in alcune discipline, come le corse di resistenza e il nuoto, le donne hanno la possibilità di tenere testa ai loro colleghi". Questa la tesi di Enrico Arcelli, il medico da noi intervistato per questo servizio dedicato allo sport. L'australiano K.F. Dyer, docente alla facoltà di genetica dell'università di Adelaide e studioso di statistiche, va oltre. Secondo lui nel 2077 i due sessi si equivarranno sul piano sportivo. E c'è anche chi dichiara che le donne supereranno gli uomini. Credere a questo che sembra tuttavia esagerato. E' vero che il margine di miglioramento è costante e tangibile ma esistono fattori costituzionali, antropometrici, funzionali, che rendono una ragazza più debole di un ragazzo. Handicappata nelle discipline dove è fondamentale la forza muscolare, la donna è invece favorita negli sport acquatici dove può sfruttare il fatto di avere gli arti inferiori più corti, un ridotto consumo massimo di ossigeno e soprattutto quella maggiore percentuale di grasso che le permette di galleggiare meglio. Anche nella marcia (vedi la Salce) e nella maratona (Laura Fogli e Rita Marchisio) è favorita, per non parlare della ginnastica dove sfrutta la sua flessibilità muscolare.

Le donne capaci di exploit di livello internazionale crescono di numero: Marita Koch, Ulrike Meyfarth in atletica; Barbara Krause e Mary T. Meagher nel nuoto ne sono gli esempi. E casi come quelli di Stella Walsh, vincitrice dei 100 metri olimpici di Los Angeles nel 1932 e primatista mondiale della distanza, riconosciuta poi come uomo dall'autopsia fatta dopo la sua morte, sono ormai rari. Alcune atlete hanno fatto uso eccessivo di ormoni (la stilleriberista tedesca Karen Metschuk e la velocista cecoslovacca Jarmyla Kratocvilova per citarne due) con conseguenze deleterie sul loro organismo, ma i progressi della maggior parte delle donne sono dovuti ad altri motivi. Al loro maggior impegno, alla tecnica di allenamento, alla caduta di pregiudizi antiquati che volevano la donna "tutta casa e chiesa". Insomma, ora che le ragazze hanno anche nello sport gli stessi diritti degli uomini, i record non mancano.

scienziati puntano molto sul cuore, lo scrutano nei minimi particolari per stabilire la sua possibilità di pompaggio sotto sforzo; che in Germania, continuano prelievi di sangue, per arrivati a stabilire a quale velocità comincia a presentarsi l'acido lattico dei muscoli e che negli Stati Uniti, équipe di specialisti lavorano da tempo sulla molecola-carburante del nostro corpo, l'Atp.

Tutti questi studiosi sono concordi nell'affermare che i margini da erodere sono ancora enormi. Nell'atletica leggera, nel pattinaggio su ghiaccio, nel ciclismo su pista, nel nuoto. Soprattutto in quest'ultimo in quanto disciplina "giovane", ancora tutta da esplorare, dove la tecnica di allenamento ha ancora molti passi avanti da fare.

NICOLETTA PENNA

Talking About Champions: Music, Techniques, Images... — 123

Nicoletta Pennati, 'Ever Stronger, Ever Faster', *Fatti e Notizie*, no. 1, 1983

Sketch for advertisement for Pirelli Marca Stella heels, 1920

US athlete Wilma Rudolph on the cover of *Pirelli. Rivista d'informazione e di tecnica*, no. 5, 1960

Advertisement for Pirelli tennis balls, 1952

to the British it is the equivalent of a passage of Shakespeare on the track: endurance and speed. The crowd roared with happiness, everyone running, cheering, hugging each other. That insurmountable barrier was gone; the wall around the mile had fallen: 3:59.4. It was like reaching the moon while staying on earth. It was like landing in another world, doubling a stormy cape.
Look at the picture. Like some great historical painting, the photo says it all: about the time, the period, about exhaustion, emotion, and a country that had just abandoned rationing. About how sport is one

It was like reaching the moon while staying on earth. It was like landing in another world, doubling a stormy cape

and everyone. Bannister, number 41, is at the centre, head back, transfigured, in the final effort. A judge in a macintosh squats, pipe in mouth, composedly taking notes. A timekeeper covers his face and bursts into tears as he presses the button to record the time. In the background his teammates with excited looks are running across the grass. And when they ask you what lies behind sport that the eye is unable to see, tell them this: Bannister caught the train from Paddington to Oxford, travelling second class. He was six weeks away from graduating from St Mary's Hospital Medical School. Shortly before, he had gone to the lab to file the spikes on his shoes. He knew it would be better to be light in his run, so much so that he didn't even wear socks. He was accompanied by his coach (though he didn't call him that) Franz Stampfl, an Austrian native who had absorbed Freud's lesson and gave him good advice: 'Don't worry, it's only pain'. If he told you that, you believed him, because he had survived shipwreck in the icy waters of the Atlantic. In Oxford, Roger had lunch with his friends; they ate ham and salad standing up and he joked with their kids. Everything was going well. But at the sports field he changed his mind. The flag on St George's Church was fluttering wildly, the wind was coming in gusts. It didn't feel like the right day. Stampfl persuaded him that sometimes it's better to set off than to live in regret. So at six o'clock that evening Bannister made his attempt. On the track he was paced by two friends, Chris Chataway and Chris Brasher, but they ran too slowly, forcing him to run the last lap under 60 seconds to leave his mark on history. At the finish he fainted and his sight failed him. Someone hurried to check he wasn't dead. They were afraid his heart had burst. In return, he muttered that he no longer wanted to live. There was no big celebration, Bannister and his two friends walked to a hilltop to enjoy the view from above and wonder what their future held. Stampfl, who had coached all three, took the first train back to London, avoiding the limelight. As a foreigner he was disliked, despite his excellent results. The brightest hour, not the darkest one, belongs to an Italian cyclist. On 13 October 2023, Vittoria Bussi, thirty-six years old, from Rome, regained the cycling

Superga: Panatta le sceglie per il tennis

Tu per vivere in libertà

SUPERGA
le tue scarpe scelte dai campioni

Adriano Panatta as brand ambassador in the advertising campaign, 'Superga. Your shoes chosen by the champions', Agenzia Centro, proof print, 1977

hour record by becoming the first woman in history to average more than 50 kph. She cycled 201 laps at the Aguascalientes velodrome in Mexico City, at almost 2000 metres above sea level. The great Belgian champion Eddy Merckx, who in 1972 set a speed of 49.432 kph, was 835 metres behind her. For an hour of love, one is prompted to say, because what is behind Vittoria's story is amazing. She studied maths, graduating from Rome's La Sapienza University with a thesis on algebraic geometry, then did a doctorate

Sport creates a family, it creates ties and relationships, even among those who are not kin. We all belong to it because our dreams occupy the same horizon

at Oxford and a postdoc at the Abdus Salam Institute of Theoretical Physics in Trieste. In Oxford the ethos was very competitive. She was a strong rider, but she gave up cycling to study. At the end of 2012 she suffered a period of crisis. Her father Walter died of a cerebral haemorrhage and she realised she could no longer waste any time. She set aside her books and returned to Italy, but above all to the saddle, to 'find a meaning again'. At the age of twenty-five, her favourite theorems became those on two wheels.

'Cycling, like sport, is a sequence of numbers'. This is especially true of time trials, where it is essential to study trajectories, speed and wind resistance, measure effort and aerodynamics. Head down and eyes fixed on the black line. The struggle was against time, which is always painfully deceptive. 'We're all afraid of being alone. That's what makes time trials so scary. It's just you on your own. I learned to live with that anguished feeling on the nights I spent at hospital caring for my father, when he could no longer speak'. In 2018 Vittoria became the fastest woman in the world and conquered the hour record on the track. She was the first woman to break the 48-kph barrier, but England's Joss Lowden (48.405 kilometres) and the Dutch rider Ellen van Dijk bettered it in 2022, bringing the record down to 49.254 kph. Vittoria reacted as if an equation had been wiped off the board. She experimented on her own because she didn't like the idea of an athlete being a slave to an organisation. She preferred not to lose her human side. 'No one can switch off my brain. I'm Vittoria Bussi, a thinking being, autonomous in reasoning. I like to choose the materials with my own expertise. I don't want the sponsors to impose them on me'. You will have understood the type: Madame Curie on a bike, someone who doesn't care to be in a group. She did everything herself. She turned to social media. Her goal was to beat the 50-kph barrier, a huge breakthrough for women. 'A record is more than just a sports performance. It's a way to open new horizons for cycling. I don't have a staff. I have to organise myself. People identify with me. It's the daily challenge facing each of us. There's a problem to be solved, so you roll up your sleeves, set to work, find out whatever you need to know, and you solve

Vittoria Bussi during the 26th UEC Road European Championships, Plouay, France, 2020

it'. Vittoria planned the adventure online. Even superwomen have to be careful to save money. The trip to Mexico would last about forty days. She had to find her accommodation and everything else. So she launched a crowdfunding campaign enabling her to raise the 12,000 euros she needed to organise her training, travel and the velodrome. She called her project Road2Record, stressing she would do it her own way. 'It has to reflect the spirit of all the people who see themselves in me, those who in everyday life have

'No one can switch off my brain. I'm Vittoria Bussi, a thinking being, autonomous in reasoning. I like to choose the materials with my own expertise'

the same tenacity, confidence and vision of existence'. There was no crowd to applaud her, and no TV. The spectators present: nine. They included two judges, the caretaker and the photographer. Because if you're a nonconformist you count for less. Vittoria also wanted to live for her father, who hadn't made it. And in the end she thanked everyone who had helped her, including Rocco, her future husband, who had always been with her, made sacrifices, and guided her with his voice. She said she felt there were a lot of people riding with her.
Sport also means innovation, technique and hard work. But what lies behind it in the end is this: storms, doubts and courage.

The Sports Workshop

by Giuseppe Lupo
-
Writer and University lecturer

Popular Heroes in the Cycle Sprint

The races were also experienced as social and cultural phenomena, as shown by the rivalry between Bartali and Coppi. It was the popular soul of record-breaking bikes

*We write our history using bicycles,
Chasing memory along narrow roads,
Up the hills without a water bottle,
And down slopes with the wind on our faces. Because
A bike doesn't care where you take it, it's all about
The balance of periods and relationships.*

— Frankie hi-nrg mc, *Pedala*, 2014

Although Pirelli's earliest production consisted of submarine cables, tyres for velocipedes and bicycles also have their own story to tell, which began, as with the cables, in the late nineteenth century. Of course, these early examples were solid cord tyres, impossible to puncture and heavy to push. But not many years went by before the company introduced tubular cord tyres, such as the 'tipo Milano' patented in 1893, whose name honoured the city where the company was based, in Via Ponte Seveso near the Stazione Centrale. Thanks to the greater lightness that this technical innovation ensured, bicycles became a new and promising means of locomotion. In fact they soon proved so successful that just a year later, in 1894, the sale of tubular tyres brought revenues of 825,000 liras, accounting for 12% of the company's total turnover. In the absence of cars, it was the two-wheelers that best expressed the character of modernity, which is essentially the myth of speed. Their efficiency, replacing carriages and horses, foreshadowed the frontier of the coming century accompanied by fanfares trumpeting progress as the only triumphant future.

Unlike the velocipede, however, considered a vehicle as elegant as it was cumbersome, suitable for short rides rather than longer trips out of town, the bicycle was much more practical and manageable, suitable for riding on rough country roads, travelling to work daily or leisure-time excursions. Then—another significant advantage—maintenance was cheap and uncomplicated. It was seen as the vehicle on which modernity was fearlessly advancing, as shown by Gian Emilio Malerba's design for the cover of the December 1908 issue of the *Rivista mensile del Touring*. In the foreground we see a gentleman dressed for winter, in cap, jacket, scarf, boots and breeches, riding along a snow-covered road. He advances safely in the cold and dark, because the rims of his bicycle are fitted with Pirelli tubular tyres of a special kind, called Semelle: non-slip, waterproof, smooth running, as we read in the caption on the right of the layout. The image projects a mythical atmosphere. Despite the state of the weather, the journey of the solitary cyclist evokes heroic values. His pedalling is an action made possible by technology. It vaguely recalls the feat of the man who founded the Italian Touring Club: Luigi Vittorio Bertarelli, a Milanese engineer and a pioneer of the

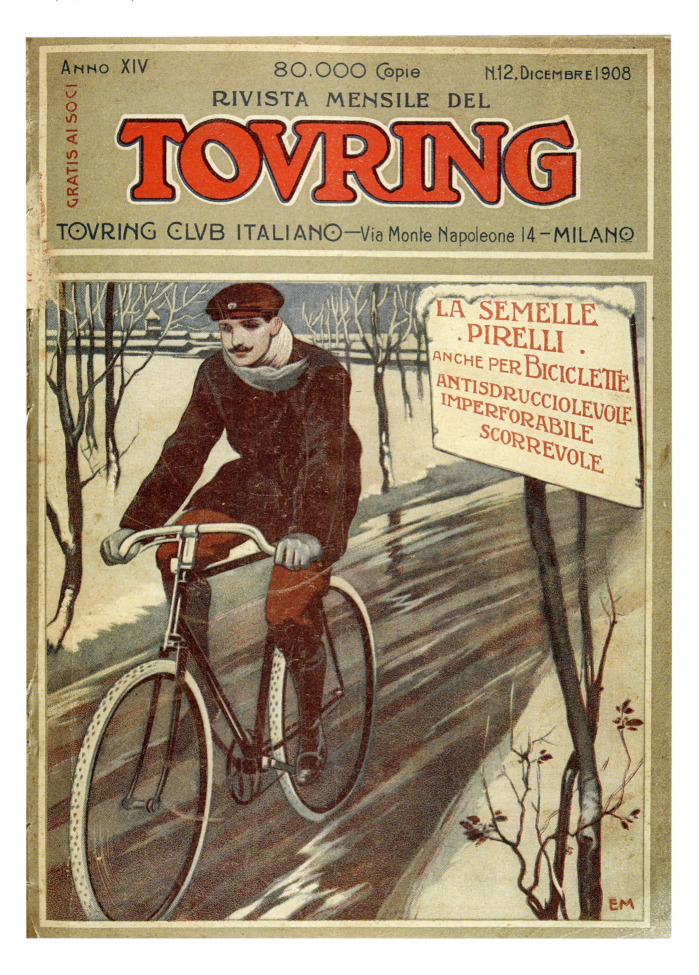

Gian Emilio Malerba, cover of the *Rivista mensile del Touring*, December 1908

new spirit of the time. In 1897, in just five days, he cycled the length of southern Italy from the tip of Calabria to Campania, on what he himself called 'my good and faithful Raleigh', a sturdy touring bike of British make, equipped with compasses, spare tyres, waterproof capes and an extra pair of shoes. Pirelli, Bertarelli and the Touring Club: a perfect triangle ushering in the twentieth century. Anyone who tried the new means of transport had to have both the daring temperament of an explorer, unafraid

sophisticated tyres for racing bikes alongside its firmly established regular models. It was the period when sports competitions were first being used to publicise the entrepreneurial qualities of a company, and the results were not long in coming. In 1907, when the Tour de France was first held on roads in the Alps, it became the ideal opportunity to promote Pirelli tubular tyres. Things got even better in May two years later, in the first Giro d'Italia organised by the *Gazzetta dello Sport* in eight stages, starting and

Anyone who tried the new means of transport had to have both the daring temperament of an explorer, unafraid of hardship, and a naive faith in technology

of hardship, and a naive faith in technology. But this only confirms how well bicycles responded—another strong point—to the needs of the philosophy of life at the turn of the century: the affirmation of the value of the individual. His ability to measure up to the rule of the self-made man, his stamina when subjected to challenges by the world. A glance at the date tells us that, when the December 1908 issue of the *Rivista mensile del Touring* was printed, the twentieth century had only begun a few years earlier, and it was pressing forward with youthful impetuosity, seeking to assert its overwhelming primacy over the slow old nineteenth century. This is why Pirelli, as early as 1899, decided to introduce more

finishing in Milan, covering a total distance of 2448 kilometres. For the occasion, Aleardo Terzi drew a postcard showing a buxom young woman in a white dress—the traditional personification of the young nation of Italy, albeit without her crown—with her left hand holding a tubular tyre inside which a cyclist in racing gear is hunched over the handlebars and pedalling, pursued by a second competitor. In this case, too, the scene alludes to something that has the flavour of individual adventure: the man alone in the lead would become a symbol of the sport. The figures are accompanied by the wind, which not only seems to be impelling the first of the two racers towards victory, but is vertiginously ruffling the

Aleardo Terzi, advertisement for Pirelli tyres, postcard issued during the Giro d'Italia, 1909

young woman's dress, adding a touch of futuristic dynamism and fluttering the tricolour flag behind her. Willpower alone does not suffice to win; you also have to rely on cutting-edge technologies. And it is no coincidence that at the foot of the postcard, in the grey area, the words 'Pirelli tyres' appear in capitals with the famous 'long P' logo.

The poster celebrates the long marriage between the company in Milan and what would become one of the most representative national sporting events. The advertisement does not say as much, but it is highly likely that the cyclist racing towards the finishing line had wheels fitted with the Stella tyres, the most reliable of the time, the most effective in performance. This is confirmed by a statistic: at the first Giro d'Italia, with 127 riders taking part, only 49 would reach the finish line in Milan, and 30 of the 49 used Stella tyres, just over 60%.

Much more than being an easily recognisable advertising logo, the 'long P' became an icon of Italy that found a significant part of its identity in cycling. A country populated by humble people, in the north as well as the south, ready to accept sacrifices but also striving to reach the goal, no matter whether it was on a hilltop or on the road to affluence. The logo could be seen everywhere, on the T-shirts of the riders in the Pneus Pirelli team in the 1910s or in the catalogues printed to publicise the products, illustrating the technical specifications of each: banded or beaded tyres, metal rim tyres such as Stella Extra or Flexor, or rubber straps for tyres. No wonder, then, that the continuous quest for innovation confirmed Pirelli's reliability for two-wheelers (shortly before four-wheelers). So much was this the case that it was again a feature of the advertisements designed about half a century later by Lora Lamm in 1959, by Riccardo Manzi in 1962 and 1963, by Massimo Vignelli and Aldo Ballo in 1966. Longevity is synonymous with classicism and reliability in market share. There is no better business card for success. That same P, in fact, would be blazoned in the following years across the chests of the legendary champions—Ottavio Bottecchia, Alfredo Binda, Learco Guerra—who battled it out after the Great War. And then it appeared again on the outfits of Gino Bartali and Fausto Coppi, the standard-bearers of the golden years of cycle racing, when a stage race or a road classic would become a social and cultural phenomenon. Or even a way of understanding politics, as happened in July 1948, when Bartali's victory in the Tour was capable of placating the Marxist revolutionary fury after the attempt to assassinate Palmiro Togliatti. Bartali and

sporting reasons that motivated, exacerbated and, at times, falsified it', commented Giuseppe Ambrosini in the May-June 1949 issue of the *Rivista Pirelli*. The magazine had a colour photo on the cover showing Coppi, with his thin face and wearing a flannel shirt, and Bartali with his big nose and wearing a double-breasted pinstripe suit. The article was entitled 'Bartali and Coppi: the secret of power'. One star wanes and another rises on the horizon.
In those years the popularity of cycling was booming, and the Italians' love affair with bicycles continued in the immediate post-war period. While projecting themselves into the dream of travelling comfortably in Fiat's economy cars (it happened, but in the 1960s),

Much more than being an easily recognisable advertising logo, the 'long P' became an icon of Italy that found a significant part of its identity in cycling

Coppi not only rewrote the history of cycling in their own way, restoring that destiny of rivalry and duality that, beginning with Romulus and Remus, has characterised the history of the Italic spirit, but they were the precursors of what was to come, in terms of mindset and anthropological approach, in the relations between the generations of fathers and sons, in the conflict between teachers and pupils. 'One could write a lot about this dualism, and it is not easy to assess the human, professional and

they continued to throng the roadsides to watch the wearer of the pink jersey riding past. And all the better if he was separated from the group, in solitary action. Everyone tried to emulate Bartali and Coppi exchanging water bottles, as on 4 July 1952, while climbing the Col du Galibier during the famous stage of the Tour from Lausanne to Alpe d'Huez. Everyone, even the amateurs who competed on Saturday mornings for their company team, dreamt of making a victorious breakaway.

The Sports Workshop

— 136

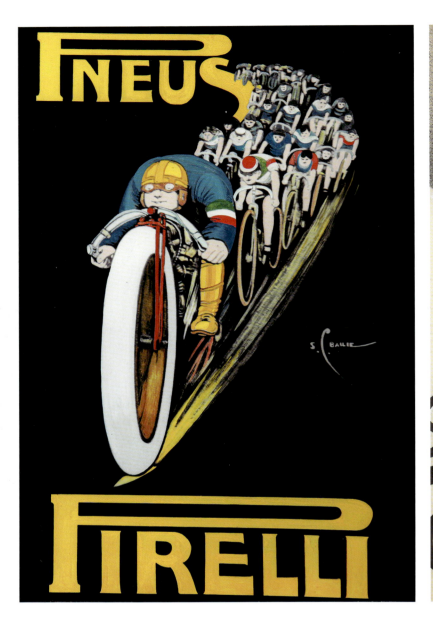

S.C. Ballie, advertisement for Pirelli bicycle tyres, 1913

Renzo Bassi, sketch for advertisement for Pirelli bicycle tyres, 1933

Fausto Coppi in the 26th Giro d'Italia, 1953, photo Publifoto

Fausto Coppi and Gino Bartali on the cover of *Pirelli. Rivista d'informazione e di tecnica*, no. 3, 1949, photo Federico Patellani

Like the character of the rebellious wingman in Giovanni Testori's novel *Il dio di Roserio* (1954), who partly succeeds, only to end up hitting his head on a stone after his captain shoves him.

Cycling remains one of the few recreational activities capable of conveying the mood of young working-class Lombardy, hopeful and dreamy. These were the people that on Saturday mornings, doffing their overalls, loved to breathe in the pure air of the Alpine foothills and throw themselves enthusiastically into the descents, pedalling from Ghisallo to the gates of Milan. Certainly, it was from this population of unknown athletes and enthusiasts that the competitors were drawn for the Pirelli Grand Prix, at the time the most important race reserved for amateurs, one of the most eagerly awaited of the year, where future champions competed. The finish line was in the velodrome built in Milan's trade fair district and named after Giuseppe Vigorelli, Pirelli's sales director. The origins of the race were recounted in an article by Lamberto Artioli, published in the May-June 1952 issue of the *Rivista Pirelli*. It all began on the morning of 30 November 1948, when the Commendatore Arturo Pozzo, the sales manager and manager of the national team, met Alfredo Binda, a cyclist in the thirties, winner of three road world championships and five editions of the Giro d'Italia, whom the French nicknamed 'La Gioconda'. 'Look, Binda', Pozzo said forthrightly, 'I'd like to develop a project for a cycle race to be held in Italy, of a national nature. The race should adopt a com-

A colour photo on the cover showing Coppi, with his thin face and wearing a flannel shirt, and Bartali with his big nose and wearing a double-breasted pinstripe suit. The article was entitled 'Bartali and Coppi: the secret of power'

pletely new formula, interesting enough to attract all the finest amateurs of the peninsula to the start. In short, I'd like it to be a competition for selecting those young talents that will then swell the ranks of the professionals'.

The *Rivista Pirelli* followed the annual event closely, especially in the 1950s, a glorious period of provincial life with its rudimentary bandages made from tow, its camphor rubs and herbal remedies. It was Testori and Pasolini's Italy that took part, as champions or spectators, in the forays along the roads connecting the Po Valley with the hills of Varese or Como. The colourful teams would go streaming past

Riccardo Manzi, advertisement for Pirelli bicycle tyres, 1962

Lora Lamm, advertisement for Pirelli bicycle tyres, window placard, 1959

Talking About Champions: Music, Techniques, Images… — 141

Final race of the 8th Gran
Premio Pirelli, 1956

The Sports Workshop

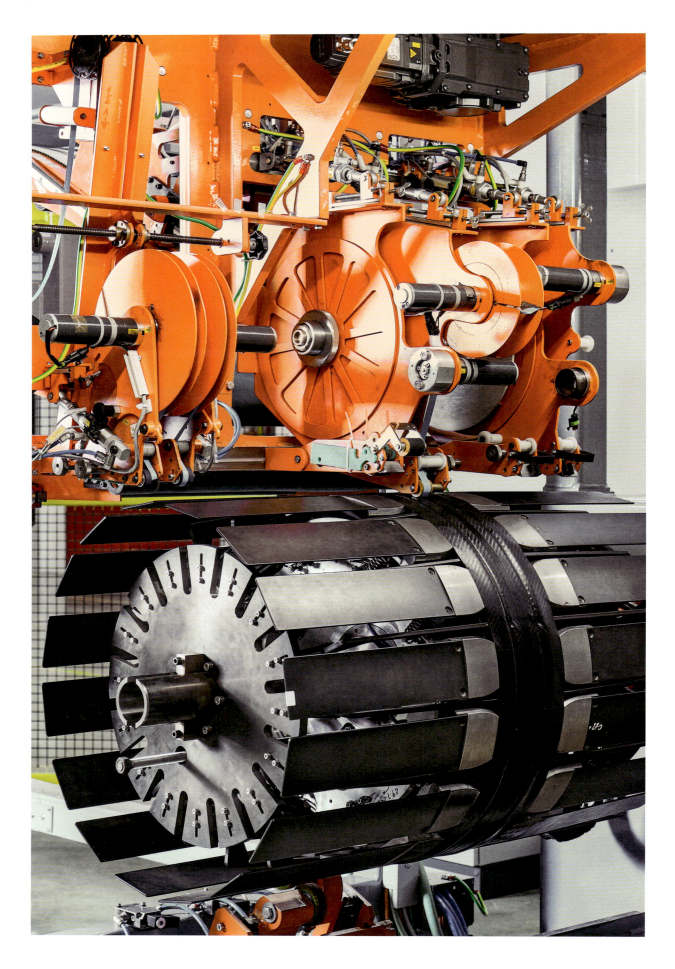

A machine in the packaging department of the Pirelli plant at Bollate (Milan), 2022, photo Carlo Furgeri Gilbert

the lakes, and there almost always appeared 'some devil on two wheels, zigzagging through the thick of the procession and disappearing round a bend', as Giansiro Ferrata wrote in his comic-style chronicle recounting the sixth Pirelli Grand Prix in the September-October 1954 issue of the *Rivista*. Then, suddenly, the years picked up speed. The evolution of progress, technological advances and even the economic boom imposed new rules on the anthropology of cycling. The impression is that the rituals of a pre-modern Italy would soon disappear forever. On 21 October 1961, the Giro di Lombardia, a race that traditionally closes the cycling calendar, started from the Pirellone. In the photos you can see the teams of runners being welcomed inside the skyscraper, and then, after the official welcome, parading on their shiny bikes through the streets past its large windows. There is no rhetoric in the language of these photographs, but a very slender unifying thread. The exertions of one of the toughest sports are related to the elegance of an architectural structure that marks a precise historical moment in the interpretation of modernity. Without forgetting that the workers in the factory making the tyres mounted on the bicycles of those champions made an effort similar to that of the cyclists on an uphill climb. Perhaps this is the reason why cycling is considered a working-class sport. It matters who wins, of course, but if there were no wingmen, like workers on the assembly line, there would be no victories either.

Also in 1961, Pirelli announced its decision to set up a new tyre plant at Villafranca Tirrena, in the province of Messina, called Pirelli Sicilia S.p.A. This was done to decentralise a whole independent production line, planned to satisfy the domestic and export markets. The plant, occupying an area of 285,000 square metres, began production in 1964 and was advanced in its degree of automation and systematic controls over each step in manufacturing. Fourteen years later, in 1975, the Azienda Pneumatici Motovelo was founded, remaining active until, in the last decade of the twentieth century, the line of bicycle tyres was discontinued. This marked the end of the long association between Pirelli and cycling all through the century of modernity. But it was only a brief interval. In 2017 the company started producing bicycle tyres again and in 2022, coinciding with the 150th anniversary of its foundation, the Bollate plant, on the northern outskirts of Milan, opened for the production of bicycle tyres for professional purposes. The scenarios change, people change, but the fable uniting grass, sweat and rubber continues.

Massimo Vignelli, advertisement for Pirelli bicycle tyres, window sticker, 1966, photo Aldo Ballo

Start of the Giro di Lombardia at the Pirelli Skyscraper in Milan, 1961, photo Publifoto

The Sports Workshop

by Giuseppe Di Piazza
-
Journalist, writer and photographer

Music and Choirs to Celebrate the Podium

The sacred value of anthems simulates victory in war, strengthens the passion of the fans and revives the spirit of participation of a whole community

*Maybe it won't be a song
That changes the rules of the game
But that's how I want to live this adventure
Without borders and with our hearts in our throats.*

— Edoardo Bennato and Gianna Nannini,
Un'estate italiana, 1990

Try listening to *You'll Never Walk Alone* sung in Anfield stadium, as Liverpool come out onto the pitch. 'The world's finest club anthem for a football team' (as ranked by *France Football*), sung by tens of thousands of fans, will send shivers down your spine. José Mourinho had the same spine-tingling experience at the Stadio Olimpico a couple of years back, when he heard for the first time sixty thousand voices in the stands singing *Roma, Roma, Roma* ('the world's second finest anthem' according to *France Football*). These emotions become the epic of a team, the soundtrack of feelings that, in the case of sport, of many sports, unite whole cities, whole nations.

The story of the love affair between sport and music is the history of the world, though it should be said that its roots are not very noble in some cases. Together we can see, starting from football, what this epic is made of. And how remote it is from the emotions that music at its broadest arouses in many other sports based on individual performances rather than team efforts. What follows is a journey through melodies, rhythms and words, earphones and deafening levels of amplification, human choruses and stadium fanfares. The love affair between sport and music is ancient and it begins—believe it or not—just outside a cave, with a piece of wood being banged against a hollow log.

Orwell and the battle
What is sport? A noble part of our life that does our body good whenever we practise it. Or, as fans, when we share in a collective passion just by cheering, adding our voice and excitement to those of countless other people in a stadium or while watching TV with friends.

But sport, whether team or individual events, is more than just passion. It is also the representation of something else. In an article entitled 'The Sporting Spirit', published in 1945, George Orwell wrote: 'Nearly all the sports practised nowadays are competitive. You play to win, and the game has little meaning unless you do your utmost to win'. The author of *Animal Farm* and *1984* added: 'At the international level sport is frankly mimic warfare'. It's a clash, a battle. Whether it's between groups (teams) or individuals (athletes). And battles, the urge to combat, since prehistoric times have had their

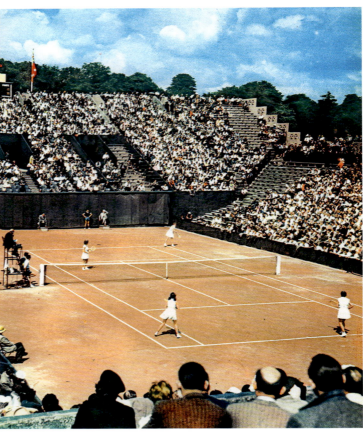

Young & Rubicam, Ronaldo in the advertising campaign 'Power is nothing without control', in *Pirelli World*, no. 21, 1999

French Open, women's doubles final at Stade Roland Garros, Paris, 1954

following pages
Fans at the Stadio Giuseppe Meazza during a match in the Italian football championship, 1967

Footballer Ivan Firotto, 1953

primordial, fearsome soundtrack: a piece of wood banged on a hollow log.
Of course, that relationship has found new forms, since we don't always fight on turf with the armies arrayed to the sound of drums and trumpets (which, remember, were used to impart orders in music, and still are). In the stadiums of the twenty-first century, the clash is mostly bloodless, and highly technical. But there are some degrading exceptions. All too often, it should be said, some extreme fans chant racist insults from the terraces, leading to complaints to the police and ASBOs. All the same, clean, rhythmic, sung support, with thrilling choruses to urge on their 'warriors' in shorts and shirts, is still strongly prevalent. And, as *France Football* wrote, this support has its ranking as well as its discography.

Passion at 33 rpm
The celebrated *You'll Never Walk Alone* was adopted by the English team in the 1963 version by Gerry and The Pacemakers, which rather betrayed the original version. Composed in 1945 by Oscar Hammerstein II and Richard Rodgers for the musical *Carousel*, it is sung to console the millworker wife of the protagonist, a fairground barker, after he is killed during a robbery. In football, as everyone knows, at most the players might sometimes steal a goal, but they don't commit real crimes, at least not on the pitch… Other famous football anthems are by composers ranging from Antonello Venditti (Roma) to Nino D'Angelo (Napoli), Elio and Graziano Romani (Inter, though in their hearts the Nerazzurri's fans cherish *Pazza Inter amala*), and Toni Malco (Lazio). The case of Inter's two anthems is emblematic. The first and earlier song has its roots in the team's unpredictability and reflects its spirit: 'Love her / Crazy Inter, love her / It's endless joy… But don't make us suffer'. The second, *C'è solo l'Inter*, composed in 2002 in honour of the team's legendary president Giuseppe Prisco, has institutional aspirations. It's clear which of the two appeals more to the Nerazzurri's impassioned fans.
The official discography of football should include Pink Floyd's *Fearless,* recorded in 1971 as the second track of the album *Meddle*. The geniuses of

progressive rock used an (English) stadium chorus to counterpoint Dave Gilmour's guitar at the thirtieth second of the song.
But the passion for the combination of music and sport goes well beyond football. Our every gesture, during an athletic action or a competitive effort, can be supported by chords, melodies, rhythm and words. The proof is offered by the study conducted in 1997 by the London team headed by Professor Costas Karageorghis ('The Psychological, Psychophysical and Ergogenic Effects of Music in Sport: A Review'). His studies have shown that music during competitions can produce effects resembling those of chemicals. So much so that the International Federations in recent years have banned earphones during competitions, considering the effects of music as almost equivalent to doping. This triggered an immediate protest in the community of athletes accustomed to training (especially in running and cycling) while using earphones to listen to their favourite tuns, or those most effective in sustaining the effort.

Our every gesture, during an athletic action or a competitive effort, can be supported by chords, melodies, rhythm and words

Compilations and the like
So what do athletes listen to when they run? What gets them psyched up, steeling them to sustain the effort? And what rhythm should the music have? At the end of the last decade, the University of Verona conducted an experiment whose results were later published in *Frontiers in Psychology*. The aim was to understand the kind of music that most helps athletes sustain physical exertion, taking a sample of nineteen women between the ages of twenty-four and thirty-one. The researchers, led by Luca Paolo Ardigò, professor of Methods and Teaching of Sports at the Department of Neuroscience, discovered that high-tempo music is the most effective in reducing the perception of physical exertion. The tests involved exercises first without music, then with tunes at low intensity (90–110 BPM), medium (130–150 BPM) and high intensity (170–190 BPM). The conclusions were clear: when listening to high-intensity music, exercise 'seems less challenging', as Ardigò wrote, 'but it is actually more beneficial in terms of improving physical fitness'. For the curious, this is the list of songs used by the researchers: Taylor Swift, *Cruel Summer* (172 BPM), Green Day, *Basket Case* (176 BPM), Pat Benatar, *Love Is a Battlefield* (181 BPM), Scissor Sisters, *Laura* (182 BPM), Caro Emerald, *You Don't Love Me* (189 BPM).
So there are close ties between what we listen to and what we're capable of doing under stress. So close that it has given rise to veritable playlists for athletics, available on all music streamers. Professor Karageorghis's research at Brunel University, London, suggests some specific works well suited for training. Three of them are surprising: *Applause* (Lady Gaga), excellent for high-intensity cardio training, according to the study; *Roar* (Katy Perry), well suited for mental preparation;

The Sports Workshop

Rome–Singapore race, Harley-Davidson with Pirelli tyres, 1975

Advertising campaign 'Superga. Your shoes chosen by the champions', Agenzia Centro, window sticker, 1978

The Monster (Eminem and Rihanna), useful for power training.

The new Beethovens
Then there is a sound that has great evocative power for those who love sports: the roar of engines. Every car has a voice, every motorcycle has its song. At Ducati for years they've been very careful not to get rid of the distinctive clatter made by the clutch as well as the roar from the exhaust on certain models, especially the most famous ones. The rumble the legendary 996 makes when it idles at a traffic light

Then there is a sound that has great evocative power for those who love sports: the roar of engines. Every car has a voice, every motorcycle has its song

is instantly recognisable… So performance isn't everything, sound counts too. The same, and perhaps even more resonant, is true of the voice of a Ferrari or the exhaust of a Harley-Davidson. Anyone who has ever watched a MotoGP race from the stands or the paddock will never forget the (shrieking, epic) music of motorcycles passing at 300 kph. Just as the sound trail left by a Ferrari chased by a Red Bull on the Monza straight will remain etched in the memory.

They are mnemonic impressions, unforgettable soundscapes, just as much as the silence of Lake Carezza at dawn muffled by a blanket of snow. The connection between music and motorsports is so strong that it has prompted hundreds of Spotify subscribers to compose music using the sound of exhausts. Just to give an example, the heart of the new Mustang SUV inspired one of Detroit's greatest electronic music composers, Matthew Dear, to transform its sound into a music track available on all platforms. The same apps have compilations devoted to the leading carmakers, first and foremost Ferrari.

Tazio Nuvolari and the Torpedo blu
In this long love affair between music and motorsport there are even some songs that have entered our collections of LPs and CDs. We can examine them, jumping from one side of the Atlantic Ocean to the other. We'll start with the Beach Boys, who in 1963 came out with *Little Deuce Coupe*, an album devoted to the 1932 Ford, a veritable legend at the time. Eleven years later, the German band Kraftwerk, pioneers of electronic music, released *Autobahn*, whose cover image featured a VW Beetle and a Mercedes 280SE. It has a long track built up out of a mix of tyre sounds, car radios and horns. This was followed shortly after, in 1982 and 1983, by *Driving In My Car* by Madness (featuring the Morris Minor) and *Eliminator* by ZZ Top, which pays homage to the 1933 Ford B coupé. In 1991 Chris Rea chose a Caterham Super Seven (he was the proud owner of one) for the cover of his album *Auberge,* while two years later Blur paid tribute to the Ferrari F40 on the cover of the CD entitled *Chemical World,* a single from the album *Modern Life Is Rubbish.*

Tazio Nuvolari competing in his last Mille Miglia, 1948

The epic of the combination of music and engines reached one of its peaks in Italy, with a sumptuous album by Lucio Dalla, aptly titled *Automobili* (1976). Written with the poet Roberto Roversi, the album contains six unmistakable tracks: *Intervista con l'Avvocato, Mille Miglia, Nuvolari, L'ingorgo, Il motore del 2000, Due ragazzi*.
The portrait of the legendary driver that emerged from Roversi's pen, caressed by Dalla's music, was epoch-making: 'Nuvolari is short in stature […] When Nuvolari races, is he scary? Because the engine is fierce as it roars across the plain'.
A few years earlier, in the middle of 1968, the genius of Giorgio Gaber had created a song that resounded (and perhaps still does) in the ears of Italians as a hymn to light-heartedness: *Torpedo blu*. It opens with the words 'I'm coming to pick you up tonight in my Torpedo / The sports car that gives me a tone of youth'. A marvel, based on simple and unforgettable rhymes.

Music that moves
Then there are graceful movements and gestures, whether human or equine. They, too, call for their own soundtrack. Take synchronised swimming, a sport of great charm, or dressage, where riders have to attain perfection from their horses. In training, girls and boys make continuous, methodical use of music. In 2013 Eremo del Castegno, ridden by Valentina Truppa, won the European Grand Prix freestyle performing impeccably to the notes of *Volare*.
In the water, the music accompanying solo synchronised swimming champions ranges from Edith Piaf singing *Non, je ne regrette rien* (chosen by the Spaniard Andrea Fuentes) to *Bohemian Rhapsody* by Queen (the soundtrack of one of the veterans of the event, the Italian Manila Flamini). How do athletes hear music underwater? How do they synchronise their movements with rhythms and melodies? The secret lies in watertight speakers called 'probes' installed in the pools where competitions are held. And water, as we know, is a good conductor of sound.
The art of moving to time and burning calories while keeping fit found its prophetess some forty years back. Jane Fonda was a legendary actress for a generation that loved the cinema of civic engagement together with her very pleasant looks. In April 1982, Henry Fonda's daughter and Peter's sister produced the first video in history (as far as we know) made by a star devoted to home fitness. The title was simple: *Jane Fonda's Workout*, a blend of warm-up, aerobics and stretching, with short introductions followed by exercises performed to the music of the time: a mixture of disco pop and flashes of pop-rock. And she, a beautiful prophetess in a glittering blue bodysuit and with hair fluffed out in *Charlie's Angels* style, kept this up for over an hour. Her *Workout* was a resounding success, spending almost five years on the chart of best-selling cassettes (VHS) in the United States. It immediately created a sort of health craze around the world: many gyms were converted into aerobics rooms, rather as now happens with Pilates and similar exercise programmes. Jane Fonda became a planetary symbol no longer for taking a stand against the Vietnam war (her image in the 1960s), but for taking a stand against body fat and flabby muscles. Even today, a beautiful octogenarian, her videos distributed piecemeal on free platforms are viewed by millions of people.

The Sports Workshop

— 156

Pirelli promotional record for Motovelo tyres: 45 rpm containing a song by Genesis and another by Steve Hackett, 1976

Ferrari F40 with Pirelli P Zero tyres, 1987

The Sports Workshop

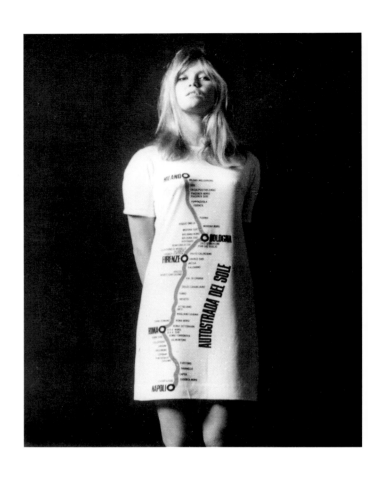

Liz Allsop photographed in the Pirelli magazine *Vado e Torno* for the release of the film *The Hare and the Tortoise*, directed by Hugh Hudson, 1966

Portrait of Lucio Dalla, from the 'Songs' column in *Fatti e Notizie*, no. 8, 1971

The banner of us all
Our journey into the indissoluble bond between music and sport can only end on a podium. What's more, it's Olympic. It is there that the winners' anthems resound, certifying the feat accomplished. When Mameli and Novaro wrote *Fratelli d'Italia* in 1847 (they originally titled it *L'inno degli italiani*), they would never have imagined that it would become a vibrant soundtrack for sporting successes. They

A war song becomes enthralling music, sweet to the ears of sporting heroes called on to vie with rivals from around the world

wanted to stir the conscience of a people, not to extol footballers or javelin throwers. The anthem was a call to battle (for freedom, independence, a national identity), just as *La Marseillaise* (1795) had been for the French for over half a century or, for almost two centuries, *God Save the King* for the British. Yet fortunately this is its destiny in peacetime. A war song becomes enthralling music, sweet to the ears of sporting heroes called on to vie with rivals from around the world, in a playful or athletic simulation of battle (Orwell was right).
So, if we limit our question to the Winter and Summer Olympics, how often have athletes had the good fortune to win gold, and so been able to hear their anthem from the top step of the podium? The most successful and therefore the best, without a doubt, from Athens 1896 to Tokyo 2021, have been the Americans. *The Star-Spangled Banner* has been performed 1174 times (the total number of gold medals won by the USA). In second place comes the Soviet Union, which before disappearing, totalled 473 performances for as many medals, followed by Germany with 305, the United Kingdom with 297, China with 284 and France with 263. Italy has taken home 258 golds, finishing seventh overall.
And which are the anthems least often performed at the Olympics? Of course, those of the countries that have never won gold. They include Barbados, Bermuda, Djibouti, Eritrea, Guyana, Iraq, Mauritius, Monaco, Macedonia and Togo. This last, truly last among the medallists (with only one bronze), has a hymn composed in 1960, after independence, which contains the following verse: 'Hail, hail the whole universe, / Let us unite our efforts in this great building work, / where a great new humanity will be born anew. / Let us bring happiness everywhere instead of sadness'.
What more can I say? We can only hope that Togo wins its first gold, so we can all listen all together to such beautiful words telecast worldwide.

Jane Fonda on the cover of *Vado e Torno*, no. 4, 1964

Fans celebrating Inter as champions of Italy, photo from the article by Gian Mario Maletto, 'Fino all'ultimo goal', in *Vado e Torno*, no. 6, 1965

Talking About Champions: Music, Techniques, Images... — 161

The Sports Workshop

by Darwin Pastorin
-
Journalist and writer

The Passion for Writing About Champions and Dreamers

The pages of great authors (Arpino, Brera, Soriano, Vergani, etc.) describe, through competitions, the qualities of women and men who have left their mark on our feelings

They're not scared of you. They're scared of what you represent to them: freedom.

— *Easy Rider*, directed by Dennis Hopper, 1969

Sport, especially football, our collective passion, definitively became literature on 2 February 1969. On that day, Guido Piovene having recommended him to the editor Alberto Ronchey, Giovanni Arpino started writing a weekly column entitled 'The Mirror of Sunday', the day the matches were played, in the Turin-based newspaper *La Stampa*. Arpino was a celebrated writer, the author of *La suora giovane* (1959), praised by Eugenio Montale and the winner of the Strega Prize in 1964 with *L'ombra delle colline*. His debut was immediately controversial. A duel of words followed with another literary giant, Pier Paolo Pasolini.

The author of *Corsair Writings* had wished for the defeat of the boxer Nino Benvenuti and further failures of the Italian team, like that against North Korea in the 1966 World Cup in England (won 1-0 by the Asian 'clowns', as Ferruccio Valcareggi, assistant to the team manager Mondino Fabbri, called them). In this way 'once and for all, we will no longer accept false consolations for low wages'.

The comment aroused Arpino's indignation, at a time when most of the intelligentsia considered not only religion, but sport a way of gulling the masses, preventing them from realising how marginalised and exploited they were. Here is Arpino's answer: 'Pasolini's words, pathetic and paradoxical, belong to a vocabulary that occasionally discharges a welter of specious interpretations over sport, as if sport were only deceptive escapism, a despicable diversion, the usual opium of the people, and not work, not a crossroads of different and important techniques, sometimes almost a science. Using sport as a target is an old weapon. It's a hackneyed argument typical of a certain strand of half-baked sociology'.

Why did that day, 2 February 1969, the year of the man on the moon and the Piazza Fontana bomb massacre, mean the end of youth and light-heartedness for many young people, a veritable revolution? Because the sports narrative had, at last found its constant point of reference, its compass, its master, who taught so many reporters to be 'poachers of stories and characters'. Of course, there was Gianni Brera. But he was a sports journalist in all respects, the finest of all, the inventor of neologisms and nicknames such as 'libero' and 'Centrocampista', which were even used by the foreign press. And it is impossible to forget 'Abatino' for Gianni Rivera (and before that for Livio Berruti, gold medallist in the 200 metres at the Rome

The Sports Workshop

The final stage of the 200 metres won by Livio Berruti at the 1960 Rome Olympics

Filming the 1960 Rome Olympics for television

Talking About Champions: Music, Techniques, Images…

Filmmaker Pier Paolo Pasolini kicking a ball during a break on the set of the film *Accattone*, Rome, 1961

Olympics), 'Rombo di tuono' for Gigi Riva, 'Rosso volante' for Eugenio Monti (bobsleigh champion), 'Schopenhauer' for the coach Osvaldo Bagnoli. Then there were important incursions into sports commentary. Like Dino Buzzati, the author of *The Tartar Steppe* and *Un amore,* who was sent on the road to review the 1949 Giro d'Italia, a few days after the death of the Torino football team in the flames of Superga ('Nothing remains, / nothing remains, or is it a glimmer? Nothing, nothing, there's nothing left, it rains / here where we speak of Rigamonti, / Castigliano, Maroso, Ballarin', wrote Mario Luzi).

in Turin, paging up the articles about the Giro d'Italia by the poet Alfonso Gatto. (Fausto Coppi tried, in vain, to teach him how to ride a bike). Or of the pages written over the years by those other great 'raiders' Orio and Guido Vergani.

Pier Paolo Pasolini also made an incursion into sports, as he loved playing football, as a right winger, the role of fantasists, dreamers and rebels. He supported Bologna and described football as 'the language of poets and prose writers'. In an interview for *L'Europeo* on 31 December 1970, he told Guido Gerosa: 'Football is the last sacred performance of our time. It's a ritual

Pier Paolo Pasolini also made an incursion into sports, as he loved playing football, as a right winger, the role of fantasists, dreamers and rebels

In this period cycling was still more popular than football, and Fausto Coppi won that edition ahead of his eternal rival Gino Bartali. They were two legends, like the heroes led by the captain Valentino Mazzola, who helped Italy emerge from the ashes of Second World War and twenty years of fascism. It was the Giro of the famous phrase of the radio commentator Mario Ferretti: 'Only one man is in the lead, his jersey is white and blue, his name is Fausto Coppi'. In his last article, Buzzati said goodbye: 'The folktale of cycling will never fade'. We like to think of the young Italo Calvino, in 1947, in the editorial office of *L'Unità*

in the depths, even if it is escapism. While other sacred performances, even the Mass, are declining, only football remains. Football is the spectacle that has replaced the theatre. The cinema couldn't replace it, but football could. Because the theatre is a relationship between a flesh-and-blood audience and flesh-and-blood characters acting on stage. Whereas the cinema is a relationship between a flesh-and-blood audience and a screen, shadows. Instead, football is again a spectacle in which a real world, of flesh and blood, on the terraces, in the stands, measures itself against real protagonists, the athletes on the field, who move and behave in keeping

Nino Benvenuti and Giuliano Gemma portrayed in the article by Giuseppe Signori, 'Cinema and the Ring', in *Vado e Torno*, no. 1, 1969

Eugenio Monti's four-man bobsleigh in training on the Cortina d'Ampezzo track, 1959

NEL MONDO DELLE DODICI CORDE

CINEMA E RING

Nino Benvenuti, il miglior peso medio che l'Italia abbia mai avuto, sta interpretando in Spagna, a fianco di Giuliano Gemma, il suo primo film, un western per la regia di Duccio Tessari. Non è la prima volta che un idolo della boxe affronta la macchina da presa; si ripete una storia vissuta da tanti campioni nel passato. Da Mario Bosisio a Enzo Fiermonte, da Mitri a Cerdan, da Tony Zale a Ray "Sugar" Robinson, da Max Baer a Rocky Marciano, sono moltissimi i pugili di fama che, con alterna fortuna, sono entrati nell'universo di celluloide

di Giuseppe Signori

Nessuno, tranne forse il suo avvocato personale, sa ciò che vuole Nino Benvenuti campione nel ring e farfalla, o pressappoco, fuori. Il ronzio delle infinite parole che il triestino spara frivolmente ovunque, lo svolazzare infaticabile qui e là, il succhiare quasi fosse nettare medaglie e premi di ogni genere, milioni di lire e colline di dollari, lo hanno fatto personaggio. Ossia Benvenuti appare ormai uno « showman », meglio il « divo » pronto anche per il cinema. La scorsa estate, puntualmente, la società Ultra-Film, con sede e capitali a Roma, ingaggiò Nino quale protagonista di una storia cinematografica scritta da Ennio Flaiano. Come titolo poco edificante, ma significativo, venne scelto: « ...*Vivi o preferibilmente morti...* ».

Il compenso per Nino Benvenuti rimase fissato in 60 milioni. Più tardi i contratti diventarono tre. Si voleva dare una continuazione al primo film. L'interesse della Ultra-Film per il pugile si spiega, in parte, con il fatto che il maggior azionista è il dottor Giuseppe Pasquale da Ferrara. Questo signore, prima di diventare presidente della Federazione Calcistica Italiana, fu apprezzato arbitro di pugilato. Personalmente lo ricordiamo negli anni Trenta dirigere importanti combattimenti con protagonisti Alberto Farabullini e Vittorio Livan, Oddone Piazza e Clemente Meroni, tutti pesi

Nino Benvenuti e Giuliano Gemma (qui presi d'assalto da giovani ammiratrici) sono attualmente in Spagna, dove stanno ultimando le riprese di « Vivi o preferibilmente morti », un western diretto da Duccio Tessari. Vestire i panni dell'attore ha richiesto al campione mondiale dei medi un duro impegno: ha dovuto infatti imparare a cavalcare e perdere molte delle sue preziose mattinate per il perfezionamento dell'inglese.

The Sports Workshop — 170

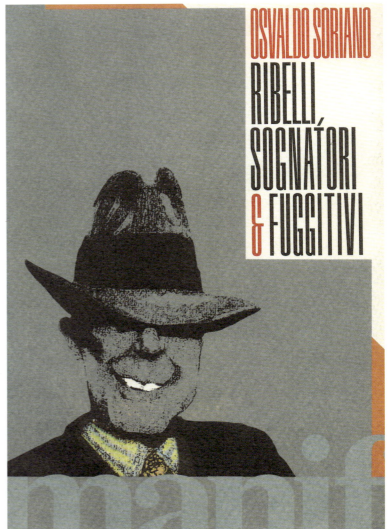

Portrait of Dino Buzzati, 1957

Cover of Osvaldo Soriano's book, *Ribelli, sognatori e fuggitivi*, Manifesto Libri, 1991

with a precise ritual. This is why I consider football to be the only great ritual left in our time'. When he made the film *Medea* starring Maria Callas (1969, based on Euripides' tragedy), Pasolini cast the triple jumper Giuseppe Gentile (former world record holder and bronze medallist in Mexico in 1968) as Jason and the discus thrower Gianni Brandizzi as Hercules. Giacomo Bulgarelli, a star player for Bologna and Pasolini's idol, turned down a part in *The Canterbury Tales*.

'El Gordo' Soriano's stories take us to the outer-city playing fields, among quirky defenders, dreamy goalkeepers, epileptic referees

Umberto Saba, advised by Carletto Cerne, the shop assistant at the Libreria Antiquaria in Trieste ('Dead people ask a dead man for dead books'), went to the stadium just twice, to see Triestina play. He brought home, so they say, his famous *Five Poems on the Game of Football*, with *Goal* above all practically an anticipation, if you think of it, of live TV broadcasts of modern football, in the foreground 'the goalkeeper fallen to the defence', the broad field for 'the crowd— united euphoria' and the teammates embracing the goal-scorer, another close-up for the goalkeeper of the team that scored 'sending kisses from afar / saying, I too am part of the celebrations'.

Thanks to Arpino, in short, writing about football, cycling, boxing and basketball was suddenly transformed into a way of assessing competition through sports: not just the technical qualities of a man and a woman, but also the character of a nation, a pretext for reasoning about poetics and sociology, anthropology and even metaphysics. Today we still owe Arpino the best novel about football: *Azzurro tenebra*, the first edition was published by Einaudi in 1977, with a picture of Giacinto Facchetti on the cover. It was set in the 1974 World Cup in Germany, with the disheartening exit of Ferruccio Valcareggi's national team in the first round. We witness an authentic human comedy, between darkness and honey, the poor in spirit, troubled or noble characters. The protagonists are Arp (the author himself) and Il Vecio (Enzo Bearzot, Valcareggi's deputy and future coach of Italy's winning World Cup team in Spain in 1982). Of his book, Arpino commented: 'I consider myself a non-Italian writer, who uses his own language ever less. *Azzurro tenebra* is untranslatable'. Arp did not restrict himself to football. We have his masterly reports, for example, on motorsports (of Enzo Ferrari: 'Yes, it's true, they call him "the Drake", but only if he's at least thirty metres away. Otherwise, everyone addresses him by the title that comes most naturally: *ingegnere*, *commendatore* or *presidente*. His face cut out of very pale marble, Enzo Ferrari either remains silent or lets himself go in deep confidences, hemming in the person he's talking to in a network of extraordinary memories'). Still other examples are the pages on Augusto Manzo, an ace of *pallapugno*, a form of handball, the sport of the Langhe loved by Beppe Fenoglio and Cesare Pavese. Or his account of the historic boxing match in Kinshasa in Zaire, on 30 October 1974, between Muhammad Ali and George

The Sports Workshop

Portrait of Enzo Ferrari, 1953

Talking About Champions: Music, Techniques, Images… — 173

Juan Manuel Fangio and Amedeo Nazzari on the set of the film *Ultimo incontro* (*Last Meeting*), Monza Circuit, 1951

The Sports Workshop

The writer Giorgio Bassani, winner of the Strega Prize with *Cinque storie ferraresi* (*Five Stories of Ferrara*), 1956

Portrait of Eugenio Montale, 1962

Foreman. It was won by the former, a champion who preferred prison to the 'dirty war' in Vietnam, disowned his white name Cassius Clay, and joined the Nation of Islam (Norman Mailer offers a ringside account of the event in *The Fight*).

In Italy we are also indebted to Giovanni Arpino (and Nico Orengo) for our knowledge of the Argentine writer Osvaldo Soriano, a picaresque narrator of stories about *fùtbol*. He made his debut in Italy in 1974, first with Vallecchi and then Einaudi, with his

Giorgio Bassani, who was a friend of Clerici's, wrote about tennis in the pages of his masterpiece, *Il giardino dei Finzi Contini*

first masterpiece *Triste solitario y final*, with Raymond Chandler and Laurel and Hardy among the characters. But it was above all the tango of football that united Arp and 'El Gordo', who among other things, in a letter from exile in Paris to his friend Giovanni, on 7 May 1979, advised Torino to sign a formidable eighteen-year-old who 'scores two goals per game': a certain Diego Armando Maradona.

Soriano played football as a boy, a centre-forward with a knack for scoring in Cipolletti's Confluencia in Patagonia. But a hard knock to his knee brought his footballing adventure to an end, opening up the broad prairies of literature. The same fate as another great writer, Jack Kerouac, the father of the Beat Generation. A promising American football player as a running back, he was stopped on the threshold of a brilliant professional career in the Columbia University team by his truculent attitude to his teammates and the coach, and above all a serious injury. A blessing, if we can call it that, for us readers, because *On the Road* became an existential manifesto for many generations.

'El Gordo' Soriano's stories take us to the outer-city playing fields, among quirky defenders, dreamy goalkeepers, epileptic referees, small, pot-bellied coaches, the 'longest penalty shot in the world', and even a 'forgotten' World Cup, in 1942 in Patagonia, with the referee the son of Butch Cassidy, who 'had to knock heads with his pistol butt to have a penalty taken in favour of Italy'. That cup was won by the Mapuches Indios.

He didn't limit himself to football (which Jean-Paul Sartre saw as 'a metaphor for life'). His pages portray Juan Manuel Fangio, the ace of the wheel, 'a quiet idol', and the rough boxer Carlos Monzón, his whole life plagued by a troubled destiny. Beside Osvaldo Soriano, we can place another formidable South American author: the Uruguayan Eduardo Galeano, who became famous with his essay *The Open Veins of Latin America*, on the value of memory and the enormous harm done by colonialism. He was also an incomparable lover of football played and written. *Splendours and Miseries of the Game of Football* and *Closed for Football* are two texts considered essential for fans of the subject. And this is one of the phrases most often quoted during conferences or lectures: 'A journalist asked the German theologian Dorothee Sölle: "How would you explain to a child what

Footballer Gianni Rivera, 1968

happiness is?". "I wouldn't explain it", she said. "I'd toss him a ball and tell him to play"'.

So Arpino is the leitmotif, the compass, the guiding star, of this narrative, helping us get to the heart of the relationship between sport, especially football, and culture, in the form of literature, cinema, theatre, television and photography (the images from the *Rivista Pirelli* in these pages are exemplary). All the possible arts, in short. Opening the dance is the Mexican World Cup semi-final between Italy and West Germany on 17 June 1970, at the Estadio Azteca in Mexico City. 1-1 at full time, Boninsegna's goal, the Azzurri's defence and the frustration of the goal scored in the dying seconds of the match by the German full-back Schnellinger, who played in Italy for AC Milan. What made that match historic was the extra time, a carousel of emotions, a heart-pounding kaleidoscope. The Germans moved ahead with the centre-forward Müller, the equaliser came from the defender Burgnich. The Italians gained the advantage with Gigi Riva's left-footed shot. Müller's scored the equaliser, with a mistake by Gianni Rivera, who let the ball pass between the post and Albertosi, the infuriated goalkeeper. A moment later, it was 4-3: Boninsegna's run down the left flank, the right-footed touch from Rivera, no longer a reprobate but the *deus ex machina* of the situation. The Italian night, in many towns and villages, was filled with cheering. The Azzurri then lost the final to the Brazil of Jairzinho, Carlos Alberto and Pelé 4-1. That match would be called, complete with a plaque at the Azteca, 'the match of the century'.

'Italiagermaniaquattroatre', as the score would be written for a long time, would become many things: a film directed by Andrea Barzini, in 1990, with Massimo Ghini, Giuseppe Cederna, Fabrizio Bentivoglio and Nancy Brilli; a reunion between schoolmates on the occasion of the live broadcast of that match (with commentary by Nando Martellini); two plays, the first by Umberto Marino and the second by Gianfelice Facchetti, son of the unforgettable Giacinto, captain of our national team in that World Cup; a series of essays by Nando Dalla Chiesa, Maurizio Crosetti and Riccardo Cucchi, one of our finest radio commentators, a worthy heir to Enrico Ameri and Sandro Ciotti, and the pair Roberto Brambilla and Alberto Facchinetti. Not to mention the poems by Fernando Acitelli (author of the successful and surprising collection of football stories, published by Einaudi, *La solitudine dell'ala destra*) devoted to several protagonists of that memorable challenge.

The same splendid fate befell another match. This was at the 1982 World Cup in Spain on 5 July at the Sarrià stadium in Barcelona, on an afternoon of absurd heat. Italy and Brazil were playing to go through to the semi-finals, after beating Maradona's Argentina 2-1 and 3-1 respectively in the Catalan group of three. The Brazilian Seleção, only needed a draw to go through because of that extra goal against the Selección, Argentina's national team.

The situation was as follows: the green and golds were the favourites, coming from four wins out of four where they literally put on a show, thanks to Júnior, Zico, Falcão (a star player with Roma), Toninho Cerezo and the captain Sócrates, the intellectual who read Antonio Gramsci.

For the Azzurri the music was completely different: they reached Barcelona after three draws in the elimination rounds and managed second place only thanks to their better goal difference over Cameroon. They were suffering from fierce criticism of Paolo Rossi,

The Sports Workshop

Actors Giuseppe Cederna and Sara Bertelà during the theatrical performance *Le parole dalla fabbrica*, Auditorium Pirelli, Milan, 2016, photo Don't Movie

who was back after an unfair disqualification because of the 1980 betting scandal, summoned by coach Enzo Bearzot after only three games and a goal with Juventus at the expense of Roma's Roberto Pruzzo, the championship's top scorer (according to Pasolini 'the finest poet of the year'). The players, after heated controversy, acrimony and accusations, took refuge in press silence. Victory over Argentina failed to calm the waters, because Pablito Rossi still hadn't scored. Italy seemed to be the predestined victim on the altar of the Brazilian *Grande Bellezza*. Instead, on that 5th of July, everything was turned upside down, as in an epic game.

The Azzurri were the protagonists of a magical–realist adventure. Another night of Italian celebrations

Bearzot's boys won 3-2. Rossi's hat-trick, the forty-year-old Zoff's decisive save against a header by Oscar Bernardi, a defender of Italian origins. And it was the start of a triumphant cavalcade: 2-0 against Poland (with Rossi scoring a brace) and, in the final at the Santiago Bernabeu in Madrid, in front of president Sandro Pertini, happy as a child, the Azzurri beat West Germany 3-1 (the scorers were Rossi, the event's top scorer and the next winner of the Ballon d'Or, Tardelli, Altobelli and a pointless goal by Breitner, a Maoist full-back). The Azzurri had won their third World Cup (the fourth came with Marcello Lippi on the bench, in Berlin in 2006, after penalties against France). Narrating that triumph in the press gallery were Giovanni Arpino, Mario Soldati, Oreste del Buono and Gianni Brera.

In 1982, the Nobel Prize for Literature went to the Colombian Gabriel García Márquez, the father of magical realism. The Azzurri were the protagonists of a magical–realist adventure. Another night of Italian celebrations, a moment of collective joy, even poignant, in the period of terrorism (by then in its ashes). And to mark the fortieth anniversary of that feat, two years after Pablito's death, books, films and docufilms have been released. The 600-page volume by Piero Trellini, published by Mondadori, was a huge success: *La partita*, the novel of Italy-Brazil. We are living in the age of myriads of TV channels, generalist or pay-per-view, of storytelling or the story of sport on video (among the finest examples, Federico Buffa and Giorgio Porrà of Sky Sport). Stories upon stories, to recover the memory of many feats, of memorable aces.

Today, football is played every day. The observance of Sunday as 'the Lord's day', at Mass in the morning and the games in the early afternoon, all at the same time, on every field, is a thing of the past. Sacred and profane are united on the same day. Now, we need to have pay TV subscriptions to watch the championship and the cups and tournaments of (almost) the whole world at our fingertips, or rather the remote control, with the advantage that we can always follow our favourite team live, wherever we are.

T. S. Eliot (winner of the Nobel Prize in 1948) was right. Football has always been a 'fundamental element of contemporary culture'. But, often, even in the Bel Paese, other sports, fortunately and for the sake

Paola Egonu in action during the Coppa Italia Frecciarossa Quarter Final match in Milan, 24 January 2024

of equity, find a place, stirring strong emotions and popular feelings. We saw this during the Olympics. And at the end of 2023 when, on 26 November, Spain was decked out in blue, as in the 1982 World Cup. First, there was the second consecutive world championship won in the MotoGP in Valencia, by the Piedmontese Pecco Bagnaia, the heir to Giacomo Agostini and Valentino Rossi. Then, with all Italy glued to the TV set, there came the second Davis Cup in our history, forty-seven years after the victory in Chile. It was won by our fantastic tennis players in Malaga, braced by a new idol of the fans, just like the celebrated aces of football: Jannik Sinner of Alto Adige, a phenomenon capable of twice beating the number one seed, the Serbian Novak Djokovic, within ten days. Sinner, Lorenzo Musetti, Lorenzo Sonego, Matteo Arnaldi, Simone Bolelli and the captain Filippo Volandri stood in the place of the 1976 aces: Adriano Panatta, Corrado Barazzutti, Paolo Bertolucci, Tonino Zugarelli and the captain-symbol Nicola Pietrangeli. In the doubles, Panatta and Barazzutti, against the Chileans Patricio Cornejo and Jaime Fillol, turned up at the Estadio Nacional in Santiago, a place of detention and torture, in red T-shirts to protest against the coup by the regime of General Augusto Pinochet. Playing against Australia in Malaga, the Azzurri once again lifted the prestigious salad bowl in a triumph for the Italian flag. With Sinner demonstrating, in a worldwide telecast, his human qualities, his kindness, his generosity, as well as having shown his qualities as an authentic ace shortly before. And many wondered how the scribe of 'white gestures' Gianni Clerici and the disruptive Gian Piero Galeazzi would recount that stellar triumph… There was much nostalgia for the possible and impossible interviews of Gianni Minà, with football declaimed starting with 'the green of the grass and the blue of the sky', for Vladimiro Caminiti and the roads of the Tour de France, amid sunflowers, wine and songs, for Gianni Mura…

Tennis also has a resounding literary appeal. Ezra Pound played it for pleasure, and enjoyed fencing. The author of the *Cantos* even learned the art of boxing from lessons with Ernest Hemingway. 'I taught him to box, and Pound taught me what should and should not be written'. Giorgio Bassani, who was a friend of Clerici's, wrote about tennis in the pages of his masterpiece, *Il giardino dei Finzi Contini*, with the protagonist Micòl's love for this elegant game. And David Foster Wallace was a tennis fan. So much so that he wrote about it in his most celebrated book, *Infinite Jest,* with an essay honouring the Swiss champion Roger Federer as a 'religious experience'.

Thanks to a society that has become, fortunately, multicultural and multiethnic, we have applauded many Italians of foreign origins, with black skins. Examples are Marcell Jacobs, born in El Paso in the United States to an Italian mother and a Texan father, a fabulous gold medallist in the 100 metres and 4 x 100 relay at the Tokyo Olympics in 2020. Then there is the splendid Paola Egonu, born at Cittadella to Nigerian parents, gold medallist at the European Championships in 2021 in Serbia, Croatia, Romania and Bulgaria, and again at the Nations League in 2022 in Ankara. And sport has entered our Constitution, thanks to the parliamentarian Mauro Berruto (Partito Democratico), coach of the national volleyball team that won bronze at the London Games in 2012.

We say goodbye again with Giovanni Arpino. The opening of *Passo d'addio*: 'Life is either style or error'. Just like sport.

The Sports Workshop

by Massimo Sideri
-
Journalist and University lecturer

Innovation Redeems the 'Blue Spot'

The pride of remembrance for victories and the rebirth of hope and participation in a collective project called the 'culture of a nation'

Isn't it amazing how much of life turns on whether the ball goes over the net or comes right back at you?

— *Match Point*, directed by Woody Allen, 2005

'I say to you, "Don't think about elephants". What are you thinking about?', asks one of the characters in Christopher Nolan's finest films, *Inception*. 'An elephant' answers the other. Exactly. Think for a moment about one of the images stored in your brain as a 'wonderful moment of 2023'. It could be a memory, a photo, an emotion, a fragment of sporting pride and patriotism that makes us forget for a moment Dante's stern admonition that we unjustly drag behind us, like a clog on our progress ('Alas poor Italy the home of woe! / Ship without pilot in an ocean wild, / No gentle lady, but a brothel thou!' *Purgatory*, Canto VI). To perform this experiment, we would actually have to inject the question directly into our subconscious. Much as Leonardo DiCaprio does in the movie. There are other, more pragmatic ways to achieve the same result. For example, at the start of this chapter I could post a photo that was presumably already tagged in your mind as a 'sign of hope' or 'collective emotion'. Otherwise, one would have to rummage unceremoniously through the neurological filing system that scientists call the 'blue spot'.

Sport, for now, has nothing to do with this. It's a small part of the brain that we all have, regardless of nationality, located right at the junction between the skull and the neck. In fact, it is called the 'blue spot', not because it works only for Italians when they see the timeless image of Marco Tardelli exulting after the goal scored on 11 July 1982 against Germany in Madrid, but because this was the name given it in 1784 by the anatomist Félix Vicq-d'Azyr, who observed the bluish pigmentation of its cells. The fact is that this curious coincidence enables us to understand why one of the many images of Jannik Sinner's victories—perhaps while lifting the Davis Cup, or just after beating the number one seed Djokovic, or winning his first Slam in Australia early in 2024—has been indelibly recorded (we could say developed and printed on paper) in our emotional memory, filling us with a sense of optimism. Scientists have discovered that the 'blue spot' is where we permanently store significant moments often associated with an image that becomes indelible. The discovery was anticipated by a surgical, almost scientific reflection by Italo Calvino: 'I spent the first twenty-five years of my life (or thereabout) inside a landscape. Without ever getting out of it. I can never lose this landscape, because only what exists entirely within one's memory is definitive'.

The Sports Workshop

— 184

Talking About Champions: Music, Techniques, Images… — 185

Poster of *Inception*, directed by Christopher Nolan, 2010

New York City Harbor and the Twin Towers

Jannik Sinner in action during the Nitto ATP Finals 2023 tennis tournament at the Pala Alpitour arena in Turin, 12 November 2023

Clearly the mechanism can also be activated by troubling events associated with strong feelings. The Twin Towers of the World Trade Center, New York, being struck by two airliners on 11 September 2001 are an obvious example. And, in passing, it is worth pointing out that science has recently shown that a similar mechanism (but located in another part of the brain) also works with our memories of smells. That's right: science has shown that Proustian memory does

The 'blue spot' is where we permanently store significant moments often associated with an image that becomes indelible

exist. It was no coincidence that the *petite madeleine* stirred such rich feelings in Proust. The nose has a time machine in it.

But let's stay focused on the 'blue spot' and images that arouse a feeling of hope. This is why sport is more than just sport. It's also sociology, economics, science and psychology. I am reminded of a sign that appeared in the stands of the ATP Finals in Turin late in 2023. It read: 'Sinner saint now'. If we could, we should add: economist now. Because, if we theorise it, the number four tennis player in the world ranking (for now) is giving us a recipe and also new indicators. We can christen them 'Sinneromics'. What does it consist of? To understand it, we need, among other things, to turn up some of the finest pages of John Maynard Keynes, the Cambridge professor who helped find the recipe for emerging from the great slump of 1929, and whose essay *The Economic Consequences of the Peace* had also warned about what would happen if excessive sanctions were inflicted on the frayed economic and social fabric of Germany after the Great War. In particular, we should read some little-known notes that can be found at the end of his *General Theory*. In these philosophical writings, Keynes went so far as to abandon numbers and say that, although there is no economic reason why an optimistic entrepreneur is more likely to succeed in business than a pessimistic entrepreneur, the optimist will be more likely to succeed. The moral: expectations influence outcomes, at least in part. The question now is to separate blind optimism—as when people believed in the late nineteenth century that horses were able to count—from reasonable optimism. Thomas Edison put it another way: innovation is 1% inspiration, 99% perspiration. And in another famous aphorism, Edison said that he had not been wrong a hundred times, but only tried ninety-nine ways to make the hundredth work. They would be just words if it weren't for the fact that he put them seriously into practice. His team in Menlo Park (not the one in California where Facebook is today, but the one in New Jersey near New York, where the famous Bell Labs are still located) took almost two years of effort to find the right material to prevent the filament inside the lamp bulb from burning out in a few seconds. After two years, he managed to make bulbs that lasted twenty-four hours. It was a resounding success and the beginning of the age of electric light.

Andre Agassi during third round Rome Masters Series Tennis Tournement, 5 November 2000

following pages
Practising at the Caprera sailing school, 1968, photo Rodolfo Facchini

So here is Sinneromics: inspiration and a lot of perspiration (it is unsurprising that in the world of startups they say that success depends on three things: the first is *execution,* the second is *execution*. The third is *execution*). We could also quote one of the twentieth century's great conductors, Sir Georg Solti, and find the same teaching-vision by reading between the lines. A journalist once asked Solti how to become like him. The master answered: 'There are three things in life, talent, luck and work. Talent is a

a competitive commitment made up of calluses & bugs. The calluses are those on his right hand (look at the images to believe it). The bugs are the ones that creep into the player's head when he hits a ball out by half an inch. The first ball doesn't go in. He missed three match points in a row (freely quoted from the Davis Cup semi-final between Sinner and Djokovic). In tennis, more than in other sports, you have to work on your body and mind. Andre Agassi in his autobiography *Open* (not written in his own words,

'There are three things in life, talent, luck and work. Talent is a gift of nature. You can't do anything about it. Luck is the same: we're all waiting for it, but who knows if it will ever come. In short, the only thing you can do is to put in the effort'

gift of nature. You can't do anything about it. Luck is the same: we're all waiting for it, but who knows if it will ever come. In short, the only thing you can do is to put in the effort'.
There are several points of contact between sport, a nation's economy, and a sense of belonging. It is no coincidence, incidentally, that the dictatorships, both the Nazi dictatorship and Stalin's USSR, instilled so much energy and hope into real or apparent sporting successes. Sinner's tennis in particular lends itself particularly well to recounting this sport-economics double helix, because, returning to the recipe, his is

but certainly his life lived and told) says that no sport is so abysmally solitary as tennis. Not even that of the marathon runner, who at least runs in a crowd (it's worth recalling that in Agassi's time players were banned from talking to their coaches during a match, a rule that has since been changed. Maybe that's why we're seeing fewer hysterical scenes). So: calluses & bugs. In Italy we often have inspiration and we boast about it, rightly so. We've always had it. It's part of our semantic capital, as the philosopher Luciano Floridi would say. When I had the opportunity to interview Steve Wozniak, the father with Steve Jobs of

The Sports Workshop — 190

Talking About Champions: Music, Techniques, Images… — 191

The Sports Workshop — 192

Portrait of Federico Fellini, 1962

Apple a few years ago, he told me: 'You Italians have inspiration, creativity'. What he meant to say was: why can't you take advantage of the digital economy that democratises the tools and requires this above all to succeed? Maybe it's because we just as often forget about the second part of the recipe: perspiration. Those who have observed Sinner's technical growth this year (not only in his service, but also in greater tactical maturity) know what we're talking about. The system also pays off for Sinner: 150 million euros over

This is why sport is more than just sport. It's also sociology, economics, science and psychology

ten years from Nike alone. Another 5 million a year from other sponsors. Plus the prize money. But that's not the point. To recap: Edison's perspiration (practising his serve to the point of maniacal exhaustion is rather like testing hundreds of new filaments in the Torricellian void of lamps to see them repeatedly explode in your hand, until you find the right one) and Keynes's optimism (Sinner said: 'I don't smile much, but I have a lot of fun'). The dialogue between tennis and economics does not end here. As a rule, only the eight best players in the world play in the ATP Finals, the end-of-year tennis event. We might think it's a sort of G8 of tennis, although the simile doesn't quite work. There are too many exceptions if we compare players and nations, starting with the Serbian number one. If it were a real G8, France would be missing now. And also the USA, which since the golden days of Andre Agassi and Sampras has been trying to glimpse a new dominant player to idolise in the pure talent of Ben Shelton (one of the most fun players to watch on the circuit, even though he is behind three other Americans in the ATP rankings at present). We cannot forget the case of Switzerland with Roger Federer. So the Finals (like the Davis Cup) are not a mirror of the G8 governments. More than anything else, they function as economic indicators of the future, of futures. There is no certainty that this will be the case, but there are some clues. In the age of fragmentation, we need new indicators. And the historic Davis Cup semi-final, along with the final won after a drought lasting forty-seven years, proves that it's working for now.

The Sinner effect is reminiscent of Alberto Tomba's effect in skiing in the 1980s. 'Tomba la Bomba' they called him. A decade of absolute domination of the white landscape between the late eighties and early nineties. His success was overwhelming, to the point of making a whole generation discover skiing, just as today, thanks to Sinner, the tennis clubs are booming. We'll talk about this later. Some videos of Tomba can still boost your adrenaline decades later. Partly because they make us feel young again if we are a few years older. As when he defied the laws of gravity, recovering with a superhuman lunge after falling on his skis at Lech, Austria, in 1994, and won, despite everything with the fastest time. Or else they give you the feeling you've missed something if you're

Alberto Tomba skis to a gold medal in the Giant Slalom event of the Winter Olympic Games at the Nakiska ski area, Canada, 25 February 1988

a few years younger. It's the Woodstock effect. The feeling you've missed out on a historic moment. Who wouldn't want to have been in Central Park, New York, when Simon and Garfunkel sang *The Sound of Silence*?

But let's return to sport itself. Looking over our shoulders, each of us has three or four great moments in which we have experienced a collective emotion. For my generation, in addition to Tardelli and Tomba, it will inevitably include that long season that began with *Azzurra* and her skipper Cino Ricci and continued with *Luna Rossa* and Paul Cayard. For a few weeks we all remembered that we were a nation of sailors, heirs to the trading fleets of the Genoese and the Venetians. Of Marco Polo and Christopher Columbus. Going a little further back in time, Sergio Leone had the same effect (inspiring a Clint Eastwood who has transformed himself from a gunslinger over the years into a monumental director) and Federico Fellini. Everyone envies us them. And we lose ourselves in the great beauty. Another was the Davis Cup final won by Adriano Panatta and Paolo Bertolucci against Pinochet's Chile in 1976. We live in a distortion of memory, a continuous flow of eclipses of what we are and what we could be. It is what Montanelli called the anti-Italian syndrome. We are our own worst enemies. We're deaf to our own merits. We can call it the Eustachio syndrome, after the great anatomist to whom we owe the discovery of the functioning of the inner ear. Admired in his lifetime, while working at the University of Padua, he was forgotten as soon as he died. It happens all the time. Until a champion rouses us from lethargy, enters the deep mechanisms of the 'blue spot' and rekindles a sense of hope, optimism, and desire to take part in a collective project called the culture of a nation. A moral constitution that comes and goes and that remains alive thanks to the only known antidote to decline: culture; our history.

Will Sinner make it? If we're writing about him now, maybe he's already made it.

The Sports Workshop

by Sandro Modeo
-
Journalist and writer

Neurosciences for Training

The speed of execution of an athlete's gestures is developed by working on kinaesthetic intelligence and precision of technique. The role of 'enhanced perceptions'

> *You have to feel what the wave is doing, accept its energy, get in sync. […] You don't need to see!*
>
> — *Point Break*, directed by Kathryn Bigelow, 1991

In 2016 Prince—yes, the singer-multi-instrumentalist of *Purple Rain*—decided to add another concert to the two just held in Oakland. This time, however, he would be performing in the larger Oracle Arena, the temple of the Golden State Warriors (GSW) and Stephen Curry, the player who has revolutionised basketball in recent years with his inimitable three-point field goals. According to more than one observer, Prince's decision as a great basketball fan was due to the magnetic attraction he felt for Curry.

That fervour, perhaps fostered by the empathy of one innovator for another, is offset by the problematic admiration of certain scholars, above all, the neuroscientist John Krakauer of Johns Hopkins in Baltimore. Contrasting him with LeBron James (a titan, a veritable behemoth: 206 centimetres and 113 kilos), Krakauer represents Curry as normally endowed physically (only 188 centimetres and 86 kilos) and athletic-technical ability (strength, basic speed, explosiveness of jump and other parameters), traits already noticed by observers at the youth level. Krakauer believes Stephen Curry is ultimately an enigma, and his greatness as a complete athlete, unimaginable at the start of his career, rests on impenetrable secrets.

In reality, Curry is only an apparent enigma and Krakauer's questioning partly rhetorical. To get to the heart of the matter, just turn to someone who knows Stephen Curry better than anyone else, namely his personal trainer since 2011, Brandon Payne, a former (modest) basketball player who has become a veritable training guru.

On the one hand, Payne reminds us how Curry's genetic, natural qualities—not particularly modest, though less immediately noticeable—called for a strenuous effort of learning, a '*crescendo* of assimilated skills' at various levels: stamina, speed of execution and reaction to stimuli, with work on the kinetic, postural and gestural continuum. Curry's training sessions are often gruelling, to the point where he ends up retching, not unlike what happened to Michels and Cruyff's Ajax on hill runs, or several players subjected to Antonio Conte's 'repetitions'.

In another way, but synergically, Payne stresses that Curry's accumulation of knowledge has proceeded in sync with the maturation of his body, or rather his

LeBron James during the 73rd NBA All Star game at Gainbridge Fieldhouse, Indianapolis, Indiana, 18 February 2024

brain–body rapport. As Payne sums it up, 'There are athletes who reach that maturity at twenty-two, twenty-three, twenty-four. Steph got there at twenty-seven'. Unsurprisingly, the trainer is referring to 2015, the year he won his first NBA Championship Ring. Again, this contrasts with LeBron, The Chosen One. At twenty he already sported an Olympic bronze, was a fair approximation of a fully developed athlete, and at twenty-two had already played in his first NBA final. The clincher for Payne is the way Curry performs better overall at thirty-four than at twenty-three/twenty-four; and how, in detail, he has improved not only in performance related to experience, such as defensive skills, but also in running speed.

'He feels things in his fingers that normal people can't feel… It's like he has longer nerve endings'

The synthesis between genetic and learned can be found in the neurosensory zoom of his three-point shot. Because there is no doubt that much depends on his sophisticated and anomalous technique of execution. Note, in particular, the release of the ball from the top of the jump, or just before, to take advantage of the force injected by the leap. All in the fastest time of the whole NBA (0.33 seconds against 0.4-0.5 of the average), so almost always avoiding the block. But the ultimate secret lies precisely in the inimitable neurosensory qualities of the ball-hand response, rather like Maradona's ball-foot contact or John McEnroe's hand-racquet-ball timing. The Warriors' manager Nick U'Ren traces this back to 'a kind of super-sensitivity in the fingertips', the ability to dominate and direct every molecular variation of the shot in a very short time: micro-adjustments on the height or direction of the ball, the intensity of push, angle and rotation. This is confirmed by Diana Taurasi, legendary former Phoenix Mercury player, when she explains those micro-corrections carried out 'in a few tenths or thousandths of a second'. 'He feels things in his fingers that normal people can't feel… It's like he has longer nerve endings'. It is a highly selective control, like that of great pianists over their fingers or even phalanges, epitomised in his ability to move his ring finger independently, denied to many of us. In this respect, Curry could be seen as the Keith Jarrett of basketball. Perhaps that's another reason why Prince was so enchanted by him.

The Curry case offers an exemplary link to the twofold irruption of neuroscience into sport: at the level of training and as an explanation for the outstanding performance of champions.

In terms of training, one of the best-known breakthroughs came in the 1980s with the Oporto school, headed by the emeritus of sports sciences Vitor Frade, a mentor of José Mourinho. In that conception, each player is understood as a 'functional unit', in the sense that their physical-athletic qualities, technique, tactics and individual and group psychology are all honed simultaneously in the mimetic training sessions for the match. This also

The Sports Workshop — 200

Talking About Champions: Music, Techniques, Images… — 201

Sports activities in the
Milano Bicocca facilities.
The athletes wear the uniforms
of the Istituto Piero Pirelli
and Superga shoes, 1970,
photo De Paoli

Head coach José Mourinho
during the Italian Serie
A soccer match between
AS Roma and AC Milan at the
Olimpico stadium in Rome,
1 September 2023

Diego Armando Maradona
playing for SSC Napoli, 1990s

translates into simultaneous training for strength and agility, endurance and speed. Central to the weekly sessions—net of the now pervasive 'playing every three days' in different matches—is tactical periodisation (PT), which touches most closely on the incidence of neuroscientific acquisitions. This is exemplified, in Mourinho's application, by the Wednesday–Thursday sessions on 'complex situations' and 'central fatigue'. These are based on a type of concentration for 'decision-making' to stimulate the extensive and metabolically expensive neural circuits, from the prefrontal cortex to the specific neural control through defensive play), so as to economise on the (neuro-)biological level. It is partly, if not mainly, by these methods that Mourinho achieved so much in the first, long part of his career with Porto, Chelsea and Inter, including the 'treble' of 2010, to the point where he became a model widely imitated. It remains to be understood why the second part of his career, especially in recent years, has been marked by an impasse in many ways reductive-regressive. It's not hard, however, to spot at least a couple of co-factors. On the one hand, other coaches and other systems or concepts have emerged, from the

Their physical-athletic qualities, technique, tactics and individual and group psychology are all honed simultaneously in the mimetic training sessions for the match

correlates of attention (posterior parietal lobe, frontal ocular fields…). By contrast the Friday sessions focus on 'automatic' exercises to stimulate only the motor and premotor cortex, sparing the prefrontal cortex and the related 'associative efforts'.

This mode of resting the cerebral metabolism (remember, in passing, that the brain of Homo Sapiens accounts for about 2% of the body weight, but consumes 20% of the energy) is then prolonged during the match, with the players alternating moments of high intensity with others of 'active recovery' (possession of the ball as an end in itself or evolution of Guardiola's 'positional play' to Jürgen Klopp's 'permanent reboot', based on *Gegenpressing* or 'counter-pressing', the immediate recapture of the lost ball; on the other, he has aged. In a famous article in the 'Financial Times', the journalist and writer Simon Kuper showed that managers give their best, in terms of both results and competitive and creative momentum, between the ages of forty and fifty. This biological thesis seems likely, being contradicted only by exceptions such as Spalletti, who won the Scudetto in Naples, with a further evolution of his football when he was sixty-four.

John McEnroe during Roland Garros Tennis Tournament, Paris, 1987

In Germany over the last decade, *Gegenpressing* has been a concentrate of innovative neurological and psychokinetic training practices, which bring us back to Curry's sessions.

The impressionistic background, to tell the truth, is Italian. This was the mythical 'cage' or 'gabion' that Corrado Orrico invented for training in Livorno, to prevent the ball from falling into the sea. Today it can be visited as an archaeo-industrial site. It preceded the uninterrupted games played in cages, such as padel and jorkyball, two-a-side football. But above all, it preceded revolutions such as Christian Gittler's

An example is eye tracking, which deciphers the focusing and visual orientation strategies of the most experienced or gifted players

Footbonaut at Klopp's Borussia Dortmund. In this magic training cage, each player received the ball from four machines in rotation, and was required to control and kick it, in response to a prompt, into one of 72 surrounding gates. The exercise required concentration, speed of execution and precision all at the same time. As Gittler recalls, it meant the player had to deal with 'more balls in fifteen minutes than a week of training'. And the Footbonaut, in turn, preceded other innovations, such as those introduced by the *deus ex machina* of the reboot, the hyper-Sacchian Ralf Rangnick, active above all as a coach in the Red Bull teams, from Salzburg to Leipzig. An example is eye tracking, which deciphers the focusing and visual orientation strategies of the most experienced or gifted players: for instance, the fact that the best goalkeepers have greater opportunities to save a penalty if they predict the striker's intentions by observing the player's trunk more than other parts of the body.

With this example, we have now slipped to the second type of neuroscientific impact on sport: deep explanations of the edge possessed by champions. If we stay in Germany for a moment—relying on the revelatory studies of Gerd Gigerenzer, a cognitive scientist at the Max Planck Institute—we learn that this edge stems in the first place from their 'intuitive decisions'. These are made by an operative unconscious, in which evolution has deposited, over millions of years, a flexible range of adaptive schemes for every type of context and situation. In the specific case of sport, this takes the form mainly of athletic-kinaesthetic variants. Describing how that unconscious intelligence works (as true 'knowing without thinking'), Gigerenzer provides examples in every sector, from medicine to economics, but the most numerous and convincing ones are from sport. Among much else, see the surprising data from an experiment with golf, in which champions were pitted against beginners. The former, unlike the latter, are much more skilled in time-restricted plays—3 seconds—than in indefinite-time plays, which were error-strewn. It is a case that clearly shows how at high levels the best emerges *earlier*, not *later*. Being over-aware compromises the consolidated and highly functional calibration between the brain and the outer world.

Such synthetic—in fact a priori—evaluations help

Poster of *300*, directed by Zack Snyder, 2006

explain the predictive abilities of great athletes already glimpsed in German goalkeepers, and which we find in various other sports. Above all tennis, in particular when returning a serve. This cannot be assimilated, as David Foster Wallace had already intuited, to deliberate technical gestures, given that today the serve, travelling at well over 200 kph, arrives in the opponent's court in just over a third of a second, leaving no time to develop conscious thought. In fact, many recent studies show that the great returners (first Nadal and especially Djokovic; now Sinner and Alcaraz) are 'Bayesian machines'. The reference is to

of the approaching trajectory, while knowing that the senses are inaccurate compared to the far too many variables. On the second level, there is the assessment of the conditional probability of seeing the ball bounce at an expected point, in relation to experience, which processes memories that are both general and specific, i.e. of the player faced on the day, whose service has been studied in detail in all its variants of direction and touch.

But there is another faculty of champions that is often studied (apart from the ability to read the 'signals from the future'). This is the ability to slow

In the decisive moments of the battle, the mental representation of the Spartan soldier is made to coincide *exactly* with that of a great athlete

Thomas Bayes (1702–61), a Presbyterian minister and English mathematician with a troubled life. The cornerstone of his writings—published posthumously by a friend—is the key concept of conditional probability between an event *a* and an event *b*: i.e. the probability that *a* will occur knowing that *b* has occurred. It is a sort of a priori knowledge based on experience or selective memory. For a tennis player returning a serve, who therefore has to judge as quickly as possible the point where the ball will bounce, this entails processing the incoming information. On the first level, there is always sensory evidence, i.e. evaluation

down or suspend time; to perform exceptional actions and plays as if in slowdown, in subjective slow motion, due—in an apparent paradox—to their very high speed of kinaesthetic execution, and above all to the speed of selection-processing of information from the environment.

To grasp its essence, we can resort to two fictions and their key sequences.

The first is Zack Snyder's film *300*, a highly simplified exaltation of the resistance of Leonidas' Spartans fighting outnumbered against Xerxes' Persians at Thermopylae. In the decisive moments of the battle,

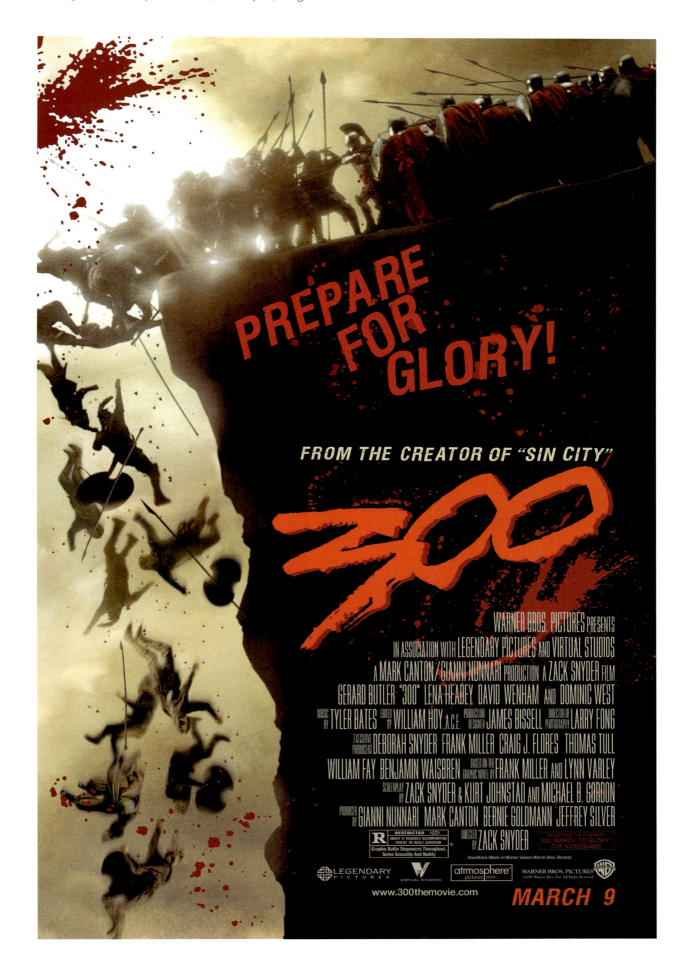

Twilight Zone, host Rod Serling, 1 January, 1963

the mental representation of the Spartan soldier is made to coincide *exactly* with that of a great athlete, so much so that one of the film's greatest attractions lies in the alternation, in these sequences, between the super-rapid fighting in the objective shots and the extremely slow representation of the subjective sequences. The second example is Greg Berlanti's TV series *The Flash*, particularly in the sequences where the scarlet speedster has to save someone or defuse a nuclear device that would annihilate a city, and hurtles effortlessly through a crowd of frozen human beings. His high-speed running and thinking make the bystanders seem motionless and the surrounding world looks stationary.

Studied by numerous neuroscientists on various champions, the process is paradoxical, being counter-intuitive. The faster the brain of a champion processes and selects information, the more the time available is dilated to guide choices in terms of technical play and kinaesthetic intelligence. Nobuhiro Hagura of University College London—one of the scientists who has studied this slowdown in most depth—provides compelling descriptions of it in various sports, from Formula 1 (the overtaking sequences) to tennis, with McEnroe 'feeling time slow as he hits the ball'. And that's not all. Hagura adds that in the dynamics, the predictive scheme reappears, and he also identifies its main neural correlates (the *insula*). When a star player tries to solve a problem *before* it arises, he generates an 'enhanced perception', as happens to certain baseball players, who see the ball 'as big as a grapefruit'.

One last point remains. It is true that the slowdown confirms how, to a large extent, the brains of champions work subliminally, through forms of unconscious intelligence. But it should also be remembered that the extensive, profound 'submerged' memory, linked to the implicit or 'working' memory, is sometimes supplemented by moments in the light of the 'emerged' memory, associated with declarative or explicit memory. Here the shots, strokes, plays and strategies are supported by other deliberate and improvised gestures, as in the case of McEnroe's volleys. He seemed to decide the trajectories of the ball not *before* hitting it, but *as* he hit it, giving the impression of holding it on his racquet a fraction of a second longer than other tennis players. And the same applies, it goes without saying, to certain of Messi's adjustments as he runs in some of his modular plays, which he varies depending on the feedback received at the moment.

Ultimately, what makes a champion is the ability to 'play amphibiously', between the levels of neural processing, in the twilight zone between determinism and free will, predetermined paths and forking paths, scripted plays and improvisation. It is this ability, after all, that is one of the main keys to many actions that compel us to suspend our disbelief in the powers of superheroes: sequences played on the confines of reality.

TESTIMONIES FROM ALL PIRELLI SPORTS

ATHLETICS

Pirelli embraced athletics in 1924, when the company's sports club officially opened its newly built facilities in Viale Sarca in Milan. In collaboration with the Pro Patria association, founded in 1883, Pirelli employees could practise specialities such as the high jump, running and the throwing events: shot put, hammer, and discus. The discus was a round, flattened object thrown some fifty metres, with rubber inserts produced by the company, for which the discus throw champion Adolfo Consolini worked. The thirty-eight-year-old athlete from Verona joined Pirelli in 1948, when he was already the holder of the Olympic gold medal, won that same year in London with a throw of 52.78 metres. He later bettered this result by setting a world record with a throw of 55.33 metres. The *Rivista Pirelli*, the company's monthly publication sold to the general public on the newsstands, could hardly fail to devote pages of passionate commentary to such a champion. As early as November 1948 he was featured in the article 'Style and Power', and then in 1950 in 'Athletes for Illustrations of Gulliver' by Corrado Pizzinelli. Together with Consolini, who meanwhile had won another gold medal at the European Championships in Brussels, there was his colleague Teseo Taddia. Taddia had also been a Pirelli employee for some time, at A.G.A., Articoli Gomma e Affini. He was a champion hammer thrower, winning a silver medal in Brussels with a throw of 54.73 metres. Consolini and Taddia were 'two giants who seem to have come out of illustrations of Gulliver's journey to Brobdingnag', wrote Pizzinelli, 'yet they do not own custom-built cars, villas or factories. Two archangels of sport, candid, innocent, pure, simple and poor'.

In the article Consolini recounted the time when he was about to spend a few days' holiday at the seaside to enjoy his world record. Instead the American Fortune Everett Gordien took the record from him. 'How could I relax? You know, I just couldn't. I tore up the ticket and went out to the circle to train'. Collecting medals and competing in the Olympics—silver in Helsinki 1952, then Melbourne in 1956—Consolini also reached a glorious maturity by playing the character of the farrier Maciste in 1953 in Carlo Lizzani's film *Chronicle of Poor Lovers*, based on Vasco Pratolini's novel of that name. Legend has it that, while filming a quarrel scene, he acted with such realism that he actually knocked out the great Marcello Mastroianni.

Consolini competed in the 1960 Rome Olympics. They particularly favoured the production of new articles in rubber and new building materials that anticipated the construction of modern sports complexes. For the Olympics, Pirelli took part in the construction of the Corso Francia viaduct, connecting the Flaminio bridge to the stadium area, with the installation of 1200 Cargo-type neoprene rubber blocks. The Aquatic

Sports Centre at the Foro Italico and some interiors of the Palazzo dello Sport were paved with Miplac from the Linoleum company. The large Leonardo da Vinci International Airport, opened in the same year, was also equipped with 230 square metres of Afolin sound-absorbing panels and 32,585 square metres of rubber flooring to welcome athletes from around the world.
Consolini died on 20 December 1969 aged fifty-two. For some time he had been in charge of the finished products warehouse in Milan Bicocca with about ten workers under him. 'You can't say he was a traditional boss', recalled the worker Alfredo in the company monthly *Fatti e Notizie*. 'We worked closely together, to the point where he would help us load and unload the goods'. Consolini's experience traced the path of hundreds of young Pirellians who, in those fabulous fifties, tackled the many track and field specialities at Bicocca: running, hurdles, javelin, high jump, pole vault. Leafing through *Fatti e Notizie* gives you some idea of the veritable army of athletes wearing Pirelli gear who used to train there.
Athletics in the 1960s also became the subject of advertising campaigns. The July 1964 issue of *Pi vendere*, Pirelli's magazine for retailers, portrayed an Olympic athlete attempting an improbable pole vault. This was the cartoon character Babbut, a clumsy caveman who, with his wife Mammut and child Figliut, was popular for a few years in Pirelli commercials on TV. It became a cartoon aired as part of *Carosello*, a programme consisting wholly of commercials aired between the late fifties and mid-seventies.
It featured a very Milanese policeman (a referee, in the Olympic version), who at the end of the cartoon admonishes the three blundering primitives, exclaiming: 'Hey cave-dwellers, we're not living in the Stone Age any more!'. He then explains that in modern times Pirelli has brought foam rubber and the Sempione tyre to the descendants of Homo sapiens.
The passion for athletics was naturally celebrated also in the Pirelli Calendar. Designed by Arthur Elgort and produced in Seville, the 1990 calendar was an ode to the spirit of Olympia and its physicality with a female interpretation. It depicted running, fencing, discus, javelin, archery and relays, with on the cover the torch on the top step of the podium. The stadium walls are grey and cyclopean, and the race is held amid dust and scrub. The prize is a laurel wreath. The women athletes on the 1990 Pirelli Calendar wore skirts decorated with symbols that seemed to evoke Olympia and the myth of the Games, but were actually the tread pattern of the Pirelli P600.
Athletics was again at the heart of Pirelli's visual communication in the 1990s. It was 1994 when the photographer Annie Leibovitz portrayed Carl Lewis at the starting

Students engaging in sports competitions at the Istituto Piero Pirelli in Milan, 1961

blocks of the 100 metres wearing the famous red stiletto shoes. The claim, created by Young & Rubicam, was: 'Power is nothing without control'. Carl Lewis was already one of the Olympic all-time greats. The long jump and the sprints were the events in which he won everything possible: four gold medals in Los Angeles 1984, two golds and a silver in Seoul 1988, two more golds in Barcelona 1992. Gold medal number nine came two years later, at the 1996 Atlanta Olympics. Four Olympics, ten medals: between Pirelli and the Five Rings, there was the race of the 'son of the wind'.
In 1995, Carl Lewis himself played the iconic character of Tyre Man in Gerard de Thame's commercial, notable for its special effects, exceptional for the time. It showed him leaping between bridges and skyscrapers in New York, running across the waters of the Hudson River, and standing poised on a gargoyle on the Chrysler Building. He enjoys total grip thanks to the sole of his foot incised with the tread of the Pirelli P6000.
In 1997, Lewis passed the baton as Pirelli's Olympic ambassador to the French sprinter Marie-José Pérec. In the commercial again made by Gerard de Thame, she continues the race begun by the 'son of the wind'. She sprints past glaciers and volcanoes, over water and sand, pursued by special effects in the form of terrible monsters. And in the end she saves herself by springing to the top of the Totem Pole, the monumental rock spire in Monument Valley, Utah, with her winged foot resting on a Pirelli tread.
That Marie-José's foot was truly winged was confirmed in the 1992 Barcelona Olympics. She won the gold medal in the 400 metres, and then in Atlanta 1996, with a double in the 200 and 400 metres. So in the 1997 commercial it was once again an Olympic athlete at the height of her success who reminded the whole world that 'power is nothing without control'.

Testimonies From All Pirelli Sports — 217

Testimonies From All Pirelli Sports — 219

Adolfo Consolini, 1956, photo Bianchi

Stand of the Pro Patria sports centre in the Milano Bicocca district, 1947

The Sports Workshop — 220

Gino and Roberto Gavioli, drawing for *Carosello*, *Mammut, Babbut, Figliut*, 1964

Gian Piero Restellini, sketch for advertisement for Pirelli soles, 1920–25

Advertising campaign 'Superga. Your shoes chosen by champions', Agenzia Centro, 1979

Young & Rubicam, Carl Lewis as brand ambassador for the advertising campaign for Cinturato Pirelli P6000 'Power is nothing without control', 1995

The Sports Workshop

MOTORSPORT

The name that marked the start of Pirelli's history in grand prix racing was Georges Boillot, a French driver who on 12 July 1913 won the Grand Prix Automobile de France at the Circuit de Picardie in Amiens aboard a 5.6-litre Peugeot. Jules Goux finished second, again aboard a Peugeot. Both raced on Pirelli tyres. It was the Italian manufacturer's first victory in an international grand prix. From there, the successes form a series, starting with the 1921 victory in the Gran Premio d'Italia in Brescia, with Joules Goux aboard a Ballot, and then in the French Grand Prix at Strasbourg in 1922, with Felice Nazzaro driving a Fiat 804. In September 1922, the Monza circuit was inaugurated with the Gran Premio of the Automobil Club d'Italia. Pietro Bordino won ahead of Felice Nazzaro, both driving 6-cylinder Fiat 804s fitted with Pirelli tyres. Those were the golden years of the Fiat–Pirelli partnership, but the Italian tyre manufacturer also worked with other carmakers, such as the historic Itala and the American Miller, engaged in races destined to become automotive classics, above all the Targa Florio. The circuit of the Madonie, with its 146 kilometres repeated three times until the finish at Campofelice, can be considered among the ancestors of the concept of gran turismo racing.
The first edition was held on 6 May 1906, fulfilling the dream of the young Vincenzo Florio, a successful entrepreneur who had long been enchanted by the wonderful modernity of motor cars. Alessandro Cagno won in an Itala 35/40 HP, which managed to complete the route in just over nine hours, at an extraordinary average speed of almost 47 kilometres per hour. For its first success in the classic Sicilian race, Pirelli had to wait until 1913, when Felice Nazzaro won in the car bearing his name. Nazzaro felt obliged to telegraph the engineer Giovanni Battista Pirelli in Milan congratulating him 'on your excellent *dérapants*', which enabled him to lower the previous record on the Madonie by four hours.
On 17 August 1924, the *Domenica del Corriere* dedicated its cover to 'an Italian automotive triumph': the victory of the Milanese driver Giuseppe Campari on the circuit in Lyon, France. Achille Beltrame's drawing depicted Campari at the wheel of the Alfa Romeo number 10 fitted with Pirelli tyres that already incorporated the cord technology, with non-woven casing fabric for better tyre fitting, hence ensuring greater reliability. Between the Quadrifoglio brand, with Vittorio Jano's legendary Alfa Romeo P2, and the 'long P', a cycle of victories began on the circuits that would endure for over thirty years.
Antonio Ascari, Giuseppe Campari and Gastone Brilli Peri were the drivers who took the Alfa Romeo–Pirelli combination to victory on the circuits of France, Italy and

Belgium during the 1920s. In 1925, Brilli Peri won the Gran Premio d'Italia at Monza and the first World Championship.

The Pirelli-Alfa Squadra Corse, whose management was entrusted to the Ferrari team, continued to win victories all through the 1930s. With Antonio Brivio, Tazio Nuvolari, Piero Taruffi and Achille Varzi, the Pirelli Stella Bianca earned the nickname of the 'victory tyre'.

Its commitment to motor racing enables the structures and tread patterns of the Stella Bianca tyres to go through a period of rapid development. As early as 1932 the Supersport version for racing cars became available, and then the Pescara tread for racing. In 1933, in the French Grand Prix, Giuseppe Campari drove to victory another car that would write a long history: the Maserati 8C. Before the outbreak of the Second World War, the Trident marque again proved victorious with Luigi Villoresi in the South African Grand Prix in 1939. Villoresi himself was confirmed champion in France in 1946, again with Maserati-Pirelli, and then once more in 1948, paired with Giuseppe Farina. The cover of the first issue of the *Rivista Pirelli* for November 1948 was devoted to Tazio Nuvolari. In the feature article 'The Monza racetrack and the problems of speed', on the reopening of the Monza circuit after the war, the magazine documented the fabulous years of automotive reconstruction. Formula 1 was officially launched, and the car to beat was again the Alfa Romeo 158 with Pirelli tyres driven by Jean-Pierre Wimille. Alfa withdrew from competition in 1952, leaving the way clear for the rising star of Maserati. Equipped with Pirelli tyres, their cars had their greatest interpreter in the Argentine Juan Manuel Fangio. Already famous with Alfa Romeo in 1950 and then winning the World Championship in the following year, Fangio drove the Maserati 250F to victory in the World Championship in 1954 and then in 1957. He won the 1957 title using Pirelli's 'warehouse remainders', after the Milanese manufacturer withdrew from competitions.

Meanwhile, a new star of motoring was starting to shine: Ferrari. Its founder, Enzo Ferrari, was a driver in the Alfa-Pirelli team, and it was on the 'long P' tyres that he had Alberto Ascari's Ferrari 125 take to the track and win in 1949.

Another inseparable trio was formed: Ascari-Ferrari-Pirelli. In 1952 and 1953 they won everything possible. In December 1956, however, came the announcement that put an end to an era: 'After its long and intense participation in motor racing and motorcycle racing, Pirelli has decided to cease production of racing tyres'. Its technological efforts were to be diverted towards that new revolutionary tyre called the Cinturato. The era of Stella Bianca and Stelvio, the tyres of victories, had come to an end.

Pirelli's return to Formula 1 came in 1981 with the Toleman–Hart TG 181 driven by Brian Henton and Derek Warwick. The previous year the same drivers had been responsible for Toleman's excellent season in Formula 2, culminating with Henton's victory in the European Championship. At Pirelli, the director of sporting activities was Mario Mezzanotte. 'The Pirelli P7s that will equip the Toleman F1 are radial tyres with an asymmetric tread pattern, hence the inner shoulder is more chamfered than the outer one. This ensures better handling of the car and a better grip of the tyre on the asphalt by compensating for the negative camber that racing radials require'. The Toleman–Candy partnership continued in the 1982 season, with the two cars entrusted to Derek Warwick and Teo Fabi and the support to Arrows–Beta with drivers Brian Henton and Mauro Baldi. Other teams included: Osella (with Jean-Pierre Jarier and Riccardo Paletti), Fittipaldi (with Chico Serra) and March (with Jochen Mass and Raul Boesel). In November 1982 came the announcement that in the 1983 season Pirelli would equip both of the Lotus JPS cars driven by Elio De Angelis and Nigel Mansell, in addition to Derek Warwick and Bruno Giacomelli's Toleman–Candy racers.

In the 1984 season, Pirelli continued to equip the Toleman team. At the wheel of the British car there was now 'an excellent test driver, who despite his youth will give us a wealth of useful information about the behaviour of the car and the tyres', said the Pirelli technicians. The youthful test driver was Ayrton Senna.

The announcement was made directly by Bernie Ecclestone in October 1984: 'We are pleased to announce that we have reached a three-year agreement with Pirelli, following which the tyre manufacturer will partner with Brabham BMW to develop and supply Formula 1 tyres starting in the 1985 season. We have followed Pirelli's progress in the 1983 and 1984 seasons with interest and we are confident that their partnership with a competitive team will enable Pirelli to gain the same results won in all the other categories of races that it has taken part in'.

The Brabham number 7 that took part in the Formula 1 World Championship in 1985 was entrusted to Nelson Piquet, the number 8 to François Hesnault and then Marc Surer. In the 1985 season Nelson Piquet won the French Grand Prix at Le Castellet. Meanwhile, the partnership with Teo Fabi's Toleman (later Benetton) continued, while Andrea De Cesaris and Jacques Laffite's Ligier and the Piercarlo Ghinzani's Osella were added.

1986 saw Pirelli collaborating with Brabham (with Elio De Angelis and Riccardo Patrese as drivers), Benetton (Teo Fabi and Gerhard Berger), Ligier (Jacques Laffite and René Arnoux), Osella (Ivan Capelli) and Minardi (Andrea De Cesaris and Piercarlo Ghinzani). Berger won the Mexican Grand Prix.

At the end of the 1986 season, Pirelli announced its retirement from Formula 1.
In the 1989 season Pirelli returned to Formula 1. The teams were Brabham, Dallara, Minardi and Zakspeed. After a year of experiments, 1990 brought a collaboration with Jean Alesi's Tyrrel.
'Benetton and Pirelli together again', headlined the February 1991 issue of the company magazine *Fatti e Notizie*. The comment was entrusted to Nelson Piquet, who was returning to Pirelli after a six-year interval: 'The agreement developed in the course of the season. Seeing the advantages that Pirelli tyres gave cars that were otherwise uncompetitive, especially on certain tracks, gave us drivers and the technical directors of the Benetton team food for thought'. The result was Piquet's victory in the Canadian Grand Prix on 2 June, with Stefano Modena second in the Tyrrel–Honda.
At the end of the season, Pirelli again announced its withdrawal from Formula 1. This did not mean, however, that it was completely abandoning racing. In fact another great tradition continued, that of gran turismo racing. A discipline that Pirelli had never really abandoned, as shown by the victories of the magnificent Lancia Beta Montecarlo driven by Riccardo Patrese and Eddie Cheever, the Osella PA8 by Lella Lombardi, the Alfa 75 Turbo by Alessandro Nannini and Giorgio Francia.
Starting with the 1995 season, the races organised by IMSA, the American International Motor Sports Association, marked the start of another period of resounding victories. It made its debut on US circuits with the Ferrari 333 SP driven by the trio Fermín Vélez, Eric van de Poele and Andy Evans, who won the final victory in the drivers' title. The following year the success was replicated with the Riley & Scott team. Pirelli was always present in endurance races on the circuits of the World Tourism Championship with winning cars, stemming from its long technological collaboration with carmakers such as Ferrari, Maserati and Porsche.
Since 2011, Pirelli has returned to Formula 1 as the sole supplier of all the teams competing, restoring a partnership that it had never permanently relinquished. This is planned to continue at least until 2028. Motoring enthusiasts have become familiar with the colours that, on the different circuits of the world, alternate to distinguish the uses of the tyre range based on the hardness of the compound. But of course the 'long P' is totally committed to motor racing, starting from the great variety of races on the circuits: Formula 2 and Formula 3, veritable stepping stones towards Formula 1, and again gran turismo: from the exclusive supply of tyres for the Blancpain GT to its historic partnership with the Ferrari Challenge, or also the Lamborghini Super Trofeo single-brand championship.

The Sports Workshop

— 228

Pavel Michael Engelmann, sketch for advertisement for the Stelvio Pirelli tyre, 1954

Pirelli technical assistance at the Monza Grand Prix, 1952

Testimonies From All Pirelli Sports

The Sports Workshop

Pirelli Racing Service at the
17th Mille Miglia, 1950, photo
Del Secco

The Sports Workshop — 232

Brochure *Pirelli vince*, 1954

Pirelli tyre check at the
San Marino Grand Prix, 1990

Testimonies From All Pirelli Sports — 233

FOOTBALL

At Pirelli, well before Ronaldo played for the Nerazzurri, football was associated with one name: Piero Pirelli. The eldest child of Giovanni Battista Pirelli, Piero Pirelli was born in 1881 and in 1904 he became co-manager of the family business together with his brother Alberto, a year his junior. He was the president of the Milan Cricket and Football Club, founded a decade earlier and already an outstanding team. And when the shareholders acclaimed him as president—as they continued to do for twenty years in a row—they said: 'Just as no one could conceive of a club without a statute and regulations, so no one can imagine Milan without its president Pirelli'. In those years Milan was constantly having to shuttle between the Sempione velodrome, the Pirelli sports facilities in Milano Bicocca and the new stadium in Viale Lombardia. It was President Pirelli himself who solved the problem by having a new stadium built for his team. Officially opened in 1926, the Giuseppe Meazza stadium, also known as the San Siro stadium, remains an icon of international football to this day.

Piero Pirelli certainly showed great insight when he recruited the manager Vittorio Pozzo in 1924. He left Turin to head the Rossoneri. At Pirelli, Pozzo took on the role of 'director of propaganda B', i.e. advertising for the rubber sector. And significantly, around the mid-1920s, there was a proliferation of advertisements for 'Pirelli footballs' and 'football bladders'. In the 1926 drawing by the artist Rino Gaspare Battaini, players in red and black striped shirts are gazing at the Pirelli ball flying over the football field. Vittorio Pozzo left AC Milan and Pirelli in 1931, having been appointed manager of the Italian national team for the third time. Victories in the World Cup in 1934 and 1938 made him the greatest manager of all time. Following the experience with Pozzo, and with the end of the Second World War, football continued to be important to Pirelli. A column in the *Rivista Pirelli* for 1949 declared: 'The future is here'. It presented the Scudetto bladder, in pure seamless latex rubber. 'These features eliminate leaks and make the bladder less likely to burst, puncture or tear, increasing its durability and extending the life of the ball'.

Football was a very popular topic in the *Rivista Pirelli* and hotly debated. The editorial staff of the magazine entrusted it to two great names of the time: Gianni Brera and Nino Nutrizio. Gianni Brera was born at San Zenone al Po in 1919. During the war he was a partisan of the Republic of Ossola after 8 September 1943. Nino Nutrizio was a Dalmatian hailing from Traù (known as Trogir since it became part of Croatia). Born in 1911, he was a prisoner of war in India until 1946. The destinies of Gianni Brera and Nino Nutrizio, perhaps, together with Orio Vergani, the greatest sports journalists of the twentieth century, intersected in the Milanese press, which was rapidly trying to raise its head again after the war. Brera had been involved in football since he was a boy and, on returning from the front, in 1945 he joined the *Gazzetta dello Sport*. Within a few years he was the editor in chief. Nutrizio had worked for *Il Secolo XIX*, but once the war ended he was forced to start all over again as a journalist. In 1952 he made the big leap: the industrialist Carlo Pesenti entrusted him with the editorship of *La Notte*, the Milan evening paper. It was a resounding success. Soon after, in 1956, Gianni Brera also went on to edit the sports page of *Il Giorno*. The paper's sales multiplied. The editors of *Il Giorno* and *La Notte*—the Day and the Night—could hardly fail to meet in the pages of the *Rivista Pirelli*, which in those lively 1950s already featured the biggest names in circulation. Football—the national sport together with cycling—was of course the responsibility of Brera and Nutrizio. And then as now, it called for notable critical insight. Nutrizio found it hard to stomach Italy's immediate elimination from the World Cup in Switzerland in June 1954, nor did he care for the fact that the seventeen-year-old Giuseppe Virgili had moved from Udinese to Fiorentina for the astronomical sum of 60 million liras. In the article 'The sick millionaire', in issue 4 of 1954, he stated that in the sports world, footballers and cyclists, motorcyclists and gymnasts, coaches and managers were all being ruined by the god of money: 'To earn a lot of money, not to work in the fields or factory, but have a nice house and a nice car, to wear fine clothes...'. He was echoed by Brera a few months later, in January 1955, in 'The hard life of a football-player': 'Perhaps because it has slowly slipped into gladiatorial combat and so into a blatant search for profit, Italian sport has not yet had worthy singers'. The article's opening summed up its contents. That same year, in issue 6 for December, Nutrizio criticised defensive football, the *catenaccio* tactic: 'An odious spectacle in at least six out of nine games every Sunday', a symptom of the 'worrying decline of Italian football'. In the January 1957 article, Nutrizio warned—among much else—that with this outlook there was a risk that the team would fail to qualify for the World Cup in Sweden, scheduled for a few months later. Italy did fail to qualify, and the 1958 World Cup was won by Brazil, who beat the Swedish hosts. It was a 'metamorphosis', as the title of the article in issue number 4 of 1958, Brera's last, put it.

In 1964, Vittorio Sereni's article 'The nerazzurro phantom' appeared in the *Rivista Pirelli*, which told the story of Giuseppe Meazza, and then of Giuliano Sarti, Luis Suárez and the banners reading: 'Whether the future's black or blue / long live Inter, long live Herrera'. Thirty years later, in 1995, Pirelli took a stake in F.C. Internazionale and printed the 'long P' on the Nerazzurri shirts. A new era began, a new story of football associated with Pirelli. In 1997 Inter signed the 'phenomenon' Ronaldo, winner of the Ballon d'Or.

The following year he became the 'Redeemer' in the famous advertisement that showed him dominating Rio de Janeiro from the summit of Corcovado, with a Pirelli P3000 tread on his foot: 'Power is nothing without control'. And then Ronaldo appeared in the *auriverde* shirt scoring under the Eiffel Tower at the 1998 World Cup in France. Fun fact: for graphic reasons, Ronaldo is shooting with his left foot.

With the 'long P' on the players' shirts (in 2006 it also appeared in a Chinese version, to celebrate the opening of the new Pirelli production site in Shandong Province), Inter managed by José Mourinho achieved the so-called 'treble' in 2010, winning the Campionato, the Coppa Italia and the Champions League. A first for Italian football. In 2018, there was another important innovation for the Nerazzurri, again with Pirelli as the sponsor on the shirts, when Inter Women was founded. In Serie A from the following year, Inter Women gradually grew in prestige until they settled steadily at the top of the table.

Pirelli withdrew as sponsor from Inter's shirts in 2021. It left behind not only the legacy of the 2010 treble—and a winning mentality certified by the Scudetto in 2021 and the exciting 2023–2024 season—but also the social initiative of the Pirelli Inter Campus. This is a partnership between the football club and the company that uses the values of sport to assist young people in the countries and communities where the company operates.

Testimonies From All Pirelli Sports — 237

Diploma of honour awarded to the Pirelli workers' club for the 2nd prize in the Football Tournament 'Coppa Donatello', first category, played in Milan from 4 December 1927 to 5 February 1928

Price list for leather balls and bladders 'for the game of football' Pirelli, 1928

CORAZZA PER IL GIUOCO DEL CALCIO
IN UN PEZZO SOLO

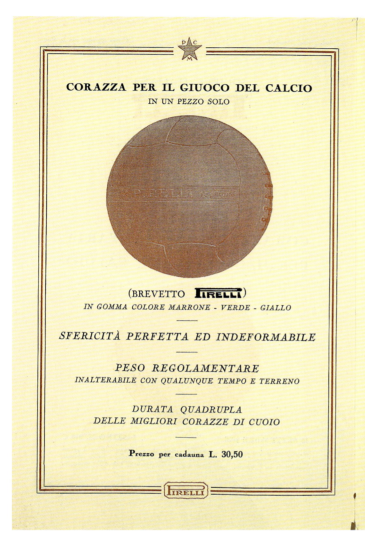

(BREVETTO **PIRELLI**)
IN GOMMA COLORE MARRONE - VERDE - GIALLO

SFERICITÀ PERFETTA ED INDEFORMABILE

PESO REGOLAMENTARE
INALTERABILE CON QUALUNQUE TEMPO E TERRENO

DURATA QUADRUPLA
DELLE MIGLIORI CORAZZE DI CUOIO

Prezzo per cadauna L. 30,50

CAMERA D'ARIA PER IL GIUOCO DEL CALCIO

IN GOMMA ROSSA

CON TUBETTO GOMMA – TIPO "928"

Numero	Peso approssimativo di cadauna	Prezzo per cadauna
1	gr. 37	2.80
2	" 41	2.90
3	" 50	3.10
4	" 60	3.40
5	" 70	3.75
6	" 85	4.10
7	" 92	4.30
8	" 100	4.50
9	" 113	4.70

Advertising postcard for Pirelli leather balls and bladders, 1920s

Salvatore Fresi, Ronaldo and Taribo West portrayed in Fabio Monti's article 'The Advertising Striker' in *Pirelli World*, no. 15, 1998

INTERVIEW

An interview with Pirelli Tyre's 1998 campaign protagonist

The Advertising Striker

Football's Golden Boy Ronaldo reveals the feelings of a 21 years old worldwide star

Inteview by Fabio Monti

To begin with, there were the speedsters of athletics: first, Carl Lewis, American, nine Olympic gold medals and eight in the World Games, who raced with high heels and on water; then Marie José Perec, French, double gold at the Atlanta Olympics, ready for the challenge and a race against a river of lava and fire. Now, Pirelli's new testimonial is a footballer, Luiz Ronaldo Nazario de Lima, known to everyone as, simply, Ronaldo, Brazilian, because "for 1998 we have chosen a man who works miracles with his feet".

Ronaldo is standing there, photographed from behind on Mount Corcovado: Inter's shirt number 10, his team since the summer of '97, arms open to the Bay of Guanabara, left foot raised and "shod". More or less like the statue that guards Rio de Janeiro and which the Brazilians have dedicated to Guglielmo Marconi, "the scientist" - according to the official description - "who was the first to connect the Eternal City (Rome) with the Marvellous City (Rio)". A powerful image, which is circumnavigating the world, created in 100 minutes ("the duration of a game of football, plus a little extra time") destined to increase a popularity which is already full to overflowing. An image accompanied by a slogan, which helps us to understand why Ronaldo was chosen: "Power is nothing without control". The goals of the Brazilian ace are just that: enormous power, linked to an extraordinary cool headedness.

Ronaldo, do you like the poster selected for the Pirelli campaign?

Yes, very much. I am Catholic and for me this is an image of greeting, like the gesture I always make when I score a goal: arms open wide, index fingers horizontal. The city is Rio, my city, where I was born and which I left when I was 15.

Why are copies and pieces of your poster, which appears at the roadsides and in the squares of Italy, disappearing like there is no tomorrow?

I believe it transmits the legitimate

CYCLING

Pirelli's association with cycling goes back a long way. After its early production of various technical and consumer products made of rubber, in 1890 the Milanese company began—on a completely experimental basis—manufacturing bicycle tyres. In 1893 it patented the 'Tipo Milano' tubular tyre, its name paying homage to the city where the company had its headquarters. In 1894 Pirelli already sold 825,000 liras' worth of these tyres, a figure that accounted for 12% of its total turnover. In 1899, road tyres were joined by racing models.
Pirelli has been to the fore in cycling competitions ever since they were first held. In 1895 the first cycle race was organised by Pirelli & C. on the Milan–Cremona–Brescia–Milan route, open to all cyclists 'riding on tyres of its own manufacture'. These were Pirelli 'Tipo Milano' tyres, equipped with beads to attach them to the rim and bearing the trademark with the star and the letters P&CM (Pirelli & Company, Milan). The best known cyclists in those years were Narciso Pasta and Gilberto Marley. Their bikes had been equipped with chain drives for some years and they had wheels of the same size. They were built by companies such as Dei, Maino, Orio Marchand and then Atala, Frera, Ganna. Another was the Legnano brand, destined to enter the legend of cycling together with its rival Bianchi. Pirelli took part in all the great road classics, such as the Giro d'Italia, the Milan–Sanremo, the Giro di Lombardia, the Giro di Romagna, and of course, the historic Tour de France. Participation in the Grande Boucle of 1907 helped promote the commercial expansion of the Italian brand on the French market. In 1909 the first Giro d'Italia was held, organised by the *Gazzetta dello Sport* in response to the Tour. The route was 2,448 kilometres in eight stages, from Milan to Milan, with 127 competitors at the start. Thirty of the forty-nine starters who arrived were fitted with Pirelli 'Stella copertura' tyres. The success excited the public and its echo conquered the racing world. Pirelli tubular tyres were used on the track at the Sempione velodrome and then on the wooden boards of the circuit created in Milan in 1935 by Giuseppe Vigorelli, who for years directed the Agenzia Lombarda Gomme Pirelli. The 'long P' logo appeared on the jerseys of champions such as Costante Girardengo, who with Pirelli in the early 1920s has gone down to history as the Campionissimo. After entering the profession in 1912, with Maino, Girardengo won stage after stage of the Giro d'Italia, and was first in the Rome–Naples–Rome grand prix of 1913. This attracted the interest of the big teams. Bianchi, naturally, and then Stucchi, which in 1921 became Stucchi-Pirelli. This Milan-based factory—a manufacturer of sewing machines, bicycles and motorised tricycles—was founded by Giulio Prinetti and Augusto Stucchi. Wearing its colours, Girardengo won the Milan–Sanremo in April 1921 and then the first four stages of the Giro d'Italia. In

the fifth stage, in Abruzzo, he was involved in a crash with other cyclists. In the end the winner was Giovanni Brunero, his rival who raced for the Legnano company.
After Bianchi and Stucchi, Girardengo won two more editions of the Milan–Sanremo in the jersey of Wolsit, the Italian licensee of the British Wolseley. In 1925 he arrived ahead of Brunero and in 1926 he beat Nello Ciaccheri, who raced for Legnano. Also in 1925, he ascended the podium of another Italian cycling championship: number nine. In the same year, at the Giro d'Italia, the six stages that he won were not enough to secure the pink jersey, awarded to a young cyclist from Cittiglio, in the province of Varese: Alfredo Binda. Binda's history with Pirelli would be even longer than Girardengo's. The late 1940s and early 1950s were an age of new champions; apart from Binda, there was the unforgettable duo Fausto Coppi and Gino Bartali. 'Do you know Bartali? Do you know Coppi?': so began the article 'How I know Gino and Fausto', which Orio Vergani wrote for the *Rivista Pirelli* in 1950. 'The question may sound silly to many', the article continued. Who didn't know Fausto Coppi and Gino Bartali at the climax of that golden season of 1950? On the other hand, it's likely that not even 'those who gave them a thumbs up', and who patiently watched them for hours in the race, knew these cycling champions as well as Vergani. In his article, Vergani compared Bartali to Ulysses and Coppi to Achilles, 'the man who carries on his shoulders the weight and responsibility of being the most phenomenal athlete that, after Binda, I have ever seen'.
An extremely careful and almost scholarly comparison between the two champions in that year had already been made by Giuseppe Ambrosini in issue 3 of the same magazine, in 1949. In that year Alfredo Binda, having 'hung up his bicycle on a nail', became the promoter of the Gran Premio Pirelli, a cycling trophy for amateurs, who competed in regional heats before going through to the final at the Vigorelli velodrome. The competition was devised by the former champion together with Arturo Pozzo, sales director of Pirelli Tyres. Binda was the organiser, Pozzo the administrator, managing the prizes which took the form of money and tyres. In the future of the participants, as amateurs, there was the gilded world of professional cycling, which in the 1950s was as popular as football. While Coppi and Bartali dominated the collective imagination, after a war that 'failed to train the last generation' of champions, it was time to start rebuilding. Nine editions of the Gran Premio were covered for the *Rivista Pirelli* by Nino Nutrizio and Gianni Brera, in addition to Alfredo Binda himself. After the death of Arturo Pozzo in October 1955, and immediately after the conclusion of the seventh Gran Premio Pirelli, now an international competition, the race continued for a couple of years, with the establishment of the Arturo Pozzo Gold Trophy. In the article in the *Rivista Pirelli* for 1957 announcing the end

The Sports Workshop — 244

of the Gran Premio, Binda stated, 'I have noticed this year, among all the young people, a particularly combative spirit. The new generation has created a typically "Italian style" of racing. It has rapidly renewed our approach and given it fresh impetus'. Also reflecting the spirit of the time is the group photo illustrating the article: 'Farmers, mechanics, errand boys or simply young people without any particular occupation but a great passion for cycling'.

From the 1960s to the late 1990s, Pirelli continued to be present with products for the new emerging sectors, such as the *Graziella*, a true status symbol of youth in the boom years, as well as other brands gradually acquired over the years. In 2017 the 'long P' marque made a return to cycling with the production—in its renovated factory at Bollate, near Milan—of a complete line of tyres, clinchers, tubular and tubeless, including models for off-road and enduro bikes, cycling competitions, commuter bikes and electric pedal-assisted bikes. This modern, technological contribution to the original know-how is fostering increasingly sustainable mobility. The firm's renewed success in the bicycle sector is showcased by its technical sponsorship of various teams, in MTB (Mountain Trail Bike) and road cycling.

Mario Duse, advertisement for Pirelli bicycle tyres, 1951

Pirelli tubular tyre of the 'Specialissimo Corsa' type, catalogue, 1932

Pirelli 'Giro d'Italia' tubular tyre, catalogue, 1939

The Sports Workshop

Programme of the 6th edition of the Pirelli international cycling Grand Prix, 1954

Fausto Coppi visits the Pirelli stand at the 29th Bicycle and Motorcycle Trade Fair in Milan, 1952, photo Cera

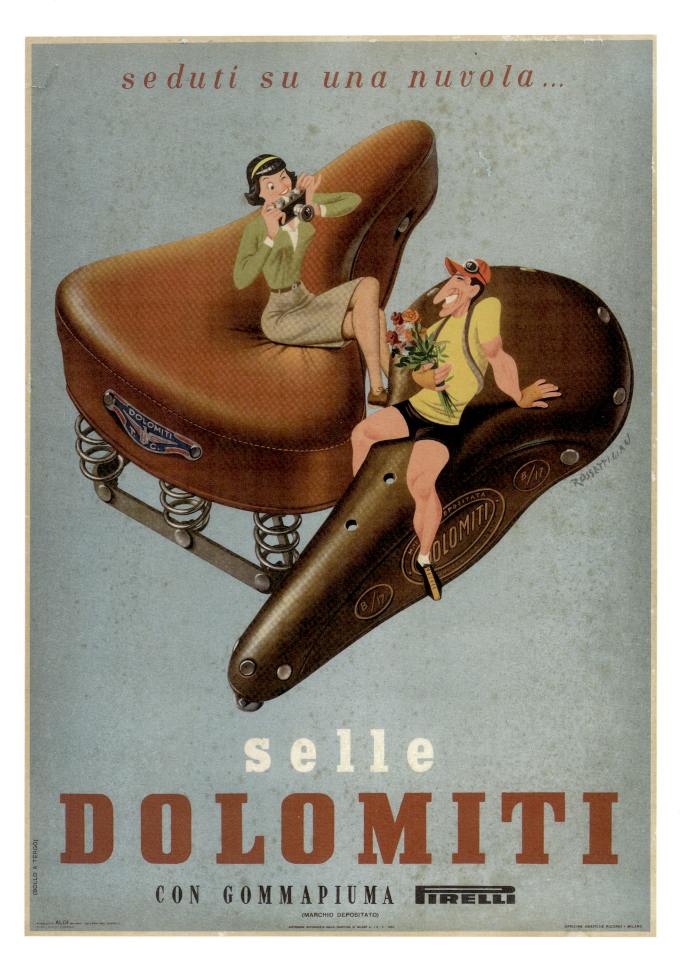

Gian Carlo Rossetti, advertisement for Dolomiti saddles with Pirelli foam rubber, 1950

Cyclist Lauretta Hanson, Lidl-Trek team, 2024, photo Jojo Harper

Testimonies From All Pirelli Sports

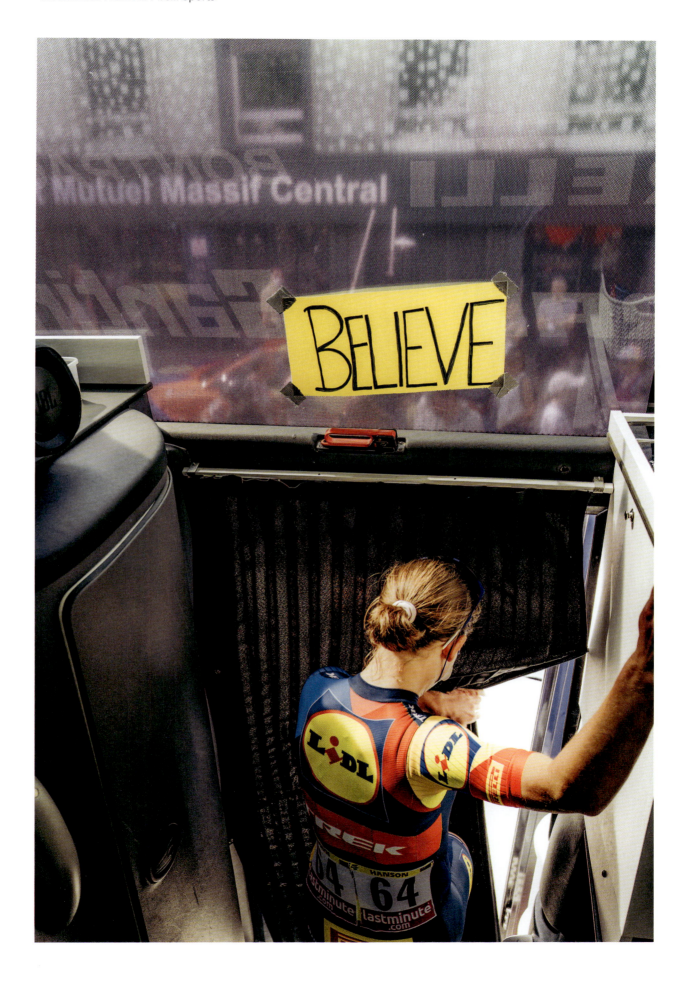

The Sports Workshop — 250

Cyclist Mads Pedersen,
Lidl-Trek team, during
the 110th Tour de France,
2023, photo Luca Bettini,
SprintCyclingAgency

Testimonies From All Pirelli Sports — 251

Cyclist Jonathan Milan, 2024,
photo Ross Bell

MOTORCYCLING

In the beginning—in the late nineteenth century, when the first 'tricycles and motorised coaches' appeared—there was no need for major technological revolutions. An engine would be mounted on a bicycle to turn it into a motorcycle, but they were still fitted with the Pirelli 'tipo Milano' beaded tyres, which ensured a snug fit to the rim. Developed soon after the company was founded, the tyres were already involved in the great sporting feats performed in both cycling and motor racing. 'Experience has now indisputably shown the great superiority of beaded edges for fitting tyres to the wheels of vehicles set in motion by mechanical energy', declared price lists of the time. The 1909 Giro d'Italia was run on Pirelli tyres, as was the 1907 Peking to Paris race. Nothing prevented the same technology from being used on the first motorcycles.

The early 1920s brought the invention of cord tyres, a fabric structure capable of efficiently supporting the power delivered by the engine. This led to a breakthrough in quality and, as with cars, it provided the impulse for the start of a veritable epic of motorcycle sport: the era of daredevils on two wheels. Riding on Pirelli Motocord tyres, the great riders of the time performed extremely dangerous feats, such as competing on the Lario circuit or in the British Tourist Trophy. The outstanding rider was Tazio Nuvolari. Riding the Bianchi Freccia Celeste, speed was always a challenge, even before he moved to four wheels with the Alfa Romeo 8C. It is hardly surprising that Enzo Ferrari considered him 'an unsurpassed prodigy of instinct at the limits of human possibilities and the laws of physics'.

'You should see him at certain moments. He's the devil incarnate', recounted the profile of the former driver written in 1949 by the journalist Orio Vergani for *Rivista Pirelli*. Observers at the time remember when Nuvolari 'used to come down the hill of Ghisallo—it must have been in 1929—and on the bends he would simply ignore the brakes. Instead he would jab his padded elbow, using it like a pivot, against the walls of the houses lining the road, abruptly changing direction and speeding off again'. With Nuvolari, other names entered the history of motorcycling and wrote pages of sport with Pirelli. Like Miro Maffeis, 'the handsome Miro', the youngest of the three Maffeis brothers. He knew by heart the more than 800 kilometres of the Raid Nord–Sud, from Milan to Naples. He won it in 1920 on an Indian 500, but even when he only came third, as in 1925, on the Bianchi 350, he always looked tough in the photos. Of course, the bike also played its part: the Bianchi Freccia Celeste fitted with Pirelli Motocord tyres. What was striking about the attitude of those pre-war riders was their confidence. They concentrated single-mindedly on getting to the finishing line without wavering, without misgivings. Like Erminio Visioli, who won on the Tre Regioni circuit in August 1921 riding a Harley-Davidson 1000 fitted with Pirelli tyres, a week after dominating the historic Como-Brunate hill climb. In 'Memories of Tenni', published in the *Rivista Pirelli* for March 1949, Renzo Biasion described (and drew) motorcyclists with the devil in their bodies 'speeding about the world as if driven by an impulse of the blood stronger than the will'. Omobono Tenni was born in Valtellina and had moved to Treviso where he became the idol of the Guzzi fans. He had died a few months earlier, while practising for the Bern Grand Prix. In 1937 he was the first non-British rider to win the Tourist Trophy. The British called him the Black Devil.

The post-war period led to a revival of motorsports on both two wheels and four. The great motorcycle races were held again and the Pirelli Motocord was renewed with them. The photos of the time preserve the memory of other riders, the sons of the first generation who had made motorcycle sporting history before the war. Raffaele Alberti appears serious and martial, portrayed in a 1948 photo with his hand on the saddle of his Guzzino, recalling the pose of an artilleryman beside his cannon. Alberti set four standing kilometre speed records in February 1948 at the Swiss circuit of Charrette-Saxon, and then another nineteen in Monza, together with Gianni Leoni and Bruno Ruffo. Records for the kilometre, for 500 miles, for the hour, for twelve hours, and so on. The Guzzi 65—boosted to 73cc but still a Guzzino—never abandoned Pirelli tyres. The Milanese Alberti had a profound understanding of motorcycle technology and was an expert collector of records, while Bruno Ruffo, his partner in setting records, only began to enjoy success when he was already in his thirties.

Rounding out the trio of Guzzi record breakers was Gianni Leoni from Como. Wearing the colours of the motorbike manufacturer based in Mandello, it was not unusual to find all three of them on the tracks of the revived world championship. For example, Ruffo and Leoni took part in the Italian Grand Prix in Monza in September 1949 on Guzzi 250s. With them was another Leoni: Guido, with the Guzzi 500. Guido Leoni was born at Castellucchio near Mantua in 1915, just a few months before his namesake Gianni. Raffaele Alberti and Guido Leoni died in Ferrara, both involved in a major pile-up during the Italian Senior Championship. It was May 1951. Gianni Leoni died in an incredible accident in the Ulster Grand Prix: a head-on crash with his teammate Geminiani. It was August 1951.

The 1960s marked a pause for reflection in the world of motorcycle sport. In the autumn of 1956, Pirelli announced it was retiring from competition to devote all its resources to the development of its revolutionary radial tyre. The same love of adventure that had inspired rallying in the early seventies—an effect of the success of the

The Sports Workshop

Motorcycle equipped with Gordon 'V' Pirelli tyres, 1976

Cinturato—ended up influencing motorcycling as well, and motocross began to boom. Pirelli's flagship product was the Campeonato Español Sevilla. Developed in 1974, this line brought a string of victories that began in the 1980s and continues to this day, with over eighty world titles collected over the years with Pirelli Cross tyres. A talent for success that continues unchanged with the competitive Scorpion MX and Scorpion Trail range for enduro. In the same way, even in the world of motorcycle racing, Pirelli's role can almost be considered institutional. The company's commitment to Superbike, dating from 2004, today means that the 'long P' marque holds the record for the longest exclusive supply in the history of motorcycle racing and makes the Diablo range the standout tyres for sports bike enthusiasts. The 2024 Pirelli Superbike season opened with the Diablo Supercorsa SP-V4, a latest-generation race replica tyre. It is a Racing SC3 bi-compound for both front and rear wheels, with profiles that combine performance on the track with pleasurable driving on the road. The tread pattern is an evolution of the Flash patent, designed to ensure the thrust is even at any lean angle. In addition, from the 2024 season, the Sportbike section of the British Superbike championship is open to riders aged sixteen and over, competing on bikes such as the Yamaha R7, Kawasaki Ninja 650, Aprilia RS660, Honda Hornet 750, Triumph Trident 660 and Suzuki GSX8S. The bikes are equipped with Pirelli Diablo Supercorsa V4 tyres and the unique Mektronic electronic control unit, with attached BoP (Balance of Performance) system to main parity of performance. Then 2024 also marks Pirelli's entry as sole supplier to the Moto2 and Moto3 championships.

Testimonies From All Pirelli Sports — 255

The rider Alberto Angiolini on a Maico motorcycle equipped with MT 16 'Campeonato Español Sevilla' Pirelli tyres, 1977, photo Guido Alberto Rossi

Bob Noorda, brochure *Vittorie Pirelli*, 1953

Agenzia Armando Testa, advertisement for Pirelli Supercorsa motorcycle tyres, 2000s

The Sports Workshop — 258

Motorcycle Grand Prix d'Italia,
Pirelli Tower, 1955, photo
Publifoto

Pirelli technicians at the Spanish motorcycle Grand Prix, 1957

The Sports Workshop — 260

Pirelli fitting area at WorldSBK (Superbike World Championship) 2023, Emilia-Romagna Round, photo Gpagency

Bilbao motorcycle Grand Prix, 1957

Testimonies From All Pirelli Sports — 261

WorldSBK Pirelli (Superbike
World Championship)
2023, French Round, photo
Gpagency

The Sports Workshop — 262

WorldSBK Pirelli (Superbike World Championship) 2023, Czech Round, photo Gpagency

Testimonies From All Pirelli Sports — 263

WorldSBK Pirelli (Superbike
World Championship) 2023,
Indonesian Round, photo
Gpagency

RALLYING

Rallying has been known by various names since it was first invented at the start of the twentieth century, with the dawn of motoring. An early version was called 'adventure racing', when the competitions crossed stony wastes, mud flats and deserts of sand. The term rally was introduced by a group of gentlemen drivers from across Europe who decided to assemble in Monte Carlo and race on the roads of the Principality. Racing standard cars on roads open to the public is as old as the idea of the car itself and the innovative technology called tyres. The completely experimental Pirelli company, which had been producing car tyres since 1901, took part in the Milan–Rome 'automotive caravan'. It was held in April 1904 and participation in the event served to test the efficiency of the Ercole tyres on the Eisenachs and the heavy Isotta Fraschinis. The Pirelli Ercole also performed well in the 'Winter Automobilisation' of February 1905, an automotive event organised by the Automobil Club Milano. And then came long-awaited victory in a Marchand car in the 1906 Settimana Automobilistica in Sanremo. It was time to look ahead.
The big step was made in 1907, with the winner in the Peking to Paris race organised by the French newspaper *Le Matin*. Pirelli shod the 40-horsepower Itala driven by an Italian team consisting of Prince Scipione Borghese, the mechanic and driver Ettore Guizzardi and the journalist Luigi Barzini of the *Corriere della Sera*. As the prince recalled in the introduction to the book *La metà del mondo vista da un'automobile*, written by Barzini at the end of the race, 'When I saw the challenge in *Le Matin* I had before my eyes this purpose: to show that a car properly manufactured, driven with caution and care, can practically replace animal traction on long journeys, on or off roads […]. And the Peking to Paris race showed I was right'. Above all, Borghese recalled, 'The Itala made the long journey without abnormal wear and tear on roads that were almost always bad, often very bad, in conditions of climate and temperature which put all the machinery to the test […]. All the parts […] were subjected to extreme stress. It was an unparalleled trial'. It was a pivotal moment in the history of the automobile. The Itala reached Paris first on 10 August 1907, having used sixteen tyres in all, on a route of 16,000 kilometres. The four on which it arrived at its destination were still capable of doing a lot more mileage. Aboard the Itala, Prince Borghese even continued the journey to Milan on the same tyres that had driven across the rocks of the Gobi desert, the mud of the Russian steppe and straddling the rails of the Trans-Siberian express.
The Mille Miglia was run on roads open to the public at night, often in bad weather. Described by Enzo Ferrari as 'the world's most beautiful race', this road racing classic

celebrated the dominance of Pirelli tyres with Alfa Romeo over the years. Already in the 1930 edition, Campari's Alfa 6C 1750 managed to overcome the historical supremacy of the Bugattis. The dominance of the 2.9-litre Alfa 8C was still evident in the late 1930s. The marque of the Quadrifoglio equipped with Pirelli Stella Bianca and Pirelli Supersport tyres won the 1937 Mille Miglia with Carlo Pintacuda and the 1938 Mille Miglia with Clemente Biondetti. The 1938 edition led to a lengthy suspension of this road-racing classic, after an accident in Bologna, where an Aprilia skidded into the spectators and killed ten people.

In December 1956, Pirelli announced it was dropping out of racing to focus on the Cinturato technology. It was feared that a history of automotive and motorcycle successes that had lasted for half a century might come to an end. Instead, the new Cinturato tyre, whose development had absorbed all the company's technological resources, led to a great new season of racing in what, in the late sixties, began to be known finally as rallies. Vehicles very similar to the standard models were tested to the limit on the road and on dirt, mud and snow. It was an almost unique and unrepeatable test bed for tyres.

And it was immediately a triumph made in Italy, with the Fiat 124 Sport and the Lancia Fulvia HF victorious fitted with the Cinturato Pirelli. The Lancia Fulvia HF 1600 driven by Sandro Munari and Mario Mannucci won the fourty-first Monte Carlo Rally on 28 January 1972. In 1973, the first World Rally Championship was held and Pirelli secured its first world championship victory in the speciality, with the Fiat 124 Abarth driven by the German Achim Warmbold. On 23 January 1975, at the finish line of the fourty-third Monte Carlo Rally, the mix of power, technology and imagination made up of the duo Munari and Mannucci aboard the Stratos number 14 in Alitalia livery and fitted with Pirelli P7s won hands down. The wizard Munari did nothing wrong in that race. The car was a miracle of reliability, and the behaviour of the tyres reminded everyone that Pirelli was making rallying history. Because it is clear that if the equipment of the Lancia Stratos represented the spearhead of Pirelli's commitment to rallying, it was equally evident that this technological know-how was being made available to much of the automotive industry. Following the Stratos number 14 in the 1975 Monte Carlo Rally came a trio of Fiat 124 Abarths, all equipped with Pirellis: number 2 driven by Hannu Mikkola and Jean Todt, number 10 by Markku Alén and Ilkka Kivimaki, number 12 by Fulvio Bacchelli and Bruno Scabini. The following year, 1976, it was again Sandro Munari—this time paired with Silvio Maiga—who drove the Stratos to victory. His number 10 was first on a podium surrounded by Lancias and Pirellis: second came

the Stratos driven by Björn Waldegård and Hans Thorszelius, third that by Bernard Darniche and Eric Mahé. And to remove any doubt, another car with Pirelli P7 tyres took fourth place: the Opel Kadett driven by Walter Röhrl and Gerhard Berger.
'We broke the bank at Monte Carlo', read the advertisement in 1977, when once again history repeated itself. In the Casino forecourt, Munari and Maiga's Stratos was again first. In second place, another jewel destined to enter the history of rallying: the Fiat 131 Abarth driven by Jean-Claude Andruet and Michèle Espinosi-Petit, aka Biche.
By this time Pirelli was absolutely dominant in the history of rallying. Since 1973, the first fourteen seasons of the world championship were raced in official partnership with the Fiat group. Five titles were won with Fiats between 1974 and 1978 and then with Lancias in 1983 and 1987, triumphing in Argentina, Canada, Greece, New Zealand, Sweden, on all types of terrain. After leaving the Fiat group, it was the turn of Pirelli's collaboration with Toyota, and the first successes in Africa in 1984, with the debut of the future champion Juha Kankkunen, and then victories by the Spaniard Carlos Sainz, who won two titles in 1990 and 1992. Another phase when Pirelli dominated the World Rally Championship began in 1994, when the 'long P' equipped the Subaru Impreza Gr. A of the 555 World Rally Team, driven by Carlos Sainz and Colin McRae. Finally the 100th victory came in 1997, again with the 555 World Rally Team and new successes with Petter Solberg at the wheel. To more recent times—the 2000s—belong Sébastien Loeb's exploits with Citroën.
Today Pirelli is present in rallies in over forty countries worldwide. Its role as sole supplier for the WRC (World Rally Championship) is the natural culmination of a commitment that has never ceased. Among much else, the company endorses the Rally Star programme, following up on its long-term commitment to supporting talented young drivers at all levels of rallying. The FIA (Fédération Internationale de l'Automobile) organises Rally Star for young people between seventeen and twenty-six years old as a natural development of Pirelli Star Driver, an initiative begun in early 2009 that launched talents such as Ott Tänak and Elfyn Evans. Craig Breen was given a head start thanks to another initiative supported by Pirelli, the WRC Academy. Young drivers are selected through a multi-stage process based on digital motorsports and real driving sessions on production vehicles.

Testimonies From All Pirelli Sports

François Chatriot and Michel Périn at the 33rd Tour de Corse—Rallye de France on BMW M3 E30, 1989

The Sports Workshop — 268

Sandro Munari and Silvio Maiga's Lancia Stratos during the 44th Monte Carlo Rally, 1976

The Sports Workshop — 270

Dani Sordo and Candido Carrera's Hyundai Shell Mobis at the 20th Rally Italia Sardegna, 2023

Testimonies From All Pirelli Sports — 271

Ott Tänak and Martin
Järveoja's M-Sport Ford at the
56th Rally de Portugal, 2023,
photo DirtFish

following pages
Takamoto Katsuta and Aaron
Johnston's Toyota Gazoo
Racing at the 70th Rally of
Sweden, 2023

The Sports Workshop — 274

Sébastian Ogier and Vincent
Landais' Toyota Gazoo Racing
at the 19th Rally Mexico, 2023

Testimonies From All Pirelli Sports — 275

Kalle Rovanperä and Jonne
Halttunen's Toyota Gazoo
Racing at the 70th Safari Rally
Kenya, 2023

SKIING AND MOUNTAINEERING

To get an idea of what Pirelli skiing equipment means, we need to go back to the 1940s. Emerging from the war, Italians still donned leather boots, picked up wooden skis and set off for the snow fields without the help of a chairlift. It was in this climate that Pirelli began to produce a series of rubber items to 'help skiers in their hard life': jackets, rubber-soled boots, handles and baskets for ski poles, belts and straps for attachments. The photographs published in the *Rivista Pirelli* for 1949 suggested that 'only those who have experienced the effort of working with gloved hands will appreciate the convenience of these small things that are easy to handle. A slight pressure suffices to free the rubber strap that binds the skis to the poles' and 'the elastic ski binding makes the operation of slipping on the skis easy and immediate. The Pirelli ski binding is always ready for use'.

'Since the first-rate sportsman is noted for the possession of refined equipment, the skier's outfit is completed by the very practical Pirelli windcheater'. Then of course there were the rubber soles, a strong point in the production of a wide range of products. 'The Alpine sole of the boots is a guarantee against dangers in the mountains'. The tradition of rubber boots continued through much of the second half of the twentieth century, leading in the seventies to the super-specialised Superga G3 ski boots.

In the 1950s, the car became the main means of transport to reach the ski slopes, and the skier's car also needed 'snow shoes'. First these were chains with rubber tensioners to prevent the wheels from skidding and then, in 1950, came the invention of the winter tyre, with a herringbone tread pattern to tackle snowy or icy roads, derived from the pre-war Artiglio model. For the Winter tyre, then a few years later for the New Winter tyre, the Dutch designer Bob Noorda designed a series of advertisments that were simply brilliant in their geometric reinterpretation of fir branches and snowflakes. Since then, the development of winter tyres has come a long way—think of the innovative BS separate tread tyre—thanks partly to experience gained in rallying. The highly specialised Pirelli Winter line continues to this day.

Another skiing invention that emerged in the 1950s was the roof-mounted ski rack. An object as simple as it was useful was the one patented by Pirelli in 1950 and then industrially manufactured by Kartell, a company to the fore in the use of plastics.

The Kartell K101 ski rack owes its invention to the engineer Carlo Barassi, a genius in the Pirelli tyre research and development department and a great enthusiast of the mountains. The need to overcome the difficulties of handling ropes and elastic straps at low temperatures prompted Barassi to invent a simple system for securing skis to the car roof. He designed a series of elements in Nastro Cord—a rubberised fabric he patented in 1948—that rested on foam pads to avoid damaging the car's paintwork. The idea appealed to the architect and designer Roberto Menghi, who joined Barassi in developing the patent.

Pirelli returned to the snow fields in the third millennium, in other forms and in the light of new technologies. In 2017, it signed a five-year partnership with the Alpine World Ski Championships organised by the FIS, the International Ski Federation, and the World Ice Hockey Championships held by the IIHF, the International Ice Hockey Federation. Already a partner of the Italian Winter Sports Federation and Swiss-Ski, in this way Pirelli strengthened its commitment to winter sports. The agreement with Infront Sports and Media accompanied the competitions on the snow involving six hundred athletes from some seventy countries around the world. In May of the same year, between Cologne and Paris, the Hockey World Championship followed.

From the support given in 2017 to the Alpine World Ski Championships, a new stage of the Pirelli Design project developed in conjunction with Blossom Skis, a technological laboratory based in Valchiavenna, to manufacture skis truly made in Italy. This is how Sport Carve Ski developed, with a design notable for the use of rubber on the upper part, the pointed 'long P' logo, a wooden core and a graphite sole. Pirelli's innovative contribution also consists in the insertion of an anti-vibration strip in vulcanised rubber made from a special compound designed to dampen the stresses the ski undergoes during descent by up to 60%.

So seventy years on we have returned to rubber as a fundamental material for improving the skier's experience. It is the guarantee that the 'racing machines' on your feet will meet the needs of the most expert consumers. Just as in 1949.

The Sports Workshop — 278

Ezio Bonini, brochure
advertising Pirelli winter tyres,
1952

Walter Bonatti on the
Matterhorn during the first
winter ascent of the Fürggen
Ridge, 1953

Bob Noorda, advertisement for Pirelli winter tyres, 1952

Cover of the Pirelli catalogue of soles and heels with deep tread patterns for footwear for the mountains and work, 1954

The Sports Workshop

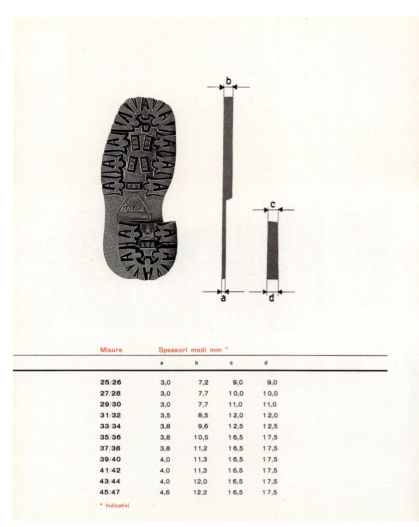

Misure	Spessori medi mm *			
	a	b	c	d
25/26	3,0	7,2	9,0	9,0
27/28	3,0	7,7	10,0	10,0
29/30	3,0	7,7	11,0	11,0
31/32	3,5	8,5	12,0	12,0
33/34	3,8	9,6	12,5	12,5
35/36	3,8	10,5	16,5	17,5
37/38	3,8	11,2	16,5	17,5
39/40	4,0	11,3	16,5	17,5
41/42	4,0	11,3	16,5	17,5
43/44	4,0	12,0	16,5	17,5
45/47	4,6	12,2	16,5	17,5

* Indicativi

Suola Alpina Roccia (m. r.)
Codice 3261

19 - A 5
4-54

Impieghi
per calzature da montagna adatte particolarmente per scalate in roccia; per pedule da roccia e da riposo; per calzature invernali da città.

Caratteristiche
La suola "Alpina Roccia" è una varietà della suola "Alpina". Perfettamente identica per disegno e qualità (cuoiacea extra), se ne differenzia soltanto per gli spessori che sono ridotti allo scopo di ottenere una suola più leggera e più flessibile.
La suola "Alpina Roccia" viene largamente adottata dagli alpinisti, con grande soddisfazione.

Pages from Pirelli catalogue of soles and heels with deep tread patterns for footwear for the mountains and work, 1954, Alpina Roccia sole

Testimonies From All Pirelli Sports — 283

Exhibition of footwear with
Alpina Pirelli soles, 1952

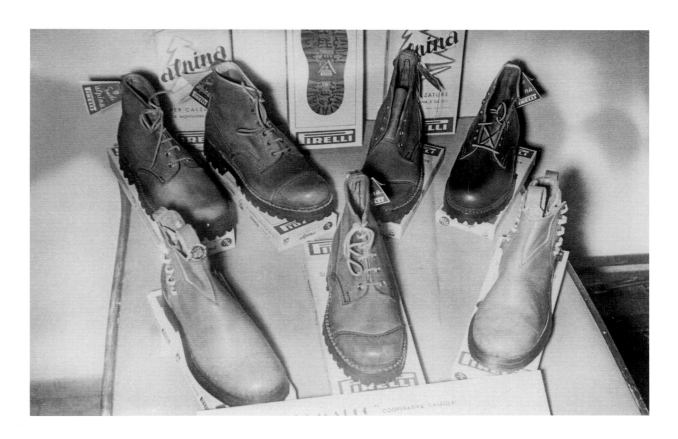

Exhibition of G3 Superga
boots, 1964

TENNIS

The private photographic legacy of Alberto Pirelli—president of the company between 1938 and 1965—contains an image of his tennis match with the journalist Tom Antongini. The umpire is Gabriele D'Annunzio, Antongini being his faithful secretary. The year was 1903. The noble sport of tennis was therefore already known and practised in the Pirelli family in the early twentieth century. But the sport only became industrialised in the 1930s. In 1930, a price list under the heading 'sporting goods' devoted half a page to 'tennis balls, cases and racquet grips'. The inner layer of the tennis ball was made from latex, the natural rubber that was a staple of Pirelli products. In 1938 the writer–tennis player Guido Cesura lent his signature to an elegant booklet—presented as a gift to customers in sports shops—which explained tennis starting from the new Pirelli Super Extra ball. It was illustrated with stills from a film clip of coach Fritz Weiss. Authorised by the Italian Tennis Federation for national and international competitions and then promoted to the Davis Cup, that ball 'that darts and bounces' took the Pirelli name into the tennis world. Further innovations followed in the 1950s. Pirelli balls were produced in the Seregno plant, 'ready to bounce on courts around the world'. In advertising, the great interpreter was the Dutch graphic designer Bob Noorda with his minimalist lines evoking a tennis court or the action of a player striking the ball. From a 1954 Pirelli advertising booklet distributed free of charge in schools, we know that 'the tennis ball consists internally of two hemispherical shapes, bonded at the edges by vulcanisation. Before being vulcanised, however, tablets are placed inside the ball which, when heated, emanate a dilating gas. And this is the explanation of the mystery of how tennis balls are inflated without the need for valves or openings. On the outside, two felt compounds form the outer layer, a kind of decoration applied to the actual ball hot-pressed in special moulds'.

From Bob Noorda to Antonio Boggeri, advertisements for Pirelli tennis balls spanned the 1960s and 1970s, between the Davis Cup and the Italian Open. The balls were produced in yellow and orange, and reinforced with nylon.

The formation of the Union between Pirelli and the British Dunlop company in 1971 gave a boost to Pirelli-branded tennis. In addition to balls made by the Dunlop brand, Slazenger racquets arrived in Union Sports shops. And the production of Superga shoes, which have been supreme on clay courts for decades, gained new momentum. In a commercial produced by the Turin-based company—a subsidiary of the Pirelli–Dunlop group—Adriano Panatta gave his face to the global line of tennis gear and equipment produced by the Union's international facilities. Recalling how that commercial came to be made, Panatta gave a charming interview to Pirelli many years later. 'I haven't kept any trophies. I swear I have got anything left, I only have a Pirelli ball with a date written on it: 30 May 1976. My sister gave it to me after moving house. She said: "Look what I found". To me, it's more a memory of my father than the game. In 1976 I beat Björn Borg in the quarter-finals at Roland Garros, then won the tournament in the final against Harold Solomon. And then there was the Davis Cup, won in Santiago against Pinochet's Chile. I had become a symbol for Italy at the time, to the point that Superga wanted me as brand ambassador for their shoes. I was in Rome and the CEO of the group called me in Turin and told me they wanted to make a shoe with my name on it'.

It was probably in Santiago, in 1976, that the dream team of Adriano Panatta, Paolo Bertolucci, Corrado Barazzutti and Tonino Zugarelli—under the guidance of Nicola Pietrangeli—created that team spirit that is again so strong today. After the recent winning seasons of Italian women tennis players, the victory by Jannik Sinner, together with his teammates, in the 2023 Davis Cup augurs well for a resurgence on the courts, whether red clay or green grass.

Adriano Panatta as brand ambassador of the advertising campaign 'Superga. Your shoes chosen by champions', Agenzia Centro, 1979

Advertisement for Pirelli tennis balls, 1950s

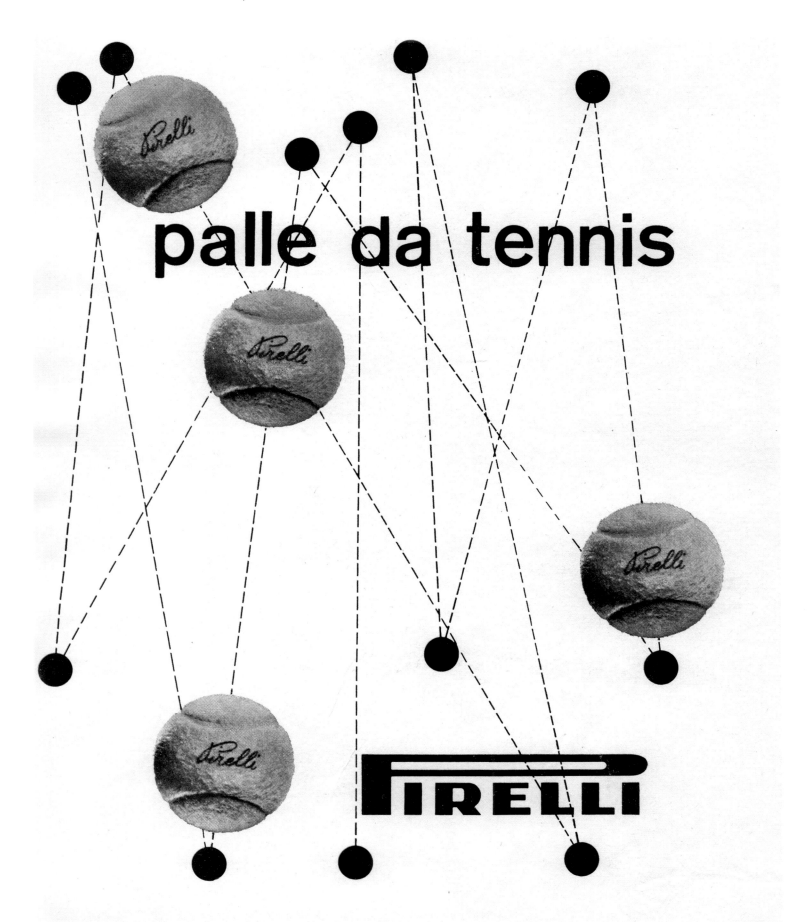

SAILING AND WATER SPORTS

'Water Is Just Another Road': this is the historic adventure of the 'long P' in the America's Cup. Pirelli began to travel the watery roads of lakes and seas in the late 1940s, when the rubber dinghy, created for military purposes and used as life-saving equipment, became popular for recreational boating. It marked the start of 'mass motoring on the waves'. Produced by the Seregno company, the Nautilus was unmistakably orange, with blue seats. It could be paddled or propelled by a small outboard engine. It was the flagship product of a Pirelli line for the Italians' seaside holidays. The Seregno company also produced inflatable loungers, which were highly adaptable, being suited either to floating in the sea or sleeping in a tent. Other iconic rubber products for Italian holidays were masks, complete with fins and spearguns. The Pirelli mask for observing reef life had an exceptional brand ambassador in Ingrid Bergman, introduced to underwater discoveries by Roberto Rossellini in 1949, while making the movie *Stromboli*. Miss Sweden also appreciated Pirelli fins. They were featured in the article 'The Miracle of Underwater Fishing' by Lamberti Sorrentino, published that year in the *Rivista Pirelli*.

In the distant 1920s, bathing caps, now rarely used after years in vogue, appeared in advertising sketches that were small masterpieces of Art Deco. And another rubber product for swimming, the Lastex stretch fabric swimsuit enjoyed peak popularity in the 1950s. Produced by the Pirelli Revere company, it was worn by none other than Marilyn Monroe on the beaches of California in 1952. For everyone, the Seregno company also offered the Tricheco scuba unit with interchangeable 10-litre cylinders, in addition to the PVC diver-down buoy complete with line and flag.

The successor of the Nautilus rubber dinghy in around the seventies was called Laros, grey with blue accessories. An icon of freedom and respect for the environment, it was used for exploring unfrequented coves and beaches, as well as extreme adventure and water sports. The Laros race from Milan to Trieste in 1968 was epic, as was the fantastic football match played on the water by rubber dinghies manufactured by the Seregno company. In 1970, Mario Valli sailed Celeusta, a large Laros 80 inflatable watercraft, across the Pacific Ocean from Peru to French Polynesia.

The same 1950s that launched rubber dinghies saw the spread of innovative technologies and materials: plastic and all its derivatives, such as tough, lightweight fiberglass. In the Monza-based company's factory, Pirelli produced a line of boats, such as Itaca, Ninfa and Levriero, made from kelesite, resivite and armorite, all trade names for fibreglass. Rowed, paddled or propelled by a motor, fibreglass boats became popular during the second half of the twentieth century. They were lightweight,

easy to load onto a car roof (a Fiat Seicento, in the original instruction booklet) or towed on a trailer. Later Pirelli kelesite boats were produced by the Celli boatyards in Venice, launching a whole new range of innovations in the field of plastics.
When it came to sailing, the *Rivista Pirelli* devoted a lot of space to the sport. As early as 1954 the yachtsman Beppe Croce—later appointed president of the Italian Yacht Club—wrote an article titled 'You Don't Need Millions to Go Sailing' for the magazine. It did much to popularise a sport still little known at the time. Subsequent contributions, such as 'Yachts on the High Seas' by Bruno Vivarello in 1960 on American offshore regattas and the '9 O'clock Sailing Lesson' by Rodolfo Facchini in 1967 on the Caprera sailing centre, were further tributes to this silent sport of the sea. All the same, it took several years for the 'long P' marque to leave the pages of a magazine and really set sail. In the year 2000, the Carlo Negri Cup returned to the regattas organised in Santa Margherita Ligure by Beppe Croce's Italian Yacht Club, after an absence of some twenty years. The new edition was held with the support of Pirelli, and dedicated to the son of Margherita Pirelli, the daughter of the founder Giovanni Battista, a pilot who died in Albania in 1943, a recipient of the gold medal for bravery. This gave rise to the Pirelli-Coppa Carlo Negri regattas, in the form of a perpetual challenge valid as a stage in the Big Boats Mediterranean Championship together with classics such as the Giraglia or the Tre Golfi of Naples.
And then came the moment of *Luna Rossa*—today *Luna Rossa Prada Pirelli*—and that epic competition known as the America's Cup. In 2018 a partnership was signed with Prada for the multi-year Luna Rossa Challenge project: 'Pirelli has chosen to be part of this project because it represents a sporting and technological challenge, capable of taking Italy and the Pirelli brand to the whole world', stated Vice-President Marco Tronchetti Provera on this occasion. This led to the thirty-sixth edition of the America's Cup, held in New Zealand in 2021. *Luna Rossa Prada Pirelli* experimented with the revolutionary foil system, a set of appendages that in the ideal configuration enables the hull to literally take off from the water and float above it. Now the launch in Cagliari of the AC75 full-foiling monohull has officially kicked off the participation of the *Luna Rossa Prada Pirelli* team in the thirty-seventh America's Cup. For made in Italy of the sea this is a story still to be written.
Alongside the upper reaches of competitive sailing, however, over the years Pirelli has also supported 'solidarity sailing', with a strong ethical and social content. The 'Matti per la Vela' (Crazy for Sailing) project dates from the 1990. It was founded in Genoa from the passion for the sea of a group of health workers, volunteers and professional

skippers. They set themselves the goal of using the sport of sailing as a therapeutic resource to assist and heal people suffering from illnesses and mental disorders.
In 2017, the WOW–Wheels on Waves project was launched by the sailor Andrea Stella, in collaboration with Pirelli, to promote awareness of the United Nations Convention on the Rights of Persons with Disabilities. The initiative is based on an 18-metre catamaran, specially designed to break down all types of architectural barriers and ensure inclusion and accessibility for people with a wide range of disabilities.
And finally, today, in this long history that links the sport of sailing to Pirelli, there is Ambrogio Beccaria, with his foil that bears the words 'Power is nothing without control' on the sail and a boat with a striking name: *Alla Grande-Pirelli*, which set sail for the first time in 2022 (it is dealt with at length on page 76). In late November 2023, the Class40 *Alla Grande-Pirelli*—skippered by Beccaria and Andrieu—won the prestigious Transat Jacques Vabre transoceanic race after sailing for 18 days 12 hours and 21 minutes. The final victory was achieved by the results of two stages. The first started from Le Havre in Normandy on 29 October 2023 and ended in Lorient in Brittany 350 miles later, and the second, begun on 6 November from France ended on the island of Martinique after Beccaria's foil had skimmed across the seas for 5,381 miles.

Testimonies From All Pirelli Sports — 291

Advertisement for Pirelli beachwear, 1965

The Sports Workshop

The Cantieri Celli stand at the
2nd Milan Winter Boat Show,
1962

Laros Pirelli rubber dinghy,
1967

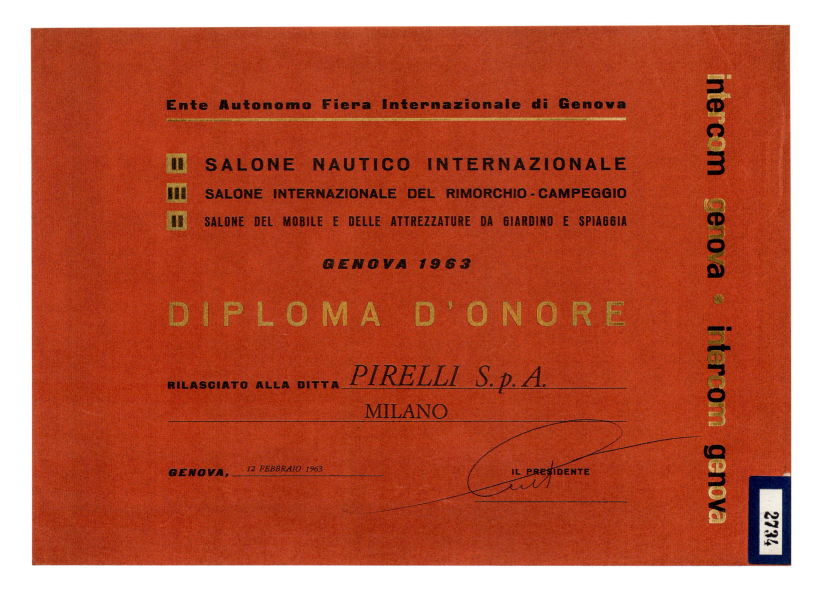

Diploma of honour awarded to Pirelli S.p.A. by the Genoa International Trade Fair Authority, 1963

Testimonies From All Pirelli Sports — 295

Laros 7 and Laros 25 on display at a Pirelli boating products stand, 1966

The Sports Workshop

Luna Rossa Prada Pirelli, 2022,
photo Studio Borlenghi

Luna Rossa Prada Pirelli, 2022

FONDAZIONE PIRELLI 'LOOKING WITHIN' TO DISSEMINATE CORPORATE CULTURE

It was June 1907 when the Itala car fitted with Pirelli tyres set off from Beijing for Paris, to win the most famous car race in history. Aboard were Prince Scipione Borghese, the journalist Luigi Barzini of the *Corriere della Sera* and the mechanic Ettore Guizzardi. A crucial event in car racing, which we celebrated already in 2007 with the photo book *Pirelli. A Hundred Years Supporting Sport*. But the link between the 'Long P' and the world of sports put down its first roots in 1877, when the company started producing rubber sports goods. And when we talk about sports, we mean more than just motor racing. Think of motorcycle racing, the great cycling classics, football, athletics, tennis and water sports, as well as those practised in the mountains.

The pairing with sport has always involved Pirelli as an integral part of the various disciplines, a technical partner attentive to the evolution of technologies in forms of competition. So telling the story of sport means talking about records and champions, teams, communities, welfare, competitiveness, conquests, challenges and overcoming one's limits; but above all it means documenting what goes on behind the scenes in competitions. The worksites, laboratories, sports products factories, the backstage of competitions. The workshops, in fact. As the engineer Luigi Emanueli, inventor of the oil-filled cable and the Pirelli Cinturato, used to say, 'Adess ghe capissaremm on quaicoss: andemm a guardagh denter' (Now we'll understand something. Let's have a look inside).

It is no coincidence that the phrase is one of the quotes that have greeted visitors at the entrance to the Fondazione Pirelli since it was established in 2008. A reference to the concreteness of the industry and the aptitude for research that have characterised the group's culture since its inception, and the twofold nature of the company, a multinational firmly rooted in Milan and its environs. Pirelli's identity has always been notable for a polytechnic corporate culture, capable of combining art, production, beauty, technology and innovation. And the Fondazione Pirelli has always been at the forefront of organising and supporting the company's cultural initiatives, in the belief that safeguarding its historical and contemporary heritage is a value for the company and its stakeholders and a fundamental asset of its competitiveness. Confirming the importance of the Pirelli Archive for the community, the Archival Superintendency proclaimed its historical interest in 1972, placing it under its protection.

The main objective of the Foundation, which is based in Building 134—now Building Stella Bianca—at the Pirelli Headquarters in Milano Bicocca, is therefore to preserve and enhance the value of this rich heritage. It has over four kilometres of documents that testify to the history of the company from its foundation in 1872 to the present, with a large section devoted to advertising and visual communication, which includes the photographic collection, the record groups of sketches, camera-ready artwork and audiovisuals.

Final notes

The photographic collection comprises more than 700,000 items including negatives on plate and film, prints and slides, whose subjects are images of factories, products, exhibitions and fairs, car, motorcycle and bicycle racing, reportages dealing with corporate welfare, including sports, fashion services intended to illustrate company magazines, product catalogues and advertising copy.
The authors include masters of photography such as Aldo Ballo, Gabriele Basilico, Rodolfo Facchini, Arno Hammacher, Annie Leibovitz, Ugo Mulas, Federico Patellani, Fulvio Roiter, Enzo Sellerio, Albert Watson, and well-known agencies such as Farabola and Publifoto.
The collection of original sketches and drawings comprises hundreds of sketches, drawings and artwork made by famous illustrators, graphic designers such as Pavel Michael Engelmann, Gerard Forster, Robert François, Lora Lamm, Alessandro Mendini, Riccardo Manzi, Bruno Munari, Bob Noorda, Massimo Vignelli, among others, and international advertising agencies such as Young & Rubicam and Armando Testa. This collection also includes the numerous works commissioned by Pirelli from artists of the calibre of Fulvio Bianconi, Renzo Biasion and Renato Guttuso, among others, to illustrate the *Rivista Pirelli*. The Pirelli Archive includes the complete collections of the company periodicals *Pirelli. Rivista d'informazione e di tecnica*, *Vado e torno*, *Pi vendere*, *Fatti e Notizie*, *Paginas Pirelli*, *Noticias Pirelli* and *Pirelli World*, among others.
The audiovisual collection contains hundreds of clips on film and magnetic tape dating from 1912 to the present. They range from films by Luca Comerio to documentaries such as *La fabbrica sospesa*, commissioned by Pirelli from the director Silvio Soldini in 1985, filmed advertising and *caroselli* by the masters of Italian animation such as Roberto Gavioli and the brothers Nino and Toni Pagot, and TV commercials from the 1990s and 2000s, with art directors such as Derek Forsyth and brand ambassadors such as the athlete Carl Lewis, the actress Sharon Stone and the footballer Ronaldo.
The Foundation also holds the private archives of the Pirelli family, which include the papers of Alberto and Leopoldo Pirelli. Alberto Pirelli's archive testifies to his work in the service of the country as a diplomat and expert in finance and international economics, and the positions he held in important national and international bodies such as the International Chamber of Commerce, Assonime and ISPI. Leopoldo Pirelli's papers, on the other hand, concern his activity as president of the group, starting in 1965, and testify to key events in the company's history, such as the Pirelli Commission for the reform of the statutes of Confindustria.
The Pirelli Archive includes collections of architectural and urban interest such as the documents of the *Bicocca Project*, which testify to the various phases of redevelopment of the site, the personal files of the company's employees, corporate, accounting and administrative papers such as the group's Annual Reports. In recent years these have been enriched by contributions from internationally renowned authors such as Peter Cameron, Emmanuel Carrère, Javier Cercas,

Luciano Floridi, Adam Greenfield, Lisa Halliday, Hanif Kureishi, William Least Heat-Moon, Nicola Lagioia, Javier Marías, Guillermo Martínez, Tom McCarthy, John Joseph 'J.R.' Moehringer.

The Archive also preserves the technical documentation relating to the design and development of products and machinery: original designs of tyre moulds, studies of treads, technical test specifications, homologation documents, price lists and catalogues.

Also of notable interest is the technical-scientific library, created by the company for its researchers and engineers, and which became part of the foundation's assets in 2010. Over 16,000 volumes on rubber and cable technology from the nineteenth century to the present day, foreign technical journals of which the Foundation holds the only copies in Italy, such as the English *India Rubber Journal*, the oldest magazine in the world on the rubber industry, founded in 1888, and the American *India Rubber World* published in New York from 1889 to 1954. A heritage that is not merely technological but also cultural.

The enhancement projects take the form of the organisation of exhibitions, the editing of publications, production of films, theatrical performances and podcasts, the management of company libraries and the creation of projects related to reading materials. They include the reconditioning, restoration, cataloguing and digitisation of documents in the Pirelli Historical Archives and the organisation of guided tours. In the field of education, the Foundation is committed to planning and producing creative and training courses for schools and institutes of different types and levels.

The dissemination of Pirelli's corporate culture also involves constant investment in improving digital resources, to optimise access to the Foundation's website and the hubs connected with it, remote access to the Historical Archives online and virtual tours enabling visitors to explore the spaces of the Foundation and the Pirelli Headquarters. A continuous challenge in all areas of innovation, a key word that has always characterised Pirelli, with its ability to 'look within' in order to look ahead.

Advertisement for 'Pneu Pirelli', lithograph, 1913

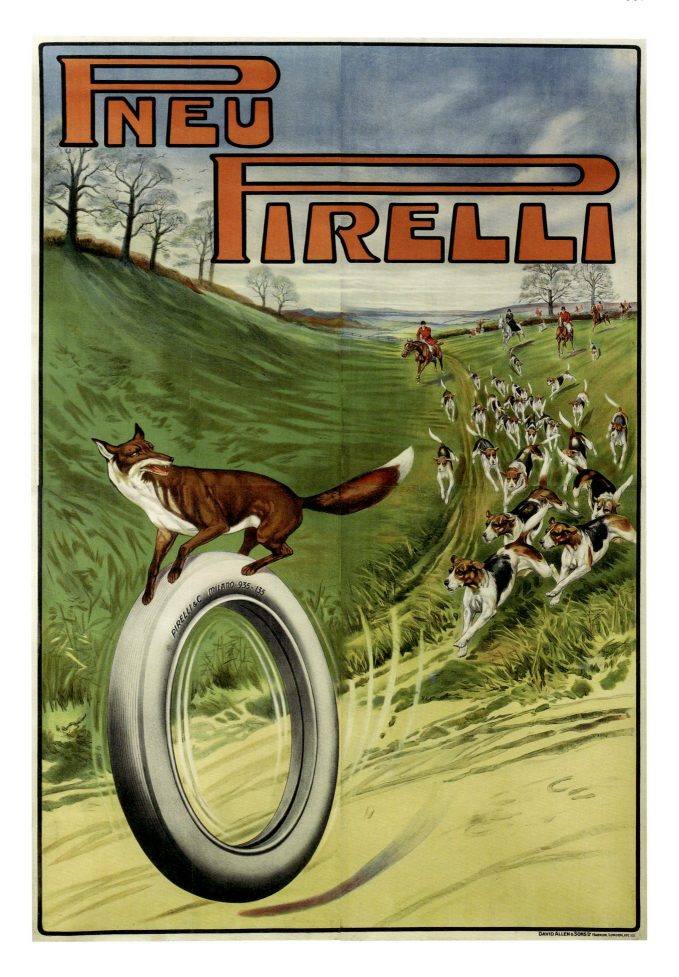

AUTHORS' BIOGRAPHIES

Emanuela Audisio

Emanuela Audisio has been working since 1976 for the daily *la Repubblica*, for which she has been a special correspondent. She is the author of three books, has directed eleven documentaries, covered ten football World Cups, eleven editions of the Summer Olympic Games (plus four editions of the Winter Games), and eighteen world championships in athletics, as well as world championships in swimming, boxing, basketball and skiing. She is the only woman to have received the Gianni Brera Prize and the Manuel Vázquez Montalbán International Prize.

Ambrogio Beccaria

Ambrogio Beccaria (32), a graduate in nautical engineering, was born and raised in Milan. After various experiences in crew and double-handed sailing, in 2013 he used his savings to buy a Mini 6.50 metre boat that had been wrecked in the Atlantic. Since then he has sailed solo and regularly won regattas in this class in Italy and France. In the 2018–19 seasons, he won a series of victories never before achieved by an Italian yachtsman, showing great promise in ocean sailing. On 15 November 2019, he won the Mini Transat, the historic single-handed transatlantic race, for the first time in the history of Italian sailing. He received the Sailor of the Year award in 2018 and 2019 and was awarded the Ambrogino d'Oro in 2020. In May 2022 he launched his new project made completely in Italy, *Alla Grande-Pirelli*, on which he will race until the end of 2024 aboard the boat of the same name, a latest generation Class40, aboard which he finished second in the Route du Rhum 2022 and first in the Transat Jacques Vabre 2023. He lives in Lorient, Brittany.

Antonio Calabrò

Antonio Calabrò (1950) is Pirelli's senior vice-president for culture and director of the Fondazione Pirelli. He is president of Museimpresa and the Fondazione Assolombarda. He is vice-president of the Unione Industriali di Torino, chairman of the Advisory Board of UniCredit Lombardia and a member of the boards of numerous institutions and foundations (Liuc/Libera Università di Castellanza, Symbola, Nomisma, Fondazione Pier Lombardo, Orchestra Sinfonica di Milano, Milano Musica, Fondazione Unipolis, etc.). A journalist and writer, he has worked for *L'Ora*, *Il Mondo* and *la Repubblica*; he was editorial director of the Il Sole 24Ore group and directed *La Lettera finanziaria* and the ApCom news agency. His most recent books include: *Orgoglio industriale*, *Cuore di cactus*, *La morale del tornio*, *I mille morti di Palermo*, *L'impresa riformista*, *Oltre la fragilità* and *L'avvenire della memoria*. He teaches at the Università Cattolica, Milan.

Eva Cantarella

Eva Cantarella is an Italian historian, jurist, sociologist and academic who studies ancient society. She has held academic positions at the universities of Camerino, Parma and Pavia, as well as at the University of Texas, Austin, and New York University. On 2 July 2002 she was appointed Grand Officer of the Order of Merit of the Italian Republic *motu proprio* by the President of the Republic Carlo Azeglio Ciampi. In 2019 she won the Hemingway Prize in the Adventure of Thought category. Her books include: *Itaca. Eroi, donne, potere tra vendetta e diritto* (Bagutta and Fort Village prizes), *L'amore è un dio. Il sesso e la polis* (Città di Padova prize for non-fiction), *Le donne e la città. Per una storia della condizione femminile*, *Sparta e Atene. Autoritarismo e democrazia* is her most recent book, issued in 2021.

Evelina Christillin

Evelina Christillin graduated in history and demographic history. A Grand Officer of the Order of Merit of the Italian Republic, she began her career in sport and culture, as well as teaching at the Università di Torino, where she was a lecturer in the course of modern history. Since 2012 she has been president of the Egyptian Museum. She has been president of ENIT, of the Teatro Stabile di Torino and of the Philharmonic Orchestra of the Teatro Regio di Torino. She was a member of the National Council of CONI, the first woman in Italy elected a sports manager with special delegation to the 2006 Olympics. In 1998–99 she was executive president of the Turin 2006 organising committee, guiding it to success in obtaining the 20th Winter Olympic Games, brought back to Italy after an interval of forty-six years, a success that earned her the Olympic Golden Collar. Since 2016 she has been UEFA's representative on the FIFA Council and a member of the board of directors of Crédit Agricole Italia. Also in 2016 she was elected Torinese dell'Anno. In November 2018 the mayor of the city of Milan appointed her the vice-president of the Smart City Association. She was president of the Steering Committee of Genova The Grand Finale, the final stage of The Ocean Race around the world 2022–23. Since April 2022 she has been a member of the board of directors of the Teatro Stabile della Città di Napoli. On 2 June 2023 she received the honour of Knight of the Grand Cross of the Order of Merit of the Italian Republic.

Giuseppe Di Piazza

Giuseppe Di Piazza, journalist, writer and photographer (Palermo 1958), is the editor of the Rome edition of the *Corriere della Sera*. In the past, he has directed the weekly magazine *Sette*, the monthly magazines *Max* and *Corriere Innovazione*, and the Agr-Cnr agency. After his beginnings at the newspaper *L'Ora* in Palermo, he worked for *Reporter* and later at *Il Messaggero*, where he was chief reporter, columnist, editor-in-chief of interiors and judiciary, and central editor-in-chief. Moving to RCS, he became director of the group's website in 2001, and then returned to print news. He has published several novels with Bompiani and HarperCollins, winning the 2019 Cortina Prize with *Malanottata*. His latest book is *O tu o lui*. His photos—landscapes and portraits—have been exhibited in Milan, Rome, Florence and New York. Married, the father of three children, he lives in Rome and Milan.

Stefano Domenicali

Stefano Domenicali was born in Imola in 1965. After studying economics and business at the University of Bologna, he fulfilled his passion for cars and in 1991 joined Ferrari at Maranello. In 1993 he was made head of Business Planning and Control & International Race director at the Mugello circuit, then responsible for personnel and sponsorship. In 1998 he was appointed Formula 1 Team Manager. In 2004 he took on the role of Ferrari's sporting director in Formula 1, and in 2008 became Team Principal of Scuderia Ferrari. In 2014 he joined Audi AG as vice-president. In 2016 he was appointed chairman and chief executive officer of Automobili Lamborghini. Chairman and CEO of Formula 1 from January 2021, he is now co-chairman of the F1 Commission and a member of the WMSC FIA. In 2019 he was a member of the UEFA Organisation Committee for the European Under-21 Football Championship. From 2019 to 2021 he was president of the Automotive Industry at Confindustria Emilia and a member of the Advisory Board for foreign investors at Confindustria. From 2020 to 2021 he was vice-president of the Fondazione Altagamma. He is currently a member of the board of directors of Brunello Cucinelli and Gruppo Ferretti. In 2022 he was appointed a member of the Sustainability Committee of the Fondazione Fratelli Tutti. In the same year he received the Collare d'Oro, the highest sporting honour awarded by CONI. In 2000 Imola awarded him the Grifo Città di Imola, and in 2023 the keys to his city. In 2002 he was awarded the honour of Officer of the Order of Merit of the Italian Republic and in 2019 that of Commander. On 2 June 2023 he was named a Cavaliere del Lavoro by the President of the Republic, Sergio Mattarella. He has given talks and held seminars at international universities, including Columbia University, Harvard Business School, Stanford University and SDA Bocconi.

Mario Isola

Mario Isola began his career at Pirelli as a test driver for road tyres, then moved to the research and development division and finally to motorsports. After overseeing various GT and rally product development projects, in 2011 he became Racing Manager, with operational responsibility for Formula 1 and the other championships in which Pirelli participates. Since 2021 he has been motorsport director with responsibility for all functions of the Business Unit. 'The passion for this sport', he says, 'is the main driver of my work, and enables me to perform my activities with the enthusiasm that I try to transmit to my team every day'.

Joe R. Lansdale

Joe R. Lansdale is the author of fifty novels and four hundred shorter works, including stories, essays, reviews, film and TV scripts, introductions and magazine articles, as well as a book of poetry. He has won numerous awards including the Edgar, Raymond Chandler Life Time Award, numerous Bram Stoker Awards, and the Spur Award. His work has been made into films, animation, comics, among them *Bubba Hotep, Cold in July*, as well as the acclaimed TV show, Hap and Leonard. His novel *The Thicket* is currently filming. He has also had works adapted to *Masters of Horror* on Showtime, Netflix's *Love, Death and Robots*, Shudder's *Creepshow*. He has written scripts for *Batman The Animated Series*, and other animation. He has received numerous awards and recognition for horror, crime, historical fiction, as well as others. He lives in Nacogdoches with his wife Karen and pit bull, RooRoo.

Giuseppe Lupo

Giuseppe Lupo was born in Lucania (Atella, 1963) and lives in Lombardy, where he teaches at the Università Cattolica di Milano. His novels, all published by Marsilio, include *L'americano di Celenne* (2000, Premio Mondello), *L'ultima sposa di Palmira* (2011, Premio Selezione Campiello), *L'albero di stanze* (2015, Premio Alassio-Centolibri), *Gli anni del nostro incanto* (2017, Premio Viareggio), *Breve storia del mio silenzio* (2019, shortlisted for the Strega Prize) and *Tabacco Clan* (2022). He is the author of several essays on twentieth-century culture, such as *La letteratura al tempo di Adriano Olivetti* (2016), *La Storia senza redenzione. Il racconto del Mezzogiorno lungo due secoli* (2021), *La modernità malintesa* (2023). He contributes to the cultural pages of *Il Sole 24Ore*.

Giovanni Malagò

Giovanni Malagò, president of CONI since 2013, was born in Rome in 1959. An entrepreneur, he gained a high school diploma in science and a degree in economics and business. As a 5-a-side football player, he won three Italian championships and four Coppa Italia. With the Italian national team, he took part in the World Cup in Brazil in 1986. Managing director and shareholder of the Sa.Mo.Car. Group, in March 2023 he was elected chairman of the board of directors, chairman, CEO and shareholder of Samofin, a holding company. President of the Aniene Rowing Club from 1997 to 2017, he is currently its honorary president. He has been a director of Air One, Banca di Roma and then of Unicredit, a member of Unicredit's Consiglio del Territorio Roma, a director of Tecnimont, Maire-Tecnimont and Advisor for Italy of HSBC. He is currently a member of the board of directors of the Fondazione Telethon, the board of directors of the Fondazione Bambino Gesù, the board of directors of the University of Verona, chairman of the Advisory Council of the Executive Master in Business of Events of SDA Bocconi, president of the jury of Sanofi's Make to Care contest, member of the Advisory Board of RCS Academy, of the jury of the Guido Carli Foundation and of the Advisory Board of Agenda Sant'Egidio, Paganini Ambassador, honorary member and councillor of AIL and councillor of Unicef Italia.

He chaired the organising committees of the 1998 and 1999 Italian International Tennis Championships, the 2005 Men's European Volleyball Championships and the 2009 World Swimming Championships in Rome. From 2001 to 2003 and from 2009 to 2013 he was a member of the National Council of CONI. In 2002 he was awarded the Gold Star for sporting merit and in 2021 the honour of Knight of the Grand Cross. A member of the International Olympic Committee since 2019, of the Olympic Programme Commission and of the Los Angeles 2028 Coordination Commission, he is president of the Fondazione Milano Cortina 2026.

Lorenzo Mattotti

Lorenzo Mattotti (Brescia, 1954) has been living and working in Paris since 1998. In the late 1970s he made his debut as a comic-book artist, drawing black and white strips inspired by the expressionism of José Muñoz and Carlos Sampayo. After attending the IUAV University of Venice, in 1983 he founded the Valvoline group in Bologna with Daniele Brolli, Giorgio Carpinteri, Igort, Marcello Joni and Jerry Kramsky. They sought to make comics engage with the languages of art, music, fashion and advertising, and edited the supplement to the magazine *Alter Alter*.

In *Alter Alter* Mattotti published his first work in colour, *Il signor Spartaco*, in 1982, and in 1984 *Fuochi* (issued in 1986 by the Parisian publisher Albin Michel), which revolutionised the language of comics and revealed some of characteristic elements of his style: sensuous, evocative and enveloping colour and markedly a markedly expressive line.

He has published numerous books for adults and children, translated into various languages, and contributes to *The New Yorker*, *Vanity Fair*, *Cosmopolitan*, *Le Monde*, *Nouvel Observateur*, *Das Magazin*, *Süddeutsche Zeitung*, *Corriere della Sera*, *Internazionale* and *la Repubblica*.

Over the years he has designed numerous book covers—for Einaudi, Garzanti, Guanda, Mondadori, Penguin, Rizzoli and Seuil—and posters for events

such as the Cannes Film Festival and Venice Film Festival.
In 1995 he illustrated an adaptation of *Bluebeard* for the French animation series *Il était une fois*.
In 2004 he created the illustrations for *Eros*, a film directed by Michelangelo Antonioni, Steven Soderbergh and Wong Kar-wai.
He participated in the collective work *Peur(s) du noir* (2008), an animated film created by six graphic designers. In 2019 his film *La famosa invasione degli orsi in Sicilia*, based on Buzzati's tale, was presented at the Cannes Film Festival in the section *Un certain regard*. In 2020, the feature film was nominated for the 45th César Awards, in the Best Animated Film category.

Sandro Modeo

Sandro Modeo (Sesto San Giovanni, Milan, 1964) is a writer, essayist and editorial consultant. He contributes to *La Lettura*, the cultural insert of the *Corriere della Sera*, and various other national and international newspapers, dealing with science, culture and sport. He has published two books on football, *L'alieno Mourinho* (ISBN, 2010, new edition 2013) and *Il Barça* (ISBN, 2011), reprinted several times and translated into numerous languages. Recently published is *I Tre. Federer, Nadal, Djokovic e il futuro del tennis* (66th, 2023). He is preparing a monograph on Jannik Sinner.

Darwin Pastorin

Darwin Pastorin was born in São Paulo, Brazil, the son, grandson and great-grandson of migrants from the Veneto. He is a professional journalist with a degree in literature. The narrator of literary football stories in numerous books, he has been editor of *Guerin Sportivo*, special correspondent and deputy director of *Tuttosport*, director of Tele+, Stream TV, new programmes of Sky Sport, La7 Sport and director of Quartarete TV.

Daniele Pirola

Daniele Pirola (67) graduated in political science after classical studies; he lives in a small town in the province of Varese. He joined Pirelli in 1986, holding the role of press officer and then, with the creation of the Fondazione Pirelli in 2008, that of researcher in the Group's Historical Archives. He has contributed to the creation of several editorial projects on the company's history and in particular the development of tyres. After leaving his position in 2021, he now concerns himself with the energy transition and environmental issues.

Massimo Sideri

Since 2001, Massimo Sideri has been a correspondent and columnist writing on science, innovation and technology for the *Corriere della Sera*, where he founded the monthly *Corriere Innovazione* and edited it for five years. He is adjunct professor of socio-economic history of innovation at the Luiss Guido Carli University in Rome. He has written several essays, including *Il visconte cibernetico. Italo Calvino e il sogno dell'AI* and *L'innovatore rampante. L'ultima lezione di Italo Calvino* (Lup) both with Andrea Prencipe, *La sindrome di Eustachio. Storia italiana delle scoperte dimenticate* (Bompiani) and *Diritto all'oblio, dovere della memoria* (Bompiani) with Umberto Ambrosoli. He has won several awards for journalism, including the Assobiotec Media Award. He teaches various Masters degree courses in popular science, including that of the University of Padua. His podcast for the *Corriere della Sera* on science and forgotten Italian discoveries is entitled *Geni Invisibili* and has obtained over 300,000 listeners.

Marco Tronchetti Provera

Marco Tronchetti Provera has been chief executive officer of Pirelli since 1992, executive vice-president and chief executive officer since 20 october 2015, and executive vice-president of the Group since 3 August 2023. Born in 1948, he graduated in economics and business in 1971 from the Università Bocconi in Milan. In the early seventies he started working in the family business, in particular its activities related to the maritime transport sector. In 1986 he joined Pirelli as a general partner. In 1992 he took over the operational leadership of the Pirelli Group, of which he is currently executive vice-president.
From December 1996 to September 2001 he was chairman of *Il Sole 24Ore* and from October 2001 to September 2005 a member of the board of directors of the Teatro alla Scala. From September 2001 to September 2006 he was chairman of Telecom Italia, from October 1996 to April 2002 he was a director of Mediobanca–Banca di Credito Finanziario, where from May 2007 to October 2017 he was a director and vice-chairman; from November 1999 to April 2002 he was a member of the board of directors of Banca Commerciale Italiana–Intesa BCI. Until May 2013 he held the position of chairman of Prelios S.p.A.
He is chairman of Marco Tronchetti Provera & C., the holding company that controls Camfin, which in turn holds approximately 14% of Pirelli & C., and a director of RCS MediaGroup.
Honorary co-chairman for the italian part of the council for relations between Italy and the United States, of which he was Italian co-president for fifteen years, he is on the general council and advisory board of Assolombarda as well as on the general council of Confindustria. He is a member of the board of directors of the Università Bocconi.

BIBLIOGRAPHY

A

AA.VV., 'The Psychophysiological Effects of Different Tempo Music on Endurance Versus High-Intensity Performances', *Frontiers in Psychology*, 2020.
Acitelli, Fernando, *La solitudine dell'ala destra* (Turin: Einaudi, 1998).
Agassi, Andre, *Open. La mia storia* (Turin: Einaudi, 2011).
Alighieri, Dante, *La Divina Commedia. Inferno*, ed. Natalino Sapegno (Scandicci, Florence: La Nuova Italia, 1957).
Ambrosini, Giuseppe, 'Bartali e Coppi: il segreto della potenza', *Pirelli. Rivista d'informazione e di tecnica*, II, 3 (1949), 19–22.
Arpino, Giovanni, *Azzurro tenebra* (Turin: Einaudi, 1977).
Arpino, Giovanni, *La suora giovane* (Turin: Einaudi, 1959).
Arpino, Giovanni, *L'ombra delle colline* (Milan: Mondadori, 1964).
Arpino, Giovanni, *Passo d'addio* (Turin: Einaudi, 1986).
Artioli, Lamberto, 'Come è nato il Gran Premio Pirelli', *Pirelli. Rivista d'informazione e di tecnica*, V, 3 (1952), 56.

B

Barzini, Luigi, *La metà del mondo vista da un'automobile. Da Pechino a Parigi in 60 giorni* (Milan: Hoepli, 1908).
Bassani, Giorgio, *Il giardino dei Finzi Contini* (Turin: Einaudi, 1962).
Baudelaire Charles, *I fiori del male* (Milan: Garzanti, 1986).
Bellavite Pellegrini, Carlo, *Pirelli. Innovazione e passione 1872-2017* (Bologna: il Mulino, 2017).
Biasion, Renzo, 'Ricordo di Tenni', *Pirelli. Rivista d'informazione e di tecnica*, II, 2 (1949), 32–33.
Binda, Alfredo, 'Nove anni con la gioventù', *Pirelli. Rivista d'informazione e di tecnica*, X, 6 (1957), 31–33.
Bonicelli, Pietro, 'Stile e potenza', *Pirelli. Rivista d'informazione e di tecnica*, I, 1 (1948), 16.
Brera, Gianni, 'Metamorfosi a Oslo', *Pirelli. Rivista d'informazione e di tecnica*, XI, 4 (1958), 48–49.
Brera, Gianni, 'Vita difficile del giocatore di calcio', *Pirelli. Rivista d'informazione e di tecnica*, VIII, 1 (1955), 50–51.
Buzzati, Dino, *Dino Buzzati al Giro d'Italia* (Milan: Mondadori, 2018).

C

Canestrini, Giovanni, 'L'autodromo di Monza e i problemi della velocità', *Pirelli. Rivista d'informazione e di tecnica*, I, 1 (1948), 9–13.
Cantarella, Eva, *Eva Cantarella racconta l'Iliade* (Turin: Einaudi Scuola, 2012).
Croce, Beppe, 'Non occorrono milioni per fare della vela', *Pirelli. Rivista d'informazione e di tecnica*, VII, 4 (1954), 18–21.

D

La Domenica del Corriere, XXVI, 33, 17 August 1924, 1.

F

Facchini, Rodolfo, 'Ore 9 lezione di vela', *Pirelli. Rivista d'informazione e di tecnica*, XX, 4 (1967), 82–87.
Ferrata, Giansiro, 'La musa tra le ruote', *Pirelli. Rivista d'informazione e di tecnica*, VII, 5 (1954), 42–44.

G

Gaia, Filippo, 'Il futuro è già fra noi', *Pirelli. Rivista d'informazione e di tecnica*, II, 3 (1949), 46–48.
Galeano, Eduardo, *Chiuso per calcio* (Rome: SUR, 2023).
Galeano, Eduardo, *Le vene aperte dell'America Latina* (Milan: Sperling & Kupfer, 1997).
Galeano, Eduardo, *Splendori e miserie del gioco del calcio* (Milan: Sperling & Kupfer, 1997).
Gerosa, Guido, interview to Pier Paolo Pasolini, *L'Europeo*, 31 December 1970.
Gigerenzer, Gerd, *Decisioni intuituitive. Quando si sceglie senza pensarci troppo* (Milan: Raffaello Cortina Editore, 2009).

H

Hagura Nobuhiro, *Ready steady slow: action preparation slows the subjective passage of time* (London: The Royal Society Publishing, 2012).
Heidegger, Martin, *Saggi e discorsi*, trans. and ed. Gianni Vattimo (Milan: Mursia, 1954).
Homer, *Iliade*, ed. Dora Marinari (Rome: La Lepre Edizioni, 2010).

I

'Inauguração da praça de esportes do Clube Atlético Pirelli, em Santo André', *Noticias Pirelli*, 1 (1956), 6.
'Insieme per vincere', *Fatti e Notizie*, XXXV, 8 (1984), 7.
Iperti Maurizio, 'Benetton e Pirelli di nuovo insieme', *Fatti e Notizie*, 1 (1991), 11.

K
Karageorghis, Costas, Terry, Peter, 'The psychophysical effects of music in sport and exercise: A review', *Journal of Sport Behavior*, 1997.
Keynes John Maynard, *The Economic Consequences of the Peace* (New York: Harcourt, Brace and Howe, 1920).
Kerouac, Jack, *On the Road* (New York: Viking Press, 1957).

L
Levi, Primo, *The Monkey's Wrench*, trans. William Weaver (New York: Penguin / London: Joseph, 1980).
Luzi, Mario, 'Ai campioni del Torino', *Il calcio è poesia*, ed. L. Surdich and A. Brambilla (Genoa: il melangolo, 2006).

M
Maggi, Maurizio, 'Ed è subito wroom', *Fatti e Notizie*, XXXV, 1-2 (1984), 9.

N
'Nessuno dimentica il gigante buono', *Fatti e Notizie*, XXX, 10 (1979), 15.
Nutrizio, Nino, 'Il dilemma del gioco', *Pirelli. Rivista d'informazione e di tecnica*, VIII, 6 (1955), 36–37.
Nutrizio, Nino, 'Il malato milionario', *Pirelli. Rivista d'informazione e di tecnica*, VII, 4 (1954), 45–48.
Nutrizio, Nino, 'Le funivie hanno aperto le porte della montagna', *Pirelli. Rivista d'informazione e di tecnica*, II, 6 (1949), 43–45.
Nutrizio, Nino, 'Lo squallido zero a zero', *Pirelli. Rivista d'informazione e di tecnica*, X, 1 (1957), 26–28.

O
Orwell, George, 'The Sporting Spirit', *Tribune*, London, 14 December 1945.

P
'Panatta, il tennis e l'arte di divertirsi', www.pirelli.com.
Pausanias, *Guida della Grecia. Libro V*, ed. Domenico Musti and Mario Torelli (Milan: Fondazione Lorenzo Valla/Mondadori, 1982).
'Piccoli Ronaldo crescono', *Fatti e Notizie*, 330 (1997), 14.
Pirelli, Alberto, *La Pirelli. Vita di un'azienda industriale* (Milan: s.n., 1946).
Pirelli. Cent'anni per lo sport, ed. Daniele Pirola (Milan: Mondadori, 2007).
Pizzinelli, Corrado, 'Atleti per illustrazione di Gulliver', *Pirelli. Rivista d'informazione e di tecnica*, III, 5 (1950), 34–35.
Pratolini, Vasco, *Cronache di poveri amanti* (Florence: Vallecchi, 1947).
La Pubblicità con la P maiuscola: la comunicazione visiva Pirelli tra design d'autore e campagne globali, anni Settanta-Duemila, ed. Fondazione Pirelli (Mantua: Corraini, 2017).

S
Saba, Umberto, *Il canzoniere* (Turin: Einaudi, 1979).
Sereni, Vittorio, 'Il fantasma nerazzurro', *Pirelli. Rivista d'informazione e di tecnica*, XVII, 5–6 (1964), 62–65.
Soriano, Osvaldo, *Fùtbol. Storie di calcio* (Turin: Einaudi, 2014).
Soriano, Osvaldo, *Triste solitario y final* (Florence: Vallecchi, 1974).
Sorrentino, Lamberti, 'Il miracolo della pesca subacquea', *Pirelli. Rivista d'informazione e di tecnica*, II, 3 (1949), 38–39.

T
Testori, Giovanni, *Il Dio di Roserio* (Turin: Einaudi, 1954).
Trellini, Piero, *La partita. Il romanzo di Italia-Brasile* (Milan: Mondadori, 2019).

U
Umanesimo industriale. Antologia di pensieri, parole, immagini e innovazioni, ed. Fondazione Pirelli (Milan: Mondadori, 2019).

V
Vergani, Orio, 'Come conosco Gino e Fausto', *Pirelli. Rivista d'informazione e di tecnica*, III, 4 (1950), 16–17.
Vergani, Orio, 'Ricordo di Nuvolari', *Pirelli. Rivista d'informazione e di tecnica*, VII, 4 (1954), 54–55.
Vivarello, Bruno, 'Yachts in altomare', *Pirelli. Rivista d'informazione e di tecnica*, XIII, 3 (1960), 38–41.

W
Wallace, David Foster, *Il tennis come esperienza religiosa* (Turin: Einaudi, 2012).
Wallace, David Foster, *Infinite Jest: a Novel* (Boston: Little, Brown and company, 1996)
Wallace, David Foster, *String Theory: David Foster Wallace On Tennis. A Library of America Special Publication* (New York: The Library of America, 2016).

Z
Zattoni Stefania, 'Pirelli ritorna con il P7', *Fatti e Notizie*, XXXII, 4 (1981), 12–13.

INDEX OF NAMES

A

555 World Rally Team, 266

Abdus Salam, Institute of Theoretical Physics, 127
Abrahams, Harold, 119, 121
Abruzzo, 242
AC75, full-foiling monohull, 289
Achilles, 107, 113, 243
Acitelli, Fernando, 176
Afolin, 215
Africa, 266
A.G.A., Articoli Gomma e Affini, 92, 214
Agassi, Andre, 189, 193
Agenzia Lombarda Gomme Pirelli, 89, 242
Agnelli, Gianni, 20
Agnelli, Umberto, 20
Agostini, Giacomo, 180
Aguascalientes, 127
Aida, 40
Albania, 289
Alberti, Raffaele, 253
Albertosi Enrico, 176
Alcaraz, Carlos, 206
Alén, Markku, 265
Alesi, Jean, 227
Alexander the Great, 108
Alfa 75 Turbo, 227
Alfa-Pirelli, 225
Alfa Romeo, 224, 225, 252, 265
Alfa Romeo 8C, 252
Alfa Romeo 158, 225
Alfa Romeo P2, 224
Alfa Romeo-Pirelli, 224
Alfredo, worker, 215
Algiers, 19
Alitalia, 19
Alla Grande-Pirelli, 12, 45, 77, 79, 80, 81, 82, 84, 85, 290
Allen, Woody, 183

Alpe d'Huez, 135
Alpina, sole, 276, 282, 283
Altobelli, Alessandro, 179
Ambrogino d'Oro, 87
Ambrosini, Giuseppe, 135, 243
America's Cup, 41, 288, 289, 290
Ameri, Enrico, 176
Amiens, 224
Andrieu, Nicolas, 83, 84, 290
Andruet, Jean-Claude, 266
Anfield, 147
Ankara, 180
Annoni, Ambrogio, 89
Antongini, Tom, 284
Apollo, 109
Apollodorus, 113
Apple, 25, 193
Aprilia, 254, 265
Aquaman, 53
Araras, 101
Ardigò, Luca Paolo, 149
Argentina, 97, 98, 176, 266
Argolis, 109
Arnaldi, Matteo, 180
Arnoux, René, 226
Aronofsky, Darren, 107
Arpino, Giovanni, 39, 162, 163, 171, 175, 176, 179, 180
Arrows-Beta, 226
Artemis, 115
Artioli, Lamberto, 139
Arturo Pozzo Gold Trophy, 243
Ascari, Alberto, 225
Ascari, Antonio, 224
Asso, 53, 55
Atala, 242
Atalanta, 115
Athens, 21, 115, 159
Atlanta, 33, 36, 216
Atlantic Ocean, 36, 124, 153
Audi, 23

Audisio, Emanuela, 39, 118
Austin, 27
Australia, 180, 183
Austria, 26, 194
Automobil Club d'Italia, 224, 264
Azienda Pneumatici Motovelo, 143
Azteca, stadium in Mexico City, 176
Azzurra, 120, 194

B

Babbut, 215, 220
Bacchelli, Fulvio, 265
Baggio, Roberto, 120
Baldi, Mauro, 226
Ballo, Aldo, 134, 144, 299
Ballon d'Or, 41, 179, 236
Ballot, 224
Baltimora, 197
Bannister, Roger, 121, 124
Barazzutti, Corrado, 180, 285
Barbados, 159
Barcelona, 33, 36, 176, 216
Barletta, 120
Bartali, Gino, 3, 39, 130, 135, 139, 166, 243
Barzini, Andrea, 176
Barzini, Luigi, 39, 40, 176, 264
Basel, 98
Basilico, Gabriele, 299
Bassani, Giorgio, 174, 175, 180
Batman, 52, 53, 55, 61
Battaini, Rino Gaspare, 234
Baudelaire, Charles, 45
Bayes, Thomas, 206
BBC, 121
Beach Boys, 153
Bearzot, Enzo, 171, 179
Beccaria, Ambrogio, 12, 45, 76, 78, 82, 290
Beethoven, Ludwig van, 153

Belgium, 224
Bell Labs, 189
Beltrame, Achille, 224
Benatar, Pat, 149
Benetton, 226, 227
Bennato, Edoardo, 147
Bentivoglio, Fabrizio, 176
Benvenuti, Nino, 163, 168
Berger, Gerhard, 226, 266
Bergman, Ingrid, 288
Berlanti, Greg, 209
Berlin, 35, 179
Bermuda, 159
Bern Grand Prix, 253
Bernardi, Oscar, 179
Berruti, Livio, 21, 163, 164
Berruto, Mauro, 180
Berta, Giuseppe, 39, 45, 46
Bertarelli, Luigi Vittorio, 131
Bertolini, Bianca, 79
Bertolucci, Paolo, 180, 194, 285
Bianchi, firm, 40, 77, 219, 242, 243, 252
Bianchi, Edoardo, 77
Bianchi-Pirelli, 40
Bianconi, Fulvio, 299
Biasion, Renzo, 253, 299
Biblioteca Ambrosiana di Milano, 36, 56
Bicocca, 88, 91, 92, 95, 97, 98, 201, 215, 234, 298, 299
Bicocca degli Arcimboldi, 89
Big Bear, 53
Big Dipper, 53
Bigelow, Kathryn, 197
Binda, Alfredo, 'la Gioconda', 39, 135, 139, 243, 244
Biondetti, Clemente, 265
Birmingham, 26
Blake, William, 119
Blancpain GT, 227
Blatter, Joseph, aka Sepp, 21
Blossom, Skis, 45, 277
Blur, 153
Boesel, Raul, 226
Boggeri, Antonio, 284
Boillot, Georges, 224
Bolelli, Simone, 180
Bollate, Milan, 143, 244
Bologna, 166, 171, 265
Boninsegna, Roberto, 176
BoP (Balance of Performance), 254
Bordino, Pietro, 224
Borg, Björn, 285
Borghese, Scipione, 40, 264, 298
Borgo Pirelli, 89
Borussia Dortmund, 205
Boston, 26
Bottecchia, Ottavio, 135

Brabham, 226, 227
Brambilla, Roberto, 176
Brandizzi, Gianni, 171
Brasher, Chris, 124
Brazil, 97, 98, 101, 176, 179, 235
Brauron, 115
Breen, Craig, 266
Breitner, Paul, 179
Brera, Gianni, 39, 162, 163, 179, 234, 235, 243
Brescia, 39, 42, 224, 242
Brilli, Nancy, 176, 224, 225
Brilli Peri, Gastone, 224
British Superbike, 254
Brittany, 290
Brivio, Antonio, 225
Brobdingnag, 214
Brunate, 252
Brunel University, 149
Brunero, Giovanni, 243
Brussels, 45, 92, 214
Buffa, Federico, 179
Bugatti, 265
Bulgarelli, Giacomo, 171
Bulgaria, 180
Burgnich, Tarcisio, 176
Bussi, Vittoria, 127, 128
Bussi, Walter, 127
Buzzati, Dino, 166, 170

C

Cagliari, 289
Cagno, Alessandro, 224
Calabria, 133
Calabrò, Antonio, 32
Calcagni, Emilio, 89
Callas, Maria, 171
Calvino, Italo, 166, 183
Cambiasso, Esteban, 101
Cambridge, 119, 186
Cameron, Peter, 299
Camerun, 176
Caminiti, Vladimiro, 180
Campania, 133
Campari, Giuseppe, 224, 225, 265
Campofelice, 224
Campriani, Niccolò, 119
Canada, 194, 227, 266
Canadian Grand Prix, 227
Cantarella, Eva, 39, 106
CAP – Club Atlético Pirelli, 97
Capelli, Ivan, 226
Cape Horn, 121
Cape Town, 19
Caprera, 189, 289
Capuava, favela, 101
Carezza, lake, 153
Carlos Alberto, 176

Carosello, 215, 220
Carousel, musical, 148
Cassidy, Butch, 175
Cassius Clay, 59, 175
Castellani, Valentino, 20
Castellucchio, 253
Castigliano, Eusebio, 166
Caterham Super Seven, 153
Cayard, Paul, 194
Ceccarelli, Riccardo, 121
Cederna, Giuseppe, 176
Celeusta, Laros inflatable watercraft, 41, 288
Celli, boatyards, 289, 292
Central Station, Milan, 131
Cercas, Javier, 299
Cerezo, Toninho, 176
Cerne, Carletto, 171
Cesura, Guido, 284
Champions League, 41, 236
Chandler, Raymond, 175
Charrette-Saxon, Swiss circuit, 253
Chataway, Chris, 124
Cheever, Eddie, 227
Chelsea, 202
Chile, 180, 194, 285
China, 159
Chivasso, 180
Christ the Redeemer, 36
Christillin, Evelina, 18
Chrysler Building, 216
Ciaccheri, Nello, 243
Ciampi, Carlo Azeglio
Ciotti, Sandro, 176
Cipolletti, 175
Circuit de Picardie, 224
Citroën, 266
Cittadella, 180
Cittiglio (Varese), 243
Class40, 80, 81, 82, 84, 85, 86
Clerici, Gianni, 175, 180
Col du Galibier, 139
Cologne, 277
Colombes, 119
Columbia University, 175
Columbus, Christopher, 194
Como, 139, 252
Comunità Nuova Onlus, 101
Confindustria, 36, 299
Confluencia, 175
CONI, 14, 16, 21
Consolini, Adolfo, 13, 45, 88, 92, 214, 215, 219
Conte, Antonio, 197
Conte, Paolo, 3
Continental, 35
Coppa Carlo Negri, 41, 101, 289
Coppa Italia, 41, 180, 236

Coppi, Fausto, 37, 40, 120, 130, 135, 136, 136, 166, 243, 246
Corcovado, 36, 41, 236
Corinth, 109
Cornejo, Patricio, 180
Corporate Social Responsibility, 101
Corradi, Egisto, 19
Corriere della Sera, 19, 40, 264
Cortina, 14, 19, 168
Croatia, 180
Croce, Beppe, 289
Croci, Sergio, 41
Crosetti, Maurizio, 176
Cruijff, Johan, 197
Cucchi, Riccardo, 176
Curie, Marie, 127
Curry, Stephen, 197, 199, 205

D

Dalla Chiesa, Nando, 176
Dalla, Lucio, 33, 154, 158, 176
Dallara, 227
D'Angeli, Fabio, 77
D'Angelo, Nino, 148
D'Annunzio, Gabriele, 284
Darniche, Bernard, 266
Daspo, 148
Davis Cup, 45, 121, 180, 183, 189, 193, 284, 285
De Angelis, Elio, 226
Dear, Matthew, 153
De Cesaris, Andrea, 226
De Chiesa, Carlo, 19
De Gregori, Francesco, 11, 39, 119
Dei, firm, 242
del Buono, Oreste, 179
Delphi, 109, 110
Dessi, Paolo, 79
de Thame, Gerard, 216
Detroit, 153
Di Piazza, Giuseppe, 39, 146
DiCaprio, Leonardo, 183
Djokovic, Novak, 180, 183, 193, 206
La Domenica del Corriere, 224
Domenicali, Stefano, 22, 40
Ducati, 153
Dunlop, 284

E

Earp, Wyatt, 55
Eastwood, Clint, 194
Ecclestone, Bernie, 226
Edison, Thomas, 186, 193
Egyptian Museum, 18, 21
Egonu, Paola, 180
Eiffel Tower, 236
Einaudi, 171, 175, 176
Eisenach, 264

Elgort, Arthur, 215
Elis, 109
El Paso, 180
Emanueli, Luigi, 298
Emerald, Caro, 149
Eminem, 153
Engelmann, Pavel Michael, 299
England, 21, 163
Environmental Accreditation Programme, 68
Eremo del Castegno, 154
Eritrea, 159
Espinosi-Petit, Michèle, aka Biche, 266
Estadio Nacional in Santiago, 180
Europe, 22, 23, 26, 27, 101, 264
Evans, Andy, 227
Evans, Elfyn, 266

F

F1 Academy, 27
F1 Arcade, 26
F1 Exhibition, 26
F1 Sprint Race, 24
Fabbri, Mondino, 163
Fabi, Teo, 226
Facchetti, Giacinto, 171
Facchetti, Gianfelice, 176
Facchinetti, Alberto, 176
Facchini, Rodolfo, 189, 289, 299
Facebook, 189
Falcão, 176
FAMS (Fundação de Amparo ao Menor de Feira de Santana), 101
Fangio, Juan Manuel, 40, 173, 175, 225
Farabola, 299
Farina, Giuseppe, 37, 40, 225
Fatti e Notizie, 97, 98, 112, 123, 215, 227, 299
Federcalcio, 21
Federer, Roger, 180, 193
Fellini, Federico, 194
Fenoglio, Beppe, 171
Ferrara, 253
Ferrari 125, 153, 225
Ferrari 333 SP, 227
Ferrari Challenge, 67, 227
Ferrari, Enzo, 171, 172, 225, 252, 265
Ferrari F40, 153
Ferrari, team, 225
Ferrata, Giansiro, 143
Ferretti, Mario, 166
FIA (Fédération Internationale de l'Automobile), 68, 71, 266
Fiat, 20, 97, 135, 224, 265, 266, 289
Fiat 124 Abarth, 265
Fiat 124 Sport, 265
Fiat 131 Abarth, 266

Fiat 804, 224
Fiat, group, 266
Fiat-Pirelli, 224
Fiat Seicento, 289
Fiera di Milano, 139
FIFA (Fédération Internationale de Football Association), 21
Figliut, 215, 220
Fillol, Jaime, 180
Financial Times, 202
Fiorentina, 235
FIS (International Ski Federation), 277
Fittipaldi, 226
Flamini, Manila, 154
Flaminio bridge, 214
Flash, patent, 53, 209, 254
Floridi, Luciano, 193
Florio, Vincenzo, 12, 40, 42, 224
FM (Formula Medicine), 121
Fogar, Ambrogio, 87
Fonda, Henry, 154
Fonda, Jane, 154
Fonda, Peter, 154
Fondazione Pirelli, 11, 12, 32, 298
Footbonaut, 205
Ford, 153, 154, 271
Ford B coupé, 154
Foreman, George, 175
Formia, 16, 120
Formula 1, 12, 22, 23, 24, 25, 26, 27, 40, 67, 68, 69, 72, 73, 98, 121, 209, 225, 226, 227
Formula 2, 226, 227
Formula 3, 227
Formula E, 68
Foro Italico, 215
Forster, Gerard, 299
Fossati, Ivano, 77
Foster Wallace, David, 180, 206
Frade, Vitor, 199
France, 77, 128, 148, 159, 179, 193, 205, 214, 224, 225, 226, 227, 236, 290
France Football, 147, 148
Francia, Giorgio, 227
François, Robert, 299
Frankie hi-nrg mc, 131
FRECA (Formula Regional European Championship by Alpine), 27
Frédy, Charles Pierre de, Baron de Coubertin (Pierre de Coubertin), 107
French Grand Prix, 224, 225, 226
French Polynesia, 41
Frera, firm, 242
Freud, Sigmund, 124
Frontiers in Psychology, 149
Fuentes, Andrea, 154

G

Gaber Giorgio, 154
Galateri, Gabriele, 20
Galeano, Eduardo, 175
Galeazzi, Gian Piero, 180
Ganna, firm, 242
García, Marta, 27
Gatto, Alfonso, 166
Gazzetta dello Sport, 133, 235, 242
Geminiani, Sante, 253
Geneva, 19
Genoa, 77, 101, 290, 294
Gentile, Giuseppe, 171
Germany, 159, 176, 179, 183, 186, 205
Gerosa, Guido, 166
Gerry and The Pacemakers, 148
Ghini, Massimo, 176
Ghinzani, Piercarlo, 226
Ghisallo, 139, 252
Giacomelli, Bruno, 226
Gibuti, 159
Gigerenzer, Gerd, 205
Gilmour, Dave, 149
Giordani, Claudia, 19, 20
Giraglia, regatta, 289
Girardengo, Costante, 38, 39, 242, 243
Giro d'Italia, 39, 40, 133, 134, 136, 166, 242, 243, 245, 252
Giro di Lombardia, 143, 144, 242
Giro di Romagna, 242
Gittler, Christian, 205
Glaucus, 107
Global Tyre Partner, 41
Gobi, desert, 264
Golden State Warriors (GSW), 197
Gordien, Fortune Everett, 214
Gotham City, 53
Goux, Jules, 224
Gramsci, Antonio, 176
Grande Boucle, 242
Great War, 135, 186
Grand Prix Automobile de France, 224
Gran Premio of the Automobil Club d'Italia, 224
Gran Premio d'Italia, 69, 72, 224, 225
Graziella, 244
Greeks, 107, 108, 115
Greece, 107, 108, 109, 112, 266
Green Day, 149
Greenfield, Adam, 299
Grenoble, 19
Griffiths, Ken, 36, 47
Guardiola, Pep, 202
Guelfi, Gianluca, 77
Guerra, Learco, 135, 186
Guinness Book, 121
Guizzardi, Ettore, 40, 264, 298
Gulliver, 214
Guttuso, Renato, 299

Guyana, 159
Guzzi, 253
Guzzi 65, 'Guzzino', 253
Guzzi 250, 253
Guzzi 500, 253

H

Hagura, Nobuhiro, 209
Halliday, Lisa, 300
Hammacher, Arno, 299
Hammerstein II, Oscar, 148
Hansen, Mogens Herman, 108
Harley-Davidson, 153
Harris, Calvin, 25
Heidegger, Martin, 47
Helen of Troy, 115
Helsinki, 92, 214
Hemingway, Ernest, 180
Henton, Brian, 226
Hera, 116
Heraia, 116
Hercules, 121, 171, 264
Herrera, Helenio, 236
Hesnault, François, 226
Hippodamia, 113, 116
Hippolytus, 107
Hollywood, 25
Homer, 113
Honda Hornet 750, 254
Hopper, Dennis, 163
Horner, Christian, 24
Hudson, river, 120, 158, 216

I

Icarus, 35
ICT (Information and Communication Technology), 35
Iffley Road, 121
IIHF (International Ice Hockey Federation), 277
Il Giorno, 235
Iliad, 107, 113
Il Secolo XIX, 235
Imola, 23
IMSA, International Motor Sports Association, 227
India, 234, 300
India Rubber Journal, 300
India Rubber World, 300
Indian 500, 252
Industrial Revolution, 89
Industrias Pirelli – Casa Central, football team, 97
Infantino, Gianni, 21
Infront Sports and Media, 277
Institute of Sports Medicine, 16
Institute of Sports Science, 16
Inter, 12, 41, 101, 148, 160, 202, 235, 236

International Olympic Committee (IOC), 14, 19, 20, 21
Inter Women, 236
Iraq, 159
Isola, Mario, 40, 66
Isotta Fraschini, 264
Istanbul, 41
Istituto Autonomo Case Popolari, 89
Isthmian Games, 109, 110
Itaca, line of fibreglass boats, 289
Itala, 40, 224, 264, 298
Italian Grand Prix, 253
Italian National team, 234
Italian Republican Constitution, 18, 19, 21, 180
Italian Tennis Federation, 284
Italian Winter Sports Federation, 277
Italy, 12, 15, 17, 21, 27, 39, 40, 41, 45, 69, 70, 72, 79, 97, 101, 120, 127, 133, 134, 135, 136, 139, 143, 154, 159, 160, 166, 171, 175, 176, 179, 180, 183, 193, 224, 225, 235, 236, 242, 243, 245, 252, 258, 270, 276, 284, 285, 289, 300

J

Jacobs, Marcell, 180
Jairzinho, 176
Jannacci, Enzo, 89
Jano Vittorio, 224
Japan, 17
Jarier, Jean-Pierre, 226
Jarrett, Keith, 199
Jason, 171
Jobs, Steve, 189
Jochen Mass, 226
Johns Hopkins, 197
Johnson, Michael, 119
Juventus, 20, 21, 179

K

Kankkunen, Juha, 266
Karageorghis, Costas, 149, 153
Kartell, firm, 276
Kartell K101, ski rack, 276
Kawasaki Ninja 650, 254
Kerouac, Jack, 175
Keynes, John Maynard, 186, 193
Killy, Jean-Claude, 19
Kinshasa, Zaire, 171
Kivimaki, Ilkka, 265
Klopp, Jürgen, 202, 205
Korea, 20, 163
Kraftwerk, 153
Krakauer, John, 197
Kuper, Simon, 202
Kureishi, Hanif, 300

L

La Notte, 235
La Rochelle, 77
Lady Gaga, 149
Laffite, Jacques, 226
Lagioia, Nicola, 300
Lamborghini, 23, 227
Lamm, Lora, 134, 140, 299
Lancia, firm, 19, 227, 265, 266, 269
Lancia Beta Montecarlo, 227
Lancia Fulvia HF, 265
Lancia Stratos, 265, 269
Langhe, 171
Lansdale, Bud, 55, 56
Lansdale, Joe R., 39, 52
Lansdale, John, 56
Lansdale, O'Reta, 56
Lanterna Verde, 53
Lario, circuit, 252
Laros, inflatable watercrafts, 41, 288, 293, 295
Lastex, stretch fabric, 288
Laurel and Hardy, 175
Lausanne, 139
Lazio, 148
Le Castellet, 226
Le Havre, 290
Le Matin, 264
Least Heat-Moon, William, 300
LeBron, James, 197, 198, 199
Lech, Austria, 193
Legnano, bicycles, 242, 243
Leibovitz, Annie, 13, 33, 34, 35, 215, 299
Leipzig, 205
Leonardo da Vinci, 36, 215
Leone, Sergio, 194
'Leoni di Potrero—Calcio per tutti', 101
Leoni, Gianni, 101, 253
Leoni, Guido, 253
Leonida, 206
L'Europeo, 166
Levi, Primo, 3
Levriero, line of fibreglass boats, 289
Lewis, Carl, 13, 32, 33, 34, 35, 36, 47, 215, 216, 222, 299
Liberty Media, 23
Libreria antiquaria in Trieste, 171
Lidl-Trek, team, 98, 249, 250
Ligier, 226
Linoleum, 215
Lippi, Marcello, 179
Liverpool, 147
Livigno, 16
Lizzani, Carlo, 214
Loeb, Sébastien, 266
Lombardy, 139, 143, 144, 234, 242
Lombardi, Lella, 227
London, 26, 45, 92, 111, 119, 124, 180, 209, 214
'long P', 36, 41, 97, 98, 101, 134, 224, 225, 227, 236, 242, 244, 254, 266, 277, 288, 289
Lorient, Brittany, 290
Los Angeles, 33, 216
Lotus JPS, 226
Lowden, Joss, 127
Luna Rossa Challenge, 289
Luna Rossa Prada Pirelli, 12, 41, 289, 296, 297
L'Unità, 166
Lupo, Giuseppe, 40, 130
Luzi, Mario, 166
Lycians, 107
Lyon, 224

M

Macedonia, 159
Macioci, Vittorio, 41
Maciste, 214
Madness, 153
Madonie, 224
Madrid, 26, 179, 183
Maffeis, Miro, 252
Mahé, Eric, 266
Maiga, Silvio, 266, 269
Mailer, Norman, 175
Maino, firm, 242
Malaga, 180
Malagò, Giovanni, 14
Malandra, Michele, 79
Malco, Toni, 148
Malerba, Gian Emilio, 131, 132
Mameli, Goffredo, 159
Mammut, 215, 220
Mandello, 253
Mannucci, Mario, 265
Mansell, Nigel, 226
Manzi, Riccardo, 134, 140, 299
Manzo, Augusto, 171
Maradona, Diego Armando, 175, 199, 202
Marchand, 242, 264
March, team, 226
Marías, Javier, 300
Marino, Umberto, 176, 232
Marley, Gilberto, 242
Maroso, Pietro, 166
Márquez, Gabriel García, 179
Mars, Bruno, 25
Martellini, Nando, 176
Martínez, Guillermo, 300
Martinique, 81, 290
Martin Luther King Library, Washington, 36
Maserati 8C, 225
Maserati 250F, 225
Maserati, firm, 75, 225, 227
Maserati MC12, 75
Mass, Jochen, 226
Masterson, Bat, 55
Mastroianni, Marcello, 214
Mattarella, Sergio, 19
'Matti per la Vela' (Crazy for Sailing), initiative, 101, 290
Mattotti, Lorenzo, 36
Mauritius, 159
Mazzola, Valentino, 166
McCarthy, Tom, 300
McEnroe, John, 199, 205, 209
McRae, Colin, 266
McWhirter, Norris, 121
Meazza, Giuseppe, 148, 234, 235
Mektronic, electronic control unit, 254
Melanion, 115
Melbourne, 92, 214
Memphis, Tennessee, 56
Mendini, Alessandro, 299
Menghi, Roberto, 277
Menlo Park, 186
Mennea, Pietro Paolo, 119, 120
Mercedes, 153
Mercedes 280SE, 153
Mercury, Phoenix, 199
Merkx, Eddy, 127
Messina, 143
Mexican Grand Prix, 226
Mexico, 41, 73, 119, 127, 128, 171, 176, 226, 274
Mexico City, 41, 73, 119, 127, 176
Mezzanotte, Mario, 226
Michels, Rinus, 197
Micòl, 175, 180
Mikkola, Hannu, 265
Milan, football team, 41, 92, 176, 201, 234, 251
Milan Cricket and Football Club, 41, 92, 234
Milan, 9, 36, 39, 41, 87, 89, 92, 97, 98, 133, 134, 139, 143, 214, 215, 224, 234, 235, 242, 243, 244, 252, 264, 288, 298
Milan–Cremona–Brescia–Milan, first road race by Pirelli & C., 39, 242
Milan–Rome 'automotive caravan', 264
Milan–Sanremo, 242, 243
Mille Miglia, 12, 19, 40, 154, 228, 264, 265
Miller, 224
Minà, Gianni, 180
Minardi, 226, 227
Miplac, 215
Modena, Stefano, 227
Modeo, Sandro, 36, 196
Moehringer, John Joseph "J.R.", 300

Mondadori, 179
Monroe, Marilyn, 288
Montale, Eugenio, 163, 174
Monte Carlo, 227, 264, 265, 266
Monte Carlo Rally, 265
Monti, Eugenio, 166, 168, 240
Monument Valley, Utah, 216
Montanelli, Indro, 194
Monza, 72, 153, 173, 224, 225, 228, 253, 288
Mónzon, Carlos
Morgan, Peter, 67
Morris Minor, 153
Moscow, 41
Motocross, 98
MotoGP, 153, 180
Mottarone, 92
Mourinho, José, 41, 147, 199, 201, 202, 236
MTB (Mountain Trail Bike), 244
Muhammad Alì, 171
Mulas, Ugo, 299
Müller, Gerd, 176
Munari, Bruno, 299
Munari, Sandro, 40, 265, 266, 269, 299
Munich, 61, 159, 264
Mura, Gianni, 180
Musetti, Lorenzo, 180
Mussabini, Sam, 119
Mustang, 153

N

Nacional, stadium in Santiago, Chile, 180
Nadal, Rafael, 206
Nannini, Alessandro, 227
Nannini, Gianna, 147
Naples, 148, 202, 205, 242, 252, 289
NASA, 118, 120
Nastro 'cord', rubberised fabric, 277
Nation of Islam, 175
Nations League, 180
Nautilus, line of inflatable watercrafts, 41, 288
Nazzaro, Felice, 42, 224
NBA, 121, 198, 199
Nemea, 109
Nemean Games, 109, 110
Netflix, 24, 25
New Jersey, 189
New York, 59, 185, 186, 189, 194, 216, 300
New Zealand, 266, 289
Ninfa, line of fibreglass boats, 289
Nobel Prize, 179
Nolan, Christopher, 183
Noorda, Bob, 256, 276, 280, 284, 299
Normandy, 290

North Sails Italia, 79
Northeast, 19
Noticias Pirelli, 299
Novaro, Michele, 159
Nutrizio, Nino, 39, 234, 235, 243
Nuvolari, Tazio, 33, 40, 153, 154, 225, 252

O

Oakland, 197
Oakley, Annie, 55
Oger, Bastian, 79
Olympia, 109, 110, 115, 116, 215
Olympic Games, 13, 16, 17, 19, 20, 21, 33, 36, 45, 92, 106, 107, 108, 109, 110, 112, 113, 116, 159, 164, 166, 180, 194, 214, 216
Olympic stadium, 19, 147, 201
Onesti, Giulio, 16
Opel Kadett, 266
Oporto, 101, 185, 202
Oracle Arena, 197
Orengo, Nico, 175
Orio Marchand, firm, 242
Orrico, Corrado, 205
Orwell, George, 147, 159
Osella, 226, 227
Osella PA8, 227
Oxford, 121, 124, 127

P

Pacific Ocean, 41, 288
Paddington Station, 124
Paginas Pirelli, 299
Paletti, Riccardo, 226
Palmeiras, football team, 98
Panatta, Adriano, 45, 120, 126, 180, 194, 284, 285, 286
Paris, 12, 40, 107, 119, 124, 148, 175, 205, 252, 264, 277, 298
Pasolini, Pier Paolo, 143, 163, 166, 171, 179
Pasta, Narciso, 242
Pastorin, Darwin, 39, 162
Patagonia, 175
Patellani, Federico, 299
Patrese, Riccardo, 226, 227
Patroclus, 113
Pausanias, 116
Pavese, Cesare, 171
Payne, Brandon, 197, 199
P&CM (Pirelli & Company, Milan), 242
Peking, 12, 40, 41, 252, 264, 298
Peking to Paris, race, 12, 40, 252, 264
Pelé, 176
Peleus, 107
Pelops, 113, 116
Peñarol, football team, 98
Pérec, Marie-José, 13, 36, 47, 216
Pernanbuco, 101

Perry, Katy, 149
Pertini, Sandro, 179
Peru, 41, 288
Pescara, tread, 225
Pesenti, Carlo, 235
Peugeot, 224
Pi vendere, 215, 299
Piaf, Edith, 154
Piazza Fontana, bomb massacre, 163
Pietrangeli, Nicola, 180, 285
Pigmei, Valentina, 79
Pindar, 108
Pink Floyd, 149
Pinochet, Augusto, 180, 194, 285
Pintacuda, Carlo, 265
Piovene, Guido, 163
Piquet, Nelson, 40, 226, 227
Pirelli, Alberto, 97, 284, 299
Pirelli-Alfa Corse, team, 225
Pirelli Argentina, 97
Pirelli, firm, 11, 12, 13, 32, 33, 35, 36, 39, 40, 41, 45, 67, 68, 71, 75, 77, 89, 92, 97, 98, 101, 131, 133, 134, 135, 139, 143, 176, 214, 215, 224, 225, 226, 227, 234, 236, 242, 243, 244, 252, 253, 254, 263, 264, 265, 266, 267, 269, 271, 275, 276, 277, 284, 285, 288, 289, 290, 291, 298, 299, 300
Pirelli Calendar, 215
Pirelli–Coppa Carlo Negri, regatta, 41, 101, 289
Pirelli Design project, 277
Pirelli–Dunlop, 284
Pirelli, Giovanni Battista, 41, 89, 92, 224, 234, 289
Pirelli Grand Prix, 139, 141, 143, 243
Pirelli Historical Archives, 12, 88, 89, 300
Pirelli Inter Campus, 41, 101, 236
Pirelli, Leopoldo, 299
Pirelli, Margherita, 289
Pirelli Nox, tennis balls, 45
Pirelli P1, tennis balls, 45
Pirelli, Piero, 234
Pirelli Revere, 288
Pirelli. Rivista d'informazione e di tecnica, see *Rivista Pirelli*
Pirelli Sicilia, 143
Pirelli Super Extra, tennis balls, 45, 284
Pirelli World, 299
Pirelli tyres, 134, 243
    Artiglio, 276
    BS, 276
    Campeonato Español Sevilla, 254
    Cinturato, 222, 225, 253, 265, 298
    Cross, 254
    Diablo Supercorsa SP-V4, 254
    Ercole, 121, 171, 264
    Flexor, 135

Motocord, 252, 253
Inverno, 276
Nuovo Inverno, 276
P7, 226, 265, 266
P3000, 13, 36, 41, 47, 236
P6000, 13, 47, 216, 222
P Zero, 75, 156
Scorpion MX, 254
Scorpion Trail, 254
Semelle, 131
Sempione, 92, 215, 234, 242
Star Driver, 266
Stella, 134, 225, 242, 265, 298
Stella Bianca, 225, 265, 298
Stella Extra, 134
Stelvio, 225, 228
Supersport, 225, 265
'tipo Milano', 39, 131, 242, 252
Pirellone, 143
Pirola, Daniele, 36, 88
Pneus Pirelli, 42, 134
Poland, 46, 179
Polo, Marco, 194
Porrà, Giorgio, 179
Porsche, 227
Porto Alegre, 101
Pound, Ezra, 180
Pozzo, Arturo, 139, 243
Pozzo, Vittorio, 41, 92, 234
Prada, 12, 41, 289, 296, 297
Pratolini, Vasco, 214
Presley, Elvis, 56
Prince, 197, 199
Principality of Monaco, 264
Prinetti, Giulio, 242
Prisco, Giuseppe, 148
Pro Patria 1883, sports club, 92, 97, 98, 214, 219
Proust, Marcel, 186
Pruzzo, Roberto, 179
Publifoto, 299

Q
Qatar Grand Prix, 71
Quadrifoglio, brand, 224, 265
Queen, 154

R
Racing SC3, 254
Raid Nord-Sud, 252
Raleigh, 133
Rally Star, 266
Rangnick, Ralf, 205
Rea, Chris, 153
Recife, 101
Red Bull, 153, 205
Republic of Ossola, 234
Ricci, Cino, 194

Rigamonti, Mario, 166
Rihanna, 153
Riley & Scott, 227
Rio de Janeiro, 36, 236
Rio Grande do Sul, 101
Riva, Gigi, 166, 176
Rivera, Gianni, 163, 176
Rivista mensile del Touring, 131, 133
Rivista Pirelli, 97, 123, 135, 139, 176, 214, 225, 234, 235, 243, 252, 253, 276, 288, 289, 299
Road2Record, 128
Robin, 53, 55
Rodgers, Richard, 148
Röhrl, Walter, 266
Roiter, Fulvio, 299
Roland Garros, 148, 205, 285
Rolling Stones, 33
Rome, 16, 21, 92, 127, 147, 148, 153, 164, 166, 176, 189, 201, 214, 242, 264, 285
Rome–Naples–Rome, Grand Prix, 242
Romania, 101, 180
Romani, Elio, 148
Romani, Graziano, 148
Romulus and Remus, 135
Ronaldo, 13, 36, 41, 47, 148, 234, 236, 240, 299
Ronchey, Alberto, 163
Rossellini, Roberto, 288
Rossi, Paolo, 'Pablito', 176, 179
Rossi, Valentino, 180
Roversi, Roberto, 154
Rudolph, Wilma, 21, 123
Ruffo, Bruno, 253

S
Saba, Umberto, 171
Saint-Exupéry, Antoine de, 41
Saint-Moritz, 45
Sainz, Carlos, 40, 266
Salzburg, 205
Sangiorgio Marine, 77
São Paulo, 97
San Siro, stadium in Milan, 41, 92, 234
Santa Margherita Ligure, 41, 101, 289
Santiago, Chile, 179, 180, 285
Santiago Bernabeu, stadium in Madrid, 179
San Zenone al Po, 234
Sapienza, University, Rome, 127
Sarrià, stadium in Barcelona, 176
Sarti, Giuliano, 235
Sartre, Jean-Paul, 175
Scabini, Bruno, 265
Schnellinger, Karl-Heinz, 176
School of Sport, 16
Scissor Sisters, 149
Scudetto, Pirelli bladder, 41, 234

Seleção, Brazil's national team, 176
Selección, Argentina's national team, 176
Sellerio, Enzo, 299
Sempione, velodrome, 92, 215, 234, 242
Senna, Ayrton, 226
Serbia, 180
Seregno, 284, 288
Sereni, Vittorio, 235
Serra, Chico, 226
Sesto Fiorentino, 119
Settimana Automobilistica in Sanremo, 264
Seul, 33, 216
Sevilla, 215
Shakespeare, William, 121, 124
Sheeran, Ed, 25
Sherlock Holmes, 53
Sideri, Massimo, 36, 182
Simeoni, Sara, 120
Simon and Garfunkel, 194
Sinner, Jannik, 121, 180, 183, 186, 189, 193, 194, 206, 285
Sisyphus, 35
Slatina, 101
Slazenger, 284
Snyder, Zack, 206, 209
Sócrates, 176
Solberg, Petter, 266
Soldati, Mario, 179
Soldini, Giovanni, 87, 299
Sölle, Dorothee, 175
Solomon, Harold, 285
Solon, 110
Solti, Sir Georg, 189
Sonego, Lorenzo, 180
Soriano, Osvaldo, 162, 170, 171, 175
Sorrentino, Lamberti, 288
South Tyrol, 19
Soviet Union, 159, 189
Spain, 26, 171, 176, 180, 259
Sparta, 115
Sportbike, 254
Sport Carve Ski, 277
Sport Club Pirelli, 89, 92
Spotify, 153
St George, church, 124
St Mary's Medical School, 124
Stadium, Turin, 21
Stampfl, Franz, 124
State of São Paulo, 101
Stearns Eliot, Thomas, 179
Steiner, Guenther, 24
Stella, Andrea, 290
Stone, Sharon, 299
Strasbourg, 224
Stratos, 265, 266, 269
Streep, Meryl, 33
Strega Prize, 163, 174

Stromboli, film, 288
Stucchi, Augusto, 242
Stucchi, firm, 242, 243
Stucchi–Pirelli, 242
Suárez, Luis, 235
Subaru Impreza Gr. A, 266
Superbike, 40, 98, 254, 260, 261, 262, 263
Superbike Pirelli, 254
Super Extra Pirelli, tennis balls, 45, 284
Superga, firm, 126, 153, 166, 201, 222, 276, 283, 284, 285, 286
Superga G3, ski boots, 276, 283
Superman, 53
Surer, Marc, 226
Suzuki GSX8S, 254
Sweden, 235, 266, 271, 288
Switzerland, 98, 193, 235
Swift, Taylor, 149
Swiss-Ski, 277

T
Taddia, Teseo, 45, 92, 214
Tänak, Ott, 266, 271
Tardelli, Marco, 179, 183, 194
Targa Florio, 12, 40, 42, 224
Taruffi, Piero, 40, 42, 225
Taurasi, Diana, 199
Tavecchio, Carlo, 21
Teatro Stabile di Torino, 21
Tenni, Omobono, aka Black Devil, 253
Terzi, Aleardo, 133, 134
Testori, Giovanni, 139, 143
Texas, 57
The Black Eyed Peas, 25
Thermopylae, 207
Thorszelius, Hans, 266
Tirrenia, 16
Todt, Jean, 265
Togliatti, Palmiro, 135
Togo, 159
Tokyo, 16, 61, 159, 180
Toleman-Candy, 225, 226
Toleman F1, 226
Toleman, team, 225, 226
Tomba, Alberto, 193, 194
Torpedo blu, 153, 154
Totem Pole, 216
Tour de France, 12, 40, 133, 180, 242, 250
Touring Club Italiano, 133
Tourist Trophy, 252, 253
Toyota, 70, 266, 271, 274, 275
Transat Jacques Vabre, transoceanic regatta, 79, 82, 84, 85, 290
Trans Siberian, 264
Traù (Trogir), 234
Tre Golfi of Naples, regatta, 289
Trellini, Piero, 179

Tre Regioni, circuit, 252
Treviso, 253
Tricheco, scuba unit, 288
Tridente, marque, 225
Trieste, 41, 127, 171, 288
Triestina, 171
Trillini, Giovanna, 120
Triumph Trident, 660, 254
Trofeo d'oro Arturo Pozzo, 243
Tronchetti Provera, Marco, 11, 41, 289
Truppa, Valentina, 154
Turin, 18, 19, 20, 21, 92, 166, 175, 186, 234, 285
Twain, Mark, 55
Twin Towers, 186
Tyre Man, 216
Tyrrel, 227
Tyrrel-Honda, 227

U
UAE Emirates, team
Udinese, 235
Ulster Grand Prix, 253
Ulysses, 35, 243
Union, 284, 285
Union Sports, shops, 284
United Kingdom, 26, 27, 159
United Nations Convention, 290
United States, 25, 26, 27, 159, 180, 193
University of Turin, 20
University of Verona, 149
University College, London
U'Ren, Nick, 199
US Grand Prix, 26
Uva, Michele, 21

V
Vado e torno, 299
Valcareggi, Ferruccio, 163, 171
Valchiavenna, 277
Valencia, 180
Vallecchi, 175
Valli, Mario, 41, 288
van de Poele, Eric, 227
van Dijk, Ellen, 127
Varese, 139, 243
Varzi, Achille, 225
Vélez, Fermín, 227
Velez Sarsfield, football team, 98
Venditti, Antonello, 148
Venerando, Antonio, 16
Venosta, Giuseppe, 89
Verdi, Giuseppe, 40
Vergani, Guido, 166
Vergani, Orio, 39, 162, 166, 235, 243, 252
Viale Sarca, 89, 92, 214
Via Ponte Seveso, 39, 131

Viareggio, 121
Vicq-d'Azyr, Félix, 183
Vienna, 26
Vietnam, 154, 175
Vignelli, Massimo, 134, 144, 299
Vigorelli, Giuseppe, 89, 139, 242
Vigorelli, velodrome, 139, 242, 243
Villafranca Tirrena, 143
Virgili, Giuseppe, 235
Visioli, Erminio, 252
Visqueen Pirelli Plast, 41
Vittori, Carlo, 119
Vivarello, Bruno, 289
Volandri, Filippo, 180
VW Beetle, 153

W
Waldegård, Björn, 266
Warmbold, Achim, 265
Warwick, Derek, 226
Washington DC, 26, 39
Watson, Albert, 299
Weiss, Fritz, 284
Wilmant, Giuseppe, 92
Wimille, Jean-Pierre, 225
'Winter Automobilisation', 264
Winter Olympics, 19, 20, 21, 159
Wolff, Toto, 24
Wolseley, 243
Wolsit, 38, 243
Wonder Woman, 53
Woodstock, 194
World Trade Center, 186
WOW - Wheels on Waves, 290
Wozniak, Steve, 189
WRC Academy, 266
WRC, World Rally Championship, 266

X
Xerxes, 206

Y
Yacht Club Italiano, 41, 289
Yamaha R7, 254
YMCA, Tyler, Texas, 57, 58
Young & Rubicam, 33, 34, 47, 148, 216, 222, 299

Z
Zakspeed, 227
Zanetti, Javier, 101
Zavoli, Sergio, 39
Zeus, 109, 115
Zico, 176
Zin, Bernardo, 79
Zoff, Dino, 179
Zugarelli, Tonino, 180, 285

FONDAZIONE PIRELLI

Marco Tronchetti Provera
Chairman

Cecilia Pirelli
Honorary Chairman

**Alberto Pirelli, Nicolò Pirelli,
Giovanni Tronchetti Provera**
Advisers

Antonio Calabrò
Managing Director

Laura Riboldi
Deputy Director

Marina Canta
Editorial Content and Research

Federico Castiglia
Project and Content Development

Martina De Petris
Responsible for Educational Activities

Mila Forlani
Valorization Initiatives,
Archives & Libraries Coordination

Chiara Guizzi
Historical Archive Responsible

Antonino Magistro
Libraries and Research

Viola Maria Mazza
Educational

Sally Peres
Secretariat

Sonia Rossoni
Institutional Cooperation and Organisation

Annalisa Tunesi
Organisation and Development of Initiatives

Eleonora Salvatti
Digital Initiatives

Aurelio Zappia
Logistics

ACKNOWLEDGEMENTS

Our special thanks go to the Motorsport, Moto & Cycling e Communication Department and to all the Pirelli colleagues who helped make the project possible.

We also wish to thank

Danny Baror
Alex Calcatelli
Alice Dinegro
Fabrizio Marchetti
Giovanni Pellerito
Valentina Pigmei
Maria Paola Romeo
Chiara Stangalino
Rina Zavagli

THE SPORTS WORKSHOP
Team Work, Research, Technology, Passion and Social Value

edited by Fondazione Pirelli

Graphic design and layout
Leftloft

Editing
Maria Giulia Montessori

Translations
Paolo Maria Noseda
Richard Sadleir

Iconographic research
Alice Montagnin

© 2024 Pirelli & C. S.p.A
© 2024 Fondazione Pirelli
© 2024 Marsilio Arte S.r.l.

First edition May 2024
ISBN 979-12-5463-184-3
www.marsilioarte.it

Available through ARTBOOK | D.A.P.
75 Broad Street, Suite 630
New York, NY 10004
www.artbook.com

All rights reserved
No part of this book may be reproduced or transmitted in any form or by any means (electronic or mechanical, including photocopying, recording or any other means of retrieving information) without the written permission of the publisher and/or the copyright holders.

Fondazione Pirelli and the publisher have searched diligently for all copyright holders of the images and are at their disposal to credit any unidentified sources.

Cover
Illustration by Lorenzo Mattotti, 2024

Texts
© 2024 Pirelli & C. S.p.A and its licensors
© 2024 Marsilio Arte S.r.l.

Images
All images © Pirelli & C. S.p.A. and Pirelli Tyre S.p.A. and their licensors, except for:
p. 54, © Christie's Images, London/Scala, Firenze, 2024
p. 56, © Veneranda Biblioteca Ambrosiana/DeAgostini Picture Library/Scala, Firenze, 2024; Mondadori Portfolio/Courtesy Everett Collection
p. 60, © photo Scala, Firenze/Hermann Landshoff, bpk, Bildagentur fuer Kunst, Kultur und Geschichte, Berlin, 2024. Inv. n. FM-2012/200.2407
p. 111, © The Trustees of the British Museum c/o Scala, Firenze, 2024. Inv. n. 18050703.43
p. 114, © photo Scala, Firenze, 2024. Su concessione del Ministero della Cultura
p. 117, © DeAgostini Picture Library/Scala, Firenze, 2024
p. 120, © Collection Christophel/Mondadori Portfolio
p. 129, photo by Luc Claessens/Getty Images
p. 167, Pierluigi Praturlon/Reporters Associati & Archivi/Mondadori Portfolio
p. 170, Courtesy of MANIFESTOLIBRI
p. 181, photo by Giuseppe Cottini/Getty Images
p. 184, Warner Bros. Pictures/Syncopy/Legendary Pictures/Album/ Mondadori Portfolio
p. 185, Underwood Archives/UIG/Bridgeman Images
p. 187, © Scala, Firenze, 2024/Ansa/Alessandro di Marco
p. 188, Reuters/Bridgeman Images
p. 195, photo by David Madison/Getty Images
p. 198, Kyle Terada-Usa Today Sports/Sipa Usa/Mondadori Portfolio Usa/Mondadori Portfolio
p. 201, © Scala, Firenze, 2024/Ansa/Fabio Frustaci
p. 203, Farabola/Bridgeman Images
p. 204, photo © AGIP/Bridgeman Images
p. 207, Warner Bros. Pictures/Album/Mondadori Portfolio
p. 208, photo by CBS Photo Archive via Getty Images

The F1 logos, F1 Formula 1 logos, F1 FIA Formula 1 World Championship logo, Formula 1, Formula One, F1, FIA Formula One World Championship, Grand Prix, F1 Grand Prix, Formula 1 Grand Prix and related marks are trademarks of Formula One Licensing BV, a Formula 1 company. All rights reserved.

The images reproduced, unless otherwise stated, come from the Pirelli Historical Archives preserved in the Fondazione Pirelli.

Colour reproduction and printing
Grafiche Antiga S.p.A., Crocetta
del Montello (Treviso)

for
Marsilio Arte S.r.l., Venezia

Up to 15% of this book may be photocopied
for personal use by readers provided they pay
the SIAE fee as per art. 68, clauses 4 and 5
of Italian Law no. 633 of April 22, 1941.
Photocopies for professional, economic,
or commercial use or in any way different
from personal use may be made, but only after
obtaining specific authorization from the Centro
Licenze e Autorizzazioni per le Riproduzioni
Editoriali (clearedi), 108 Corso di Porta Romana,
20122 Milan, e-mail autorizzazioni@clearedi.org
and web site www.clearedi.org.